The Struggle for a Better World

Advanced Studies in Political Economy

Series Editors: Virgil Henry Storr and Stefanie Haeffele

The Advanced Studies in Political Economy series consists of republished as well as newly commissioned work that seeks to understand the underpinnings of a free society through the foundations of the Austrian, Virginia, and Bloomington schools of political economy. Through this series, the Mercatus Center at George Mason University aims to further the exploration of and discussion on the dynamics of social change by making this research available to students and scholars.

The
STRUGGLE
for a
BETTER WORLD

PETER J. BOETTKE

MERCATUS CENTER
George Mason University
Arlington, Virginia

About the Mercatus Center

The Mercatus Center at George Mason University is the world's premier university source for market-oriented ideas—bridging the gap between academic ideas and real-world problems.

A university-based research center, the Mercatus Center advances knowledge about how markets work to improve people's lives by training graduate students, conducting research, and applying economics to offer solutions to society's most pressing problems.

Our mission is to generate knowledge and understanding of the institutions that affect the freedom to prosper, and to find sustainable solutions that overcome the barriers preventing individuals from living free, prosperous, and peaceful lives.

Founded in 1980, the Mercatus Center is located on George Mason University's Arlington and Fairfax campuses.

© 2021 by Peter J. Boettke and the Mercatus Center at George Mason University.
All rights reserved. Printed in the United States of America.

978-1-942951-86-5 (hardcover)
978-1-942951-87-2 (paper)
978-1-942951-88-9 (electronic)

Mercatus Center at George Mason University
3434 Washington Blvd., 4th Floor
Arlington, VA 22201
www.mercatus.org
703-993-4930

Cover design: Jessica Hogenson
Editorial and production: Publications Professionals LLC

Library of Congress Cataloging-in-Publication data are available for this publication.

To Dave Prychitko, Steve Horwitz, Emily Chamlee-Wright, and Virgil Storr

My fellow students of our beloved teacher Don Lavoie, who have provided, and continue to provide, much needed assistance in the struggle. May our efforts continue to honor the memory of Don and the path he prepared us to follow.

The power of abstract ideas rests largely on the very fact that they are not consciously held as theories but are treated by most people as self-evident truths which act as tacit presuppositions. That this dominant power of ideas is so rarely admitted is largely due to the oversimplified manner in which it is often asserted, suggesting that some great mind had the power of impressing on succeeding generations their particular conceptions. But which ideas will dominate, mostly without people ever being aware of them, is, of course, determined by a slow and immensely intricate process which can rarely reconstruct in outline even in retrospect. It is certainly humbling to have to admit that our present decisions are determined by what happened long ago in a remote specialty without the general public ever knowing about it, and without those who first formulated the new conception being aware of what would be its consequences, particularly when it was not a discovery of new facts but a general philosophical conception which later affected particular decisions. These opinions not only the "men in the street," but also the experts in the particular fields accept unreflectingly and in general simply because they happen to be "modern."

—F. A. Hayek
Law, Legislation and Liberty

Contents

Acknowledgments

I n pursuing a career as a scholar, one accumulates many debts to the teachers who taught, to the family members who supported, to the colleagues who collaborated, and to unknown scholars past, present, and future who were sources of inspiration. I consider myself very fortunate; I had professors who changed my life and gave me a mission and ample intellectual resources to start me on my quest. I have a lovely and willing life partner in Rosemary, who since we were teenagers has been my best friend and strongest supporter, as well as the love of my life. And I had amazing classmates in graduate school, and then wonderful colleagues and students at every stop along the way in my career. And finally, I have my "friends" through the ages that I am in constant dialogue with and learning from in the form of books and articles that occupy my bookshelves, pile up on my desk and office floor, and tend to spread throughout the house—or more recently, eat up storage space on various electronic devices. Books, in particular, have played a big part in Rosemary's and my life together, as she spent the last decade of her career in education as a school librarian and is an avid reader.

Reading, writing, and teaching has occupied my professional life for close to 40 years. It has enabled me to travel throughout the world from the edge of Patagonia in Argentina to the cold of winter in Moscow, Russia, and almost everywhere in between.

The essays in this collection are in most instances invited lectures that I was honored to have given for learned societies and organizations. Full attribution to the organizer, the date, and subsequent publication details may be found on the first page of each essay. I gratefully acknowledge these opportunities, and am especially grateful for the permission to include in this volume these lectures from Atlas Network, Liberty Fund, New Zealand Business Roundtable, *Constitutional Political Economy*, *The Independent Review*, *The Insider*, the *Journal of Private Enterprise*, *Policy: A Journal of Public Policy and Ideas*, the *Review of Austrian Economics*, and the *Southern Economic Journal*.

I have been closely associated with the following organizations throughout my career: the Association of Private Enterprise Education (APEE), the Mont Pelerin Society (MPS), the Society for the Development of Austrian Economics (SDAE), and the Southern Economic Association (SEA). I have consistently attended the meetings and served in various capacities for each of these organizations, and have had the honor of serving as president of each of these organizations as well (APEE, 2013–2014; MPS, 2016–2018; SDAE, 2000–2001; SEA, 2015–2017).

I could not have served in this capacity without a tremendous support team at my home institution of George Mason University and at the Mercatus Center. Individuals such as Peter Lipsey, Eric Celler, McKenzie Robey Ackermann, Stephen Zimmer, Karla Moran Segovia, and Jessica Carges have been indispensable to my ability to balance my teaching, research, and organizational efforts.

The Mercatus Center is celebrating its 40th anniversary at Mason in 2020; I have been lucky to be along for the ride for 26 of those years (1984–1988 as a grad student; 1998–present as faculty). This is my home base, and this is where I draw my inspiration for the continuing struggle to understand the world in the hope that improved understanding can lead to betterment. Thank you to all who have made Mercatus such a special place for all these years, with the hope that we will continue our quest for understanding the human condition, and, based on that understanding, that we will fight the good fight for respect for universal human rights and economic, political, and civil freedom.

Economic and Political Liberalism: Yesterday, Today, and Tomorrow

The essays that constitute *The Struggle for a Better World* come from various opportunities I have been afforded since 2000 to summarize my research and discuss the implications of this work for a broader project in political economy and social philosophy. I mean the term *struggle* in a few senses. As a scholar, I am struggling to understand the world and its governing dynamics. As a concerned citizen, I am struggling to make sense of the senseless inhumanity that constantly creeps into our economic lives, social interactions, and political engagement. And as an advocate of liberal cosmopolitanism, I recognize that there is a historical struggle for the fulfillment of that program—a program grounded in the basic recognition that we are one another's dignified equals—that is ongoing and unending.

As I sit down at my computer to write these words (summer 2020), the United States is confronted with a "legitimation crisis."[1] Trust in public institutions of governance, private institutions of finance and commerce, and social institutions of community is under a severe stress test.

Since March 2020, much of the economy has been locked down by government decree in order to confront the public health crisis of a pandemic. Hundreds of thousands of lives have already been tragically lost to COVID-19 even with the lockdown policies in place, and we still do not know the final tally as the virus continues to spread, let alone the collateral damage in terms of the accurate accounting of excess deaths during this period due to the restrictions imposed on the healthcare system that resulted in undiagnosed illness, postponed surgeries, or fear-induced delays in seeking

I gratefully acknowledge the comments and criticisms on an earlier draft by Rosemary Boettke, Rosolino Candela, Jessica Carges, Chris Coyne, Jayme Lemke, Jordan Lofthouse, and Virgil Storr. The usual caveat applies.

1

medical attention. History will be better able to do a full accounting than we are able to accomplish in real time.

The economic consequences are also significant, as the economy was basically placed in a state of suspended animation from March to June. In a "normal" economic crisis, business either adjusts or adapts to changing circumstances, and labor and capital are reallocated to more valued uses as guided by price signals and profit-and-loss statements. Economic crises are moments of *recalculation* of opportunities to meet imagined futures and redeployed labor and capital in that endeavor. But as a consequence of the lockdown, many businesses were unable to experiment with mitigation strategies and engage in the sort of risk assessment and risk management that would normally be required to address such an exogenous shock to ordinary business of life. Mandates and restrictions were issued, not public health guidelines and recommendations. Stay-at-home and stay-safe orders substituted for adapt-or-fail adjustments on multiple margins. Necessity can be the mother of invention, but only if the pressures of necessity are felt, not if they are suspended.

Various aggressive policies have been pursued by the Federal Reserve, by the Treasury, and by Congress to address the economic situation of keeping businesses afloat during these difficult times and providing unemployment payments to keep workers from economic ruin. The economic policy steps taken to enable this suspended animation for much of the US economy (and global economy, since most countries followed a similar path) will be discussed by economists and economic historians for years to come. But needless to say, extraordinary measures were enacted and foundational economic institutions that govern fiscal policy, monetary policy, trade and immigration policy, and regulation of economic activity were transformed in the process. We will see how quickly, if at all, they will be able to bounce back.

Then, just as it appeared there might be some light at the end of this tunnel for the public health crisis, a tragic and senseless act of violence and disregard of human life against a black man—George Floyd—was committed once again by those who supposedly are entrusted to serve and protect us.[2]

Within a liberal democratic society, citizens are *not* and must not *ever* be seen as enemy combatants by the police that service their communities, and police *should not* be armed as military commanders ready to wage such a war as they patrol the streets of our society. *But they do, and they are.* Thus, this display of brutality calls into question not just the legitimacy, but the very existence of our country as a liberal democracy. These blatant displays of disregard of the fundamental principle of equal treatment of equals serve to highlight that we live in a society where those in positions of power govern *over* us, not *with* us, and those in control systematically deny voice to the voiceless and power to the powerless. These practices, this history, are not worthy of the label *liberalism*. It is a grotesque display of inhumanity and injustice.

These senseless acts of violence and disregard of human life targeted at people of color and women simply reinforce why the title of this work has the word *struggle* in it. The liberal project, I have argued repeatedly throughout my career, was born as an *emancipation project*—freeing individuals from subjugation by the Crown, from the dogma of the Altar, from the violence and oppression of the Sword, from the bondage of Slavery, from the miserable poverty of the Plough and from the special privileges granted to the Mercantile Interests.

We learn from the history of the struggle of the wars for religious toleration, from the long struggle for constitutionally limited democratic government and the rule of law, from the long process of economic development that delivered humanity from crushing poverty and improved the material conditions of billions who were able to live longer and more satisfying lives. Along the way, hard-fought battles for the abolition of slavery, for suffrage for women, for the right of individuals to love whom they want and as they want, had to be won. All of that did happen over the course of history. In fact, it might be impossible to understand the development of the disciplines of economics and political economy without understanding that it evolved simultaneously with the political institutions of liberalism in the 18th and 19th centuries, and that it must continually evolve in the context of 20th- and 21st-century understanding of liberal cosmopolitanism.

But as discussions have highlighted well before the crisis brought on by the COVID-19 pandemic and this latest example of police brutality, the liberal project was never universally achieved, and significant segments of the population were left out because of legal barriers due to religion, ethnicity, gender, race, and sexual orientation. Frederick Douglass's words in his famous speech "What to the Slave Is the Fourth of July?" (1852) must be read and understood. Oppression, Douglass told his audience, makes a wise man mad. But brave men, he argued, always find a remedy for oppression. Such was the Declaration of Independence. An act of madness pursued by brave men to demand equality, liberty, and justice. But then Douglass pivots in his speech, and challenges his audience with the grotesque hypocrisy of the American experience:

> What, to the American slave, is your 4th of July? I answer: a day that reveals to him, more than all other days in the year, the gross injustice and cruelty to which he is the constant victim. To him, your celebration is a sham; your boasted liberty, an unholy license; your national greatness, swelling vanity; your sounds of rejoicing are empty and heartless; your denunciations of tyrants, brass fronted impudence; your shouts of liberty and equality, hollow mockery; your prayers and hymns, your sermons and thanksgivings, with all your religious parade, and solemnity, are, to him, mere bombast, fraud, deception, impiety, and hypocrisy—a thin veil to cover up crimes which would disgrace a nation of savages. There is not a nation on the earth guilty of practices, more shocking and bloody, than are the people of these United States, at this very hour. . . .
>
> The existence of slavery in this country brands your republicanism as a sham, your humanity as a base pretence, and your Christianity as a lie. It destroys your moral power abroad; it corrupts your politicians at home. It saps the foundation of religion; it makes your name a hissing, and a bye-word to a mocking earth. It is the antagonistic force in your government, the only thing that seriously disturbs and endangers your Union. It fetters your progress; it is the enemy of improvement, the deadly foe of education; it fosters pride; it breeds insolence; it promotes vice; it shelters crime; it is a curse to the earth that supports it; and yet, you cling to it, as if it were the sheet anchor of all your hopes. Oh! be warned! be warned! a horrible reptile is coiled up in your nation's bosom; the venomous creature is nursing at the tender breast of your youthful republic; for the love of God, tear away, and fling from you the hideous monster, and let the weight of twenty millions crush and destroy it forever!

The sense of shame over the inhumanity of oppression should invoke madness in the wise and the brave if the liberal project is to live up to its promises. Too often, current political leadership at the local, state, and federal levels seems completely tone-deaf to the concerns of the unheard, the discarded, and the dispossessed. The "liberal democratic" order of the 1950s was not "great" for a person of color, or for a woman, or for the LGBTQ+ community. There is no "great" to go back to; there is only a "great" to move forward to as a truly *humane* liberal democratic project is refined and perfected.

Liberalism must be offered as a promise to future generations to eradicate the shameful sins of the past. We must come to a truthful and honest public recognition of our difficult past and our troubling present. The liberal cosmopolitan project is reflected in a hand out to welcome strangers—across national borders, among multiple languages, of different races, religions, and creeds—into friendship through the mutually beneficial relationships of trade and commerce. But this project also represents—through the mechanism of modern economic growth that results from the expansion of trade and commerce—a hand to lift up the discarded, the dispossessed, and the desperate from the misery of poverty. A continuing theme in the essays in this volume is the intellectual refinements in economics and political economy that are required to establish a system that exhibits neither dominion nor discrimination, and the resolving of the intellectual tensions involved in thinking through that institutional task. The ideal is a system *absent of all privileges*. The vision of the "Good Society" that I hope to convey is one envisioned by Adam Smith in *The Wealth of Nations* when he wrote of the liberal program of "equality, liberty and justice" and argued:

> All systems either of preference or of restraint, therefore, being thus completely taken away, the obvious and simple system of natural liberty establishes itself of its own accord. Every man, as long as he does not violate the laws of justice, is left perfectly free to pursue his own interest his own way, and to bring both his industry and capital into competition with those of any other man, or order of men. *The sovereign is completely discharged from a duty, in the attempting to perform which he must always be exposed to innumerable delusions, and for the proper performance of which no human wisdom or knowledge could ever be sufficient*; the duty of superintending the industry of private people, and of directing it towards the employment most suitable to the interests of the society. ([1776] 1976, 208, emphasis added)

Smith also famously argued:

> The statesman, who should attempt to direct private people in what manner they ought to employ their capitals, would not only load himself with a most unnecessary attention, but assume an authority which could safely be trusted, not only to no single person, but to no council or senate whatever, and *which would no-where be so dangerous as in the hands of a man who had folly and presumption enough to fancy himself fit to exercise it*. (478, emphasis added)

Readers would be very mistaken, however, if they understood Smith's demand that individuals should be free from the domination and discrimination of those in positions of power as justifying the material possessions of the wealthy. Smith's great book was a critique of mercantilism, that set of economic ideas and policies that granted special privileges to the commercial elites. He was a consistent critic of the privileged elite class, and a champion of the virtues of the shopkeeper and workmen. Smith was keenly aware that "no society can surely be flourishing and happy, of which the far greater part of the members are poor and miserable" (88).

Recognition of this aspect of Smith's argument in *The Wealth of Nations* led James Buchanan (one of my teachers who, along with another one of my teachers, Kenneth Boulding, taught me so much about Smith while I was in graduate school) to argue that while the emphasis on economic efficiency is surely to be found in Smith, it is only broadly correct if "the efficiency norm is not given exclusive place. Smith's purpose was that of demonstrating how the removal of restrictions on free market forces, how the operation of his 'system of natural liberty,' would greatly increase the total product of the economy and, more importantly, how this would generate rapid economic growth thereby improving the lot of the laboring classes" (1976, 6). In short, economic liberalism, just like the struggle for political liberalism, is an effort at freeing individuals from the restrictions of the ruling elite.

F. A. Hayek—who in many ways is the most focused developer of Smith's liberal project in the 20th century—identified the project explicitly as the abolition of all privileges bestowed on the few at the expense of the many by those in positions of power.[3] As he states in the preface to the 1956 edition of *The Road to Serfdom*: "The essence of the liberal position, however, is the denial of all privilege, if privilege is understood in its proper and original meaning of the state granting and protecting rights to some which are not available on equal terms to others" ([1944] 2007, 46). And in *The Constitution of Liberty*, he further explained, "The true contrast to a reign of status is the reign of general and equal laws, of the rules which are the same for all, or, we might say, of the rule of *leges* in the original meaning of the Latin word for laws—*leges*, that is, as opposed to the *privi-leges*" (1960, 154).

Liberalism is a doctrine of economic and political life grounded in the recognition that we are one another's dignified equals, and that justice demands equal treatment of equals. No exceptions, no excuses. As Deirdre McCloskey—probably the strongest contemporary voice for the Smithian plan of equality, liberty, and justice—puts it in her book *Why Liberalism Works*:

No slaves at all. Equality of status. No pushing around. Sweet talking. Persuasive. Rhetorical. Voluntary. Minimally violent. Humane. Tolerant. No racism. No imperialism. No unnecessary taxes. No domination of women by men. No casting couch. No beating of children. No messing with other people's stuff or persons. (2019, 10)

Freedom of thought, freedom of expression, freedom of commerce. "Like liberty unsupervised in the arts and sciences, or in music and journalism," McCloskey argues, "such modern liberty unsupervised in the economy worked wonders." And the history of economic liberalism demonstrates again and again that "mainly, the ordinary people, when freed, ventured out, and showed their un-ordinariness" (2019, 23). Power to the people, not only to the privileged elites. All can partake in and enjoy the fruits of freedom, not just the select few.

While the essays in this collection consist of opportunities I was afforded based on my previous research efforts, conspicuously absent from them is work discussing in detail my formative years of research and scholarship on the Soviet and post-Soviet experience.[4] That work, however, is never far from view methodologically, analytically, and social philosophically. Socialism is a doctrine I have tried to study from every conceivable angle, and with the utmost of interpretative charity and intellectual respect. As Ludwig von Mises put in a passage I quoted as the epigraph of my first book:

It must be admitted that the idea of Socialism is at once grandiose and simple. . . . We may say, in fact, that it is one of the most ambitious creations of the human spirit. The attempt to erect society on a new basis while breaking with all traditional forms of social organization, to conceive a new world plan and foresee the form which all human affairs must assume in the future—that is so magnificent, so daring, that it has rightly aroused the greatest admiration. (1922, 41)

But like Mises, I believe that the great social experiment of the 20th century was also the greatest failure of the 20th century. I will return to this in my concluding essay, but due to its infeasibility, socialism should be eliminated from the menu of potentially desirable organizational forms of economic, political, and social life. There is no justice to be achieved from socialism, only equality in misery and despair as daily life devolves into one of economic deprivation and political terror.

We are far from a widespread intellectual consensus of the main lessons to be drawn from socialism, this bold yet failed social experiment of the 20th century. And it has been one of my main professional struggles to demonstrate those lessons to professional peers, colleagues across disciplinary divides, and students in the most intellectually responsible and scientifically careful manner. If my conjectures about the inherent contradictions in the socialist project are true, then the struggle for a just and good society is to be found in the reconstruction and fulfillment of the liberal project. However imperfect that project has been pursued in our problematic past—and it has indeed been imperfectly pursued—the struggle remains to understand and pursue a coherent and consistent vision of a society of free and responsible individuals, who can prosper through the voluntary participation in a market society, and live and be actively engaged in caring communities with their family and friends. Humane liberalism, cosmopolitan liberalism, true radical liberalism—this should be the promise of the liberal society to everyone regardless of race, religion, ethnicity, gender, and sexual orientation. People are people, and liberalism is *liberal*. We are, after all, one another's dignified equals. Open and tolerant, peaceful and prosperous, and dynamic and evolving—these are the hallmarks of a humane liberal economic, political, and social arrangement of human affairs.

The essays build on centuries of liberal thought, mainly from within my own disciplines of economics and political economy. I am, in these essays, in a constant conversation with Adam Smith and David Hume, with Jean-Baptiste Say, and John Stuart Mill, with Frank Knight and Ludwig von Mises, and especially with F. A. Hayek, Lionel Robbins, James Buchanan, Murray Rothbard, and Israel Kirzner.[5] John Locke, Alexis de Tocqueville, Robert Nozick, as well as Douglass North, Elinor and Vincent Ostrom, Vernon Smith, Don Lavoie, and Deirdre McCloskey are always in the background as well. But it is from my constant engagement with the ideas of Mises, Hayek, and Buchanan that I have formed the core of my own approach to the quest for understanding the human condition that will be most easily identified in the essays in this collection.

In Mises's classic work *Socialism* (1922) his commitment to liberal cosmopolitanism leaps off the pages for those who will read carefully, and this means a commitment to peaceful social cooperation. Look closely at some passages:

> In the Liberal Social Philosophy the human mind becomes aware of the overcoming of the principle of violence by the principle of peace. In this

philosophy for the first time humanity gives itself an account of its actions. It tears away the romantic nimbus with which the exercise of power had been surrounded. War, it teaches, is harmful, not only to the conquered but to the conqueror. Society has arisen out of the works of peace; the essence of society is peacemaking. Peace and not war is the father of all things. Only economic action has created the wealth around us; labour, not the profession of arms, brings happiness. Peace builds, war destroys. Nations are fundamentally peaceful because they recognize the predominant utility of peace. They accept war only in self-defence; wars of aggression they do not desire. It is the princes who want war, because thus they hope to get money, goods, and power. It is the business of the nations to prevent them from achieving their desire by denying them the means necessary for making war.

The love of peace of the liberal does not spring from philanthropic considerations, as does the pacifism of Bertha Suttner and of others of that category. It has none of the woebegone spirit which attempts to combat the romanticism of blood lust with the sobriety of international congresses. Its predilection for peace is not a pastime which is otherwise compatible with all possible convictions. It is the social theory of Liberalism. Whoever maintains the solidarity of the economic interests of all nations, and remains indifferent to the extent of national territories and national frontiers, whoever has so far overcome collectivist notions that such an expression as "Honour of the State" sounds incomprehensible to him, that man will nowhere find a valid cause for wars of aggression. Liberal pacifism is the offspring of the Liberal Social Philosophy. That Liberalism aims at the protection of property and that it rejects war are two expressions of one and the same principle. (59)

Prior to this, Mises had argued that the very idea of *social science* was born in the recognition of an undesigned social order, and the disposal of the perceived conflict between individualism and collectivism. The doctrine of the harmony of interest enabled theorists to grasp how, out of the purposive behavior of individuals and the pursuit of beneficial exchange, a social order could emerge that served the common interest of society. It is the recognition of Adam Smith's "invisible hand" thesis that led to the development of what Mises termed at that time *sociological thought*. The social philosophy of liberalism flows from this knowledge of sociology.

And this teaching places liberalism at the core of the emancipation of individuals from serfdom, from dogma, from violence, from poverty. And the liberal project is committed, Mises argues, to democratic government—the primary function of which is to ensure peace. "Liberalism demands the fullest freedom for the expression of political opinion and it demands that the State shall be constituted according to the will of the majority," he writes. Mises states clearly, "It demands legislation through representatives of the people, and that the government, which is a committee of the people's representatives, shall be bound by the Laws."

To Mises, "political democracy necessarily follows from Liberalism" (60). But, he elaborates, treating one another as dignified equals is not the same as saying that all are physically and materially equal. Human beings come in all shapes and sizes, and with various talents and abilities. We are all unique in this respect. Diversity is one of our greatest attributes, and marshaling and coordinating that diversity is one of the most critical aspects of the liberal project. For the strict social purposes of the law, however, Mises argues that our differences rooted in biology and aptitude are not the relevant argument.

> Society is best served when the means of production are in the possession of those who know how to use them best. The gradation of legal rights according to accident of birth keeps production goods from the best managers. We all know what role this argument has played in liberal struggles, above all in the emancipation of the serfs. The soberest reasons of expediency recommend equality to Liberalism. Liberalism is fully conscious, of course, that equality before the Law can become extremely oppressive for the individual under certain circumstances, because what benefits one may injure another; the liberal idea of equality is however based on social considerations, and where these are to be served the susceptibilities of individuals must give way. Like all other social institutions, the Law exists for social purposes. The individual must bow to it, because his own aims can be served only in and with society. (66)

To conceive of the law differently, Mises argued, is to misunderstand its social function. "The equality Liberalism creates is equality before the Law; it has never sought any other. From the liberal point of view, therefore, criticism which condemns this equality as inadequate—maintaining that true equality is full equality of income through equal distribution of commodities—is unjustified" (66). It was just this perceived tension in the liberal plan for equality, liberty, and justice that socialist thinkers sought to exploit in promoting their ideas, and which they continue to exploit to this day. But if socialism is infeasible as an economic system, not just difficult, then it cannot be a desirable social philosophy. In working toward a vision of a "Good Society," the desirable must also be feasible, and the feasible must ultimately be viable.[6] The teachings of economic science cannot be discarded when they are inconvenient to philosophical dream quests.

In *The Constitution of Liberty*, Hayek has a poignant observation that is relevant for this discussion of equality before the law and the Smithian humane liberal concern with improving the lot of the least advantaged:

> It is curious that, while in the case of a primitive country every detached observer would probably recognize that its position offered little hope so long as its whole population was on the same low dead level and that the first condition for advance was that some should pull ahead of the others, few people are willing to admit the same of more advanced countries. Of course, a society in which only the politically privileged are allowed to rise, or where those who rise first gain political power and use it to keep the others down, would be no better than an egalitarian society. But all obstacles to the rise of some are, in the long run, obstacles to the rise of all; and they are not less harmful to the true interest of the multitude because they may gratify its momentary passions. (1960, 49)

Liberalism, Hayek reminds his readers in his essay "Why I Am Not a Conservative," advocates for a society that never stands still. Economic growth is a moral imperative. But so is the advancement of ideas that expand the reach of liberal principles of justice and deepen our understanding of the common sense of progress. As he writes:

> But the main point about liberalism is that it wants to go elsewhere, not to stand still. Though today the contrary impression may sometimes be caused by the fact that there was a time when liberalism was more widely accepted and some of its objectives closer to being achieved, it has never been a backward-looking doctrine. There has never been a time when liberal ideas were fully realized and liberalism did not look forward to further improvement of institutions. Liberalism is not averse to evolution and change; and where spontaneous change has been smothered by government control, it wants a great deal of change of policy. So far as much of current governmental action is concerned, there is in the present world very little reason for the liberal to wish to preserve things as they are. It would seem to the liberal, indeed, that what is most urgently needed in most parts of the world is a thorough sweeping-away of the obstacles to free growth. (1960, 399)

Reading Mises and Hayek is a great antidote to the current discussion that puts so much stress on Democratic Socialism, because you realize that the current argument has actually been the argument ever since 1848, just in different variations on the core theme. The question that must be asked is the social scientific one of whether the two ideas—democracy and socialism—are in fact compatible with each other. The conclusion for Mises—just as for Hayek—is a resounding no; not without draining democracy of its social function completely. At least the Marxist revolutionaries understood this, which is why they defended the dictatorship of the proletariat during the transition period. "Obviously," Mises concludes, "the socialist community will have no room for democracy for centuries to come" (1922, 70).

I should also add that both the revolutionary Marxism of Lenin and also the more cultural Marxism of Antonio Gramsci and the long march through the institutions avoid advocating for democratic freedom. Instead, they call for the hollowing out of the liberal institutions of democracy and the creation of a legitimation crisis of liberalism. True freedom in these socialist visions is a complete break from bourgeois notions of the liberal project of freedom of thought and expression, freedom of association, and freedom of contract.

Now contrast that vision with the true radical liberalism of Mises:

> Always and everywhere Liberalism demands democracy at once, for it believes that the function which it has to fulfil in society permits of no postponement. Without democracy the peaceful development of the state is impossible. The demand for democracy is not the result of a policy of compromise or of a pandering to relativism in questions of world-philosophy, for Liberalism asserts the absolute validity of its doctrine. Rather, it is the consequence of the Liberal belief that power depends upon a mastery over mind alone and that to gain such a mastery only spiritual weapons are effective. Even where for an indefinite time to come it may expect to reap only disadvantages from democracy, Liberalism still advocates democracy. Liberalism believes that it cannot maintain itself against the will of the majority; and that in any case the advantages which might accrue from a liberal regime maintained artificially and against the feeling of the people would be infinitesimal compared to the disturbances that would stay the quiet course of state development if the people's will were violated. (1922, 71)

Read that passage carefully—true radical liberalism affirms its commitment to democracy even when it is inconvenient, perhaps especially when it is inconvenient, and seeks only to influence the structure of government through ideas. Economists, for example, are never to be granted a position as privileged experts immune from democratic processes of deliberation. The economist is merely another citizen freely expressing their ideas, drawing on the accumulated knowledge from science and scholarship, in an effort to persuade fellow citizens of the power of those ideas and how those ideas can promote the common welfare. Economics in the liberal tradition is first and foremost a tool of social understanding, and secondly a tool used in forming social criticism of various proposals. What the economist can never assume within a liberal democratic order is that of the expert on call to play the role of savior to society.

The role of the economist is not that of an adviser to a benevolent despot. We are not engaged in what Carl Menger and Mises referred to as "Prussian Police Science." The utilitarian calculus of social welfare functions conducted by expert social engineers trained at elite institutions of higher education is not the vocation of the humane liberal economist. It has, however, been the vocation of modern economists since World War II, and who Hayek, in his Nobel Prize address, warned (a) had made a mess of things, (b) had committed a serious philosophical error he dubbed scientism, and (c) by not correcting this error, had threatened to become tyrants over fellow citizens and destroyers of civilization. The litany of books just published in recent years—such as *The Economists' Hour* (2019) by Binyamin Appelbaum, that seeks to question the pretensions of economists and to place blame for a variety of social ills plaguing the United States—speaks to this problem even if one can counter Appelbaum's specific arguments as ill-conceived and poorly argued.

We really don't want to be tyrants and destroyers, do we? Let alone charlatans practicing a faux science. The rents are nice no doubt, but the consequences of this path are a loss of the soul of the discipline and the moral compass of practitioners. Better, I argue, to fess up to our fellow scholars and citizens in our democratic society and accept our fate as lowly philosophers of society, rather than continue to hold onto the status that our tools and techniques of analysis currently permit us to be in, including the claim that our science enables us to predict the dynamics of a complex system and design optimal controls to fine-tune the operation of that system.

The alternative vision is of an economist in a free society who is a philosopher and critic, who must be content in their role as a student of society and teacher of the accumulated wisdom from the long history of the worldly philosophy, and someone who through careful study has mastered the ability to adjudicate between the contested and contending perspectives that constitute the vibrant science of economics and the art of political economy. If in their efforts in communicating with fellow citizens, the economist fails to persuade, then they have no recourse but to reformulate their argument by further study, improving the arguments and marshaling more compelling evidence. It is a struggle, but a necessary struggle, in the quest to understand the human condition and the possibilities for a better world.

Mises makes the important argument that democracy can only serve its social function of peaceful cooperation among contentious parties within the general framework of Liberalism. A functioning democracy works within the framework of the rule of law, and the rule of law (rather than law by rules) operates on the basis of the absence of political and legal privileges. This is a point Hayek would repeatedly stress as well. Liberalism gives content to what the law should be, without which democratic procedures can be utilized to promote illiberal ends.

The critical point I would like to stress—and what I hope comes through in these essays—is that liberalism's deep commitment to democracy implies not only democratic institutions but *democratic ways of relating* to one another as dignified equals before the law. This liberal commitment permeates our economic, political, and social interactions and relationships. If we forget that, we risk corrupting and abandoning not only democratic institutions but the liberal order itself, and thus peaceful social cooperation among diverse and often physically and socially distant individuals. Instead of emancipation from oppression, we will devolve into the violence trap of a war of all against all.

Liberalism, Deirdre McCloskey (2019) has recently argued, encourages an adult conversation between citizens who are equals. We are not to treat others as children in need of instruction; we are not to compel anyone by force to do our bidding for us. We are engaged in an ongoing conversation, and that requires that we *really listen to one another*. It is in listening, really listening, that voice will be given to the voiceless.

In the "Good Society" I envision, the arrangements will be such that freedom will be granted to all, not just the anointed. The economic and political system will be absent of special privileges for a few at the expense of the many. The institutions of property, contract, and consent will be arranged so that individuals will be able to pursue productive specialization and realize social cooperation. Such an order will maximize the chances for mass flourishing and minimize the pain of human suffering. Power over their lives will be rightfully granted to the powerless.

The Struggle for a Better World is an attempt to bring the teachings of economics—in cooperation with the art of political economy—to bear in an unending quest to understand the human condition. With that knowledge earned in careful study, it has always been my hope to contribute to the continuing articulation of ideas that when consistently and persistently pursued result in fulfilling the emancipatory promise of liberalism to overcome subjugation, repression, oppression, and misery, and instead see humanity flourish in peace and prosperity. The liberal plan of equality, justice, and liberty continues to be the best hope for a better world. It is a hope worth the struggle.

Notes

1. I have been influenced in addressing the causes and consequences of this legitimation crisis by the works of both Jürgen Habermas (1973) and Vincent Ostrom (1973). A legitimation crisis results when a social system lacks the administrative capacity to sustain or achieve its agreed-upon goals. Habermas correctly identified the crisis, but not necessarily the cause. Vincent Ostrom, in my opinion, was closer to the correct diagnosis in his *The Intellectual Crisis in American Public Administration*, and in his proposed remedial recommendation for the scholarly quest. The assessment emerging from these essays is that we have neither adequately addressed the intellectual crisis nor the practical institutional and organizational crisis, and as a result the legitimation crisis has festered for decades, aided in critical ways by the modern practice of economics at a theoretical and applied public policy level. It is my hope that readers will see the connection between the intellectual crisis and the institutional crisis, and thus come to understand the severity of the problem and the urgency of addressing the crisis at a methodological, analytical, and social philosophical level.

2. It is important to stress that George Floyd was not an isolated incident, but another case in an insanely long list of similar incidents where police used deadly force on unarmed individuals often *already in their custody*. Following in the research work of Elinor Ostrom, I have published several papers addressing fundamental problems in policing, including the failure to understand the difference between measuring police services and ensuring public safety in neighborhoods and cities. See Boettke, Lemke, and Palagashvili (2013, 2016) and Boettke, Palagashvili, and Piano (2017).

3. I have used the term *mainline* to describe this Smithian project as it has been pursued from Adam Smith to Vernon Smith. Its main intellectual style of thought is to derive

"invisible hand" explanations from the rational-choice postulate via institutional analysis. Normatively, this project is one of analytical egalitarianism and seeks to develop methodologically, analytically, and normatively an economics of natural equals. See Boettke (2012); Boettke, Haeffele, and Storr (2016); Levy and Peart (2019); and Mitchell and Boettke (2017). Also see Boettke (2018) for a discussion of the evolution of Hayek's research program over the 20th century and the intimate connection between his technical economics and his efforts both to challenge the prevailing wisdom in philosophy of science with respect to economics and the social sciences, and to restate the liberal principles of justice and political economy for the 20th century.

4. See Boettke (1990, 1993, 2001).

5. Kenneth Boulding (1971) wrote a fantastic essay, "After Samuelson Who Needs Adam Smith?," that I read in my first semester of graduate school; the next year, Boulding joined the faculty and I was able to attend his class Great Books in Economics. This essay, and that experience, had a profound effect on me and the way I approach scholarship in economics, as well as the way I think about contemporary theory construction in economic analysis (see Boettke 2000).

6. In my work in comparative economic systems, I tend to stress some methodological ground rules that I argue must be followed. First, one cannot compare the ideal theory of one system with the working reality of another system. To do so is an unfair comparison. Instead, one must compare theory with theory, reality with reality, or theory of a system with the reality of *that* system. Second, in assessing social systems, there are two critical tests: a coherence test and a vulnerability test. The coherence test refers to a strict logical analysis of chosen means to given ends. If, on the one hand, means chosen can be demonstrated to be incoherent with respect to ends sought due to knowledge problems, then that system must be eliminated from the menu of options. If, on the other hand, the chosen means could—if all the actors were richly informed—achieve the desired ends, *but* the incentives in the system were such that opportunistic behavior would undermine the achievement of those goals, then the system would be possible but impractical due to vulnerabilities. Political economy and social philosophy work together and strive to weed out the incoherent and the vulnerable, and leave only those social systems of exchange and production that are logically coherent and robust against opportunism. See Hayek's discussion in *Individualism: True and False* (1948, 11–14); see also Lavoie (1985, 214–15) and Boettke (1993, 4–6).

References

Appelbaum, Binyamin. 2019. *The Economists' Hour: False Prophets, Free Markets, and the Fracture of Society*. New York: Little, Brown.

Boettke, Peter J. 1990. *The Political Economy of Soviet Socialism: The Formative Years 1918–1928*. Norwell, MA: Kluwer Academic.

———. 1993. *Why Perestroika Failed: The Politics and Economics of Socialist Transformation.* New York: Routledge.

———. 2000. "Why Read the Classics in Economics?" Library of Economics and Liberty, February 24.

———. 2001. *Calculation and Coordination: Essays on Socialism and Transitional Political Economy.* New York: Routledge.

———. 2012. *Living Economics: Yesterday, Today, and Tomorrow.* Oakland, CA: The Independent Institute.

———. 2018. *F. A. Hayek: Economics, Political Economy and Social Philosophy.* New York: Palgrave Macmillan.

Boettke, Peter J., Stefanie Haeffele, and Virgil Henry Storr. 2016. *Mainline Economics: Six Nobel Lectures in the Tradition of Adam Smith.* Arlington, VA: Mercatus Center at George Mason University.

Boettke, Peter J., Jayme S. Lemke, and Liya Palagashvili. 2013. "Riding in Cars with Boys: Elinor Ostrom's Adventures with the Police." *Journal of Institutional Economics* 9 (4): 407–25.

———. 2016. "Re-Evaluating Community Policing in a Polycentric System." *Journal of Institutional Economics* 12 (2): 305–25.

Boettke, Peter J., Liya Palagashvili, and Ennio E. Piano. 2017. "Federalism and the Police: An Applied Theory of 'Fiscal Attention.'" *Arizona State Law Journal* 49 (3): 907.

Boulding, Kenneth E. 1971. "After Samuelson Who Needs Adam Smith?" *History of Political Economy* 3 (2): 225–37.

Buchanan, James M. 1976. "The Justice of Natural Liberty." *Journal of Legal Studies* 5 (2): 1–16.

Douglass, Frederick. 1852. "What to the Slave Is the Fourth of July?" Extract from an Oration, Rochester, New York, July 5.

Habermas, Jürgen. 1973. "What Does a Crisis Mean Today? Legitimation Problems in Late Capitalism." *Social Research* 40 (4): 643–67.

Hayek, F. A. [1944] 2007. *The Road to Serfdom: Text and Documents—The Definitive Edition.* Edited by Bruce Caldwell. Chicago: University of Chicago Press.

———. 1948. *Individualism: True and False.* Chicago: University of Chicago Press.

———. 1960. *The Constitution of Liberty.* Chicago: University of Chicago Press.

Lavoie, Don. 1985. *National Economic Planning: What Is Left?* Washington, DC: Cato Institute.

Levy, David M., and Sandra J. Peart. 2019. *Towards an Economics of Natural Equals: A Documentary History of the Early Virginia School.* Cambridge: Cambridge University Press.

McCloskey, Deirdre N. 2019. *Why Liberalism Works: How True Liberal Values Produce a Freer, More Equal, Prosperous World for All.* New Haven, CT: Yale University Press.

Mises, Ludwig von. 1922. *Socialism: An Economic and Sociological Analysis.* Jena, Germany: Gustav Fischer Verlag.

Mitchell, Matthew D., and Peter J. Boettke. 2017. *Applied Mainline Economics: Bridging the Gap between Theory and Public Policy*. Arlington, VA: Mercatus Center at George Mason University.

Ostrom, Vincent. 1973. *The Intellectual Crisis in American Public Administration*. Tuscaloosa: University of Alabama Press.

Smith, Adam. [1776] 1976. *An Inquiry into the Nature and Causes of the Wealth of Nations*. Chicago: University of Chicago Press.

Chapter 1

The Battle of Ideas: Economics and the Struggle for a Better World

I n *An Inquiry into the Nature and Causes of the Wealth of Nations*, Adam Smith ([1776] 1976) argued that a virtuous circle led to increased prosperity.[1] The source of economic growth and development was the gains from specialization and trade realized through the greater division of labor and the expansion of the market economy. The division of labor was limited by the extent of the market. But as the market expands, the division of labor is refined even further and the gains from specialization increase productivity further again. There are, in other words, increasing returns to the expansion of the market arena. This Smithian virtuous circle counteracts any tendency toward being caught in the Malthusian trap of subsistence levels of production and represents, instead, the progressive march of modernity.

In the lectures and notebooks that he used in writing his great treatise, Smith summarized his position in the following manner: "Little else is requisite to carry a state to the highest degree of opulence from the lowest form of barbarism, but peace, easy taxes and a tolerable administration of justice: all the rest being brought about by the natural course of things" ([1776] 1976, xl). Smith goes further and argues in the next passage: "All governments which thwart this natural course, which force things into another channel or which endeavor to arrest the progress of society at a particular point, are unnatural, and to support themselves are obliged to be oppressive and tyrannical" (xl).

Evidence from the history of economic development supports Smith— in terms of both the path to successful development and the consequences of steering off that path.[2] But one must unpack the basic institutional infrastructure that serves as the background to Smith's policy prescription.

Speech given as the 12th Sir Ronald Trotter Lecture at the New Zealand Business Roundtable in Wellington, New Zealand, 2006. Published in 2007 by the New Zealand Business Roundtable, PO Box 10-147, The Terrace, Wellington, New Zealand.

Smith's system of natural liberty (or David Hume's of property, contract, and consent) consists of a network of complementary institutions that all serve to minimize the threat of predation from both public and private actors.

Once stated in this manner, the "paradox of government" becomes apparent. Government is called on to ward off the threat of private predation; but in the government being so empowered, the problem of public predation is created. As James Madison put it in *The Federalist Papers*:

> If men were angels, no government would be necessary. If angels were to govern men, neither external nor internal controls on government would be necessary. In framing a government which is to be administered by men over men, the great difficulty lies in this: You must first enable the government to control the governed; and in the next place, oblige it to control itself. ([1788] 1963, 164)

Neither appeals to the wisdom of nobility, nor to romantic dreams of the perfectibility of mankind, address this paradox. Instead, institutional arrangements must be forged that will check the ambitions of some against the ambitions of others to ward off predation by private and public actors.

The systems that Smith and Hume built to understand the political economy of growth and development did not rely on behavioral assumptions to generate the conclusions concerning the beneficial consequences of the "invisible hand." Self-interest is postulated as a universal aspect of human nature, but the pursuit of self-interest is not the causal factor that is relied on to explain how beneficial social order can emerge. In Smith's comparative political economy, the self-interest of businesspeople (reflected in their special-interest pleading), the self-interest of the clergy and academics (reflected in the laziness demonstrated when in protected positions), and the self-interest of politicians (reflected in their arrogance and grabs for power) are all contrasted with situations where the self-interest of buyers and sellers produces a social order that is both unintended and desirable. To put it another way, both the "invisible hand" and the "tragedy of the commons" explanations of social phenomena use the self-interested motivational assumptions, but the driving force in the analysis is the alternative institutional context, not the behavioral assumptions.

The intellectual projects of Hume and Smith were to discover, through analytical inquiry and historical investigation, the institutional environment that could produce peace and prosperity despite the foibles of man. F. A. Hayek summed up the Smith project as follows:

> The main point about which there can be little doubt is that Smith's chief concern was not so much with what man might occasionally achieve when he was at his best but that he should have as little opportunity as possible to do harm when he was at his worst. It would scarcely be too much to claim that the main merit of the individualism which he and his contemporaries advocated is that it is a system under which bad men can do least harm. It is a social system which does not depend for its functioning on our finding good men for running it, or on all men becoming better than they now are, but which makes use of men in all their given variety and complexity, sometimes good and sometimes bad, sometimes intelligent and more often stupid. . . . The chief concern of the great individualist writers was indeed to find a set of institutions by which man could be induced, by his own choice and from the motives which determined his ordinary conduct, to contribute as much as possible to the need of all others; and their discovery was that the system of private property did provide such inducements to a much greater extent than had yet been understood. (1948, 11–13)

In the reading that Hayek provides, the classical political economy of Smith was grounded in comparative institutional analysis. It is my contention that this comparative institutional approach remained the method of political economy throughout much of the 18th and 19th centuries, and it was only with the direction that economics as a discipline took in the early 20th century that the institutional context of economic action ceased to be the primary focus. From about 1900 to the 1960s, the discipline moved away from a focus on institutional context and, instead, concentrated on refinements of the behavioral assumptions. Whereas the late classical and early neoclassical traditions focused on the subject matter of economics as exchange and the institutions within which exchange takes place, the refinements of neoclassicism focused on the subject matter of economics as being the allocation of scarce resources among competing ends and the efficiency properties associated with an ideal allocation.

In this chapter, I explain why this intellectual development occurred in the 20th century, and I outline the consequential shifts in scientific thought and public policy. The story begins simply enough and is at first isolated to intellectual debates as disciplines were striving to establish themselves within the pecking order of an emerging academic structure. But the consequences of this intellectual development were ultimately a contributory factor to why the 20th century was arguably the bloodiest in recorded human history.[3] This statement might be dismissed as hyperbole, but that means I must accept the challenge of convincing readers that this position is more reasonable than it first appears, and that there are good reasons to remain deeply concerned that the lessons of the 20th century relating to unconstrained government have yet to be learned, even though so many millions paid the ultimate price.

The culprits in my narrative are going to be scientism on a philosophical level, formalism and excessive aggregation at the analytical level, and the alliance of statism with Keynesianism and socialism at the public policy level. The solutions will be found in scientific humility and methodological dualism at the philosophical level, methodological individualism and the theory of the market process on an analytical level, and laissez-faire capitalism and limited government at the public policy level.

How Did Economics Lose Its Way?

In the beginning, the discipline was called political economy and it was a branch of moral philosophy. But those who practiced political economy did so by building arguments based on reason and evidence, and not necessarily on moral intuition. The art of political economy was in the application of theory to address practical problems of public policy; thus the discipline was perceived as a guide to statesmen. However, from the beginning of the discipline, the advice it offered to those in power was routinely dismissed soon after it was heard. The reason for this is straightforward: it is extremely rare that those in power are willing to follow advice that minimizes their ability to exercise authority over either domestic or foreign subjects.

Adam Smith warned:

> The statesman, who should attempt to direct private people in what manner they ought to employ their capitals, would not only load himself with a most unnecessary attention, but assume an authority which could safely be trusted, not only to no single person, but to no council or senate whatever, and which would nowhere be so dangerous as in the hands of a man who had folly and presumption enough to fancy himself fit to exercise it. ([1776] 1976, 478)

The teachings of political economy were disregarded by an alliance of the sophistry of the businessperson engaged in special-interest pleading and the power-wielding preferences of politicians. The great French political economist Frédéric Bastiat chose satire as his way to expose the sophistry when he penned his petition of the candlestick makers for protection against the unfair competition from the sun in 1845 (Bastiat 1996). And his countryman Jean-Baptiste Say soberly discussed the problem of political power and economic efficiency that results from government-sanctioned monopolies in his *Treatise on Political Economy* ([1820] 1971, 146–47). As Say put it, "The public interest is their plea, but self-interest is evidently their object" (161). In so doing, he provides another example of how the assumption of self-interest is not what drove the classical analysis of the benefits of the invisible hand of the market economy. The system of government privileges that sought to control trade was "pregnant with injustice" and created serious mischief throughout the economy (164).

John Stuart Mill argued in his *Principles of Political Economy* ([1848] 1967, 881–83) that the first principle of social order is the protection of persons and property. Without this protection, the social order breaks down into uncertainty and violence. Mill was quick to point out that government was not the only source of this protection, though a government that habitually violated these protections would destroy society. The prosperity experienced by the free cities of Italy, Flanders, and the Hanseatic League in an age of "lawlessness" demonstrates that a certain level of insecurity can be managed through means of self-protection. As Mill put it:

> Insecurity paralyzes only when it is such in nature and in degree that no energy of which mankind in general are capable affords any tolerable means of self-protection. And this is a main reason why oppression by the government, whose power is generally irresistible by any efforts that can be made by individuals, has so much more baneful an effect on the springs of national prosperity, than almost any degree of lawlessness and turbulence under free institutions. Nations have acquired some wealth, and made some progress in improvement in states of social union so imperfect as to border on anarchy: but no countries in which the people were exposed without limit to arbitrary exactions from the officers of government ever yet continued to have industry and wealth. A few generations of such a government never fail to extinguish both. Some of the fairest, and once the most prosperous, regions of the earth have, under the Romans and afterwards under the Turkish dominion, been reduced to a desert, solely by that cause. ([1848] 1967, 882–83)

At the beginning of the 20th century, Max Weber summarized these arguments to explain why capitalism had developed in the West but not in China. In his *General Economic History* (1927), Weber enumerated the defining characteristics of modern capitalism. Although there is no doubt that the value system in a society was a significant contributing factor, according to Weber, it was not—as so many have concluded—just the existence or lack of the Protestant work ethic that provided the explanation as to why there was no capitalism in China. Weber, instead, put great emphasis on the arbitrariness in the law and the tax system that was practiced in China and that was inconsistent with the development of a modern economy. Modern capitalism was, instead, characterized by rational accounting, freedom of the market, modern scientific technology, the rule of law, free labor, a rationalization of the conduct of life consistent with market activity, and the commercialization of economic life. These factors all worked to provide a rational ethic for enterprise, and a political and legal environment that was predictable and that guaranteed market participants a semiautonomous area in society. In short, the basic lesson was once again one that provided that peace, easy taxes, and a reasonable administration of justice prevailed and that economic development would follow in the natural course of things.

When one reads these different authors' arguments, what is striking is the consensus that was evident on the fundamental question of the causes of the wealth and poverty of nations. But this consensus was extremely fragile. Classical political economy proved to be quite vulnerable to critiques that focused on (a) instability, (b) monopoly, and (c) inequality.[4] Karl Marx was the most thorough critic along these lines, but several others contributed along the way by pecking holes in the classical system through emphasizing the problems of recurring business cycles, the concentration of market power in the hands of a few or a single seller, and the unequal distribution of income. To counter the perceived problems of capitalism, critics of the classical system argued that the role of government had to change from that of a "night watchman" to the more active guardian of the public interest.

Even though John Stuart Mill saw an expanded role for government interference, he argued: "Whatever theory we adopt respecting the foundation of the social union, and under whatever political institutions we live, there is a circle around every human being which no government, be it that of one, of a few, or of the many, ought to be permitted to overstep" ([1848] 1967, 943). Violation of this principle ran the risk of the loss of human freedom and dignity. As such, Mill argued that "the onus of making out a case always lies on the defenders of legal prohibitions" (943). Mill even argued more forcefully when he stated later in this chapter, "Laissez-faire, in short, should be the general practice: every departure from it, unless required for some great good, is a certain evil" (950). Despite this line of argument, Mill made a case for government interference in the economy to address problems of unsafe work environments, consumer ignorance, education, collective action, and inequality and injustice.

Obviously, there were intellectual gaps in the classical presentation of laissez-faire, but eventually these would be addressed to a considerable extent by the emerging neoclassical theory of value and price. For example, the neoclassical theory of factor pricing challenged theories of exploitation. But as Hayek has pointed out, by the time those theoretical revisions were made, the public mind had already been swayed to the other side:

> It takes a long time to rebuild the structure of a science if one starts by revising the fundamental concepts. And the modern revision of theoretical economics has occupied sufficient time to allow what was at first the heretical view of a number of radical economists—who had to fight what was then the conservatism of the practical men who were still under the influence of economic liberalism—to pervade the thought of the public and to establish itself as the dominating doctrine, not only among advanced social reformers, but even among the most conservative businessmen. The public mind in all leading countries of the world is now completely under the domination of the views which spring from the revolt against the classical economics of seventy years ago. (1931, 24)

Despite the fact that the early neoclassical economists increasingly came to the consensus that classical economists had arrived at essentially the correct conclusions with cruder instruments, the classical presumption toward freedom of choice gave way to a demand for government action, and the concern with the abuse of political power was dismissed as the groundless fear of a predemocratic era. Theory and experience sided with the general thrust of the classical political economists, but the public mind and the political elite resisted that conclusion and were, instead, under the sway of interventionism guided by democratic consensus.[5] The classical presumption against interventionism was reversed, and now those who argued for laissez-faire were dismissed as anachronistic.

In addition to this intellectual development in economics, it is important to emphasize two critical developments that crystallized the intellectual and policy consensus in the 20th century. First, institutions of higher education were growing in importance as sources for research and policy as the German model of the research university spread throughout Europe and the United States. At the same time, academic disciplines started to become professionalized. Second, the great success in the physical sciences during this period was attributed to enhanced technologies of measurement. The idea evolved quickly that science was measurement, and any discipline that desired the status of science would have to entail measurement. The neoclassical economists who were striving to make the discipline of economics a scientific enterprise were no less enamored with measurement than anyone else in the zeitgeist—political economy was renamed economics. No longer a branch of philosophy and a handmaiden to history, economics was now a branch of social physics and deployed higher mathematics to bring rigor to the analysis of social order.[6]

Mathematical reasoning would not come to dominate economic analysis until the 1940s and 1950s, but the basic justification was already in place in the intellectual world in the late 19th century. The problem with verbal reasoning, it was argued, was that ambiguity results from either using the same words to mean different things or using different words to mean the same thing. Assumptions could remain hidden, and moral intuitions could sneak into the analysis. It was believed that, by putting arguments in mathematical form, all of this would be avoided. Formal presentation required all assumptions to be made explicitly, and definitions to be precise.

The formalist victory in economic science was secured with the publication of Paul Samuelson's *Foundations of Economic Analysis* (1947) and reflected in the axiomatic presentation of the general competitive equilibrium theory in the work of Kenneth Arrow, Gérard Debreu, and Frank Hahn. Even though Kenneth Boulding (who at the time was a recent John Bates Clark Medal winner and not the iconoclastic thinker he would later become) sent an early warning signal when, in his *Journal of Political Economy* review of Samuelson, he wrote: "Conventions of generality and mathematical elegance may be just as much barriers to the attainment and diffusion of knowledge as may contentment with particularity and literary vagueness. . . . It may be that the slovenly and literary borderland between economics and sociology will be the most fruitful building ground during the years to come and that mathematical economics will remain too flawless in its perfection to be very fruitful" (1948, 199). But the concerns of Boulding and others were ignored as relics of an unscientific age.

Boulding pinpointed something of great importance that was dismissed too quickly, in favor of the focus on whether or not a thinker was sufficiently skilled in higher mathematics. The mathematical method resulted in draining the institutional context from economic analysis. Ludwig von Mises and Hayek raised a similar concern about the shift of analytical attention away from the process of exchange and the impact of alternative institutional arrangements on that process. Human choice was reduced to an exercise in constrained optimization, and the force of competition was redefined as a state of affairs rather than a set of active engagements. Core theory no longer addressed the adjustments made in the market "not by any accurate measure, but by the higgling and bargaining of the market" (Smith [1776] 1976, 35–36). Instead, equilibrium properties— the state where all adjustments have been completed—came to dominate economic theory.

In general equilibrium theory, no trades outside of equilibrium were permitted, otherwise the "false trades" could derail the theoretical attainment of equilibrium. Instead, plans were prereconciled prior to permitting trade and then the system of simultaneous equations could be constructed and a unique price and quantity vector that would clear all markets could be discovered. Absent the prereconciliation of plans among agents, the unique price and quantity vector could not emerge within the system. The only way to get the equilibrium solution was to presuppose one was already in equilibrium. No path to equilibrium could be constructed.

The reason is not that the equilibrium theory served no purpose. It did communicate the delicate interconnectedness that an advanced economic system exhibits. And it did demonstrate the characteristics of the end state toward which economic activity would result in the absence of changing circumstances. But it clouded our understanding of the processes by which economic actors adapt creatively on the margin to changing circumstances and learn how to coordinate their plans better with others to realize the mutual gains from trade. Moreover, the theory eliminated from economic analysis how alternative institutional arrangements either impede or encourage that learning by economic actors.

The formal theory of the 1950–1970 period strove to be institutionally antiseptic, and succeeded to a considerable extent. The mantle of science was attributed to economists because of the form in which they presented their arguments, but the cost of obtaining that prestige was to "cheapen" the content of economics. James Buchanan often challenged his students with the question "What more do we know today about the nature of markets than Adam Smith knew in 1776?" If not much progress was evident, Buchanan concluded, then perhaps the formalist emperor has no clothes, and someone needs to play the role of the innocent child and reveal the truth of the matter to our fellow economists.[7]

The problem would not be so troublesome if it just affected economics, but economic policy debates were greatly influenced by the changing nature of economics in the 20th century. The debate over socialism among economists is perhaps the most obvious example. But market failure theory, in general, and the policy response through tax and regulation were equally affected by a consensus among formal theorists that institutions of private property, freedom of contract, and constitutional constraints cease to play a definitive role in economic outcomes.[8]

Scientism, formalism, and statism dominated economic thinking in the 20th century. In addition, the main generation of scientists and intellectuals in the 20th century came of political consciousness during the Great Depression, finished their graduate education either during or after World War II, rose to professional prominence in the 1950s and 1960s, and became elder statesmen of the profession in the 1970s and 1980s. This generation of elite economists, while having lost faith in unbridled capitalism, believed deeply in the ability of democratic governments to address the social ills of poverty, racism, sexism, and other forms of social injustice, and took great pride in the new science of economics they had helped create, which could serve as a tool for social control to meet those challenges. This generation defeated Hitler in their youth and put a man on the moon by middle age. Only the most cynical and superstitious of that generation, it was believed, could doubt the progressive thrust of new science and democratically elected government, and, instead, demand a return to the older teachings of classical political economy that emphasized the institution of private property, freedom of contract, and constitutional constraints on the power of government.

The Counterrevolution in Economic Thought

By 1950, economic thought and policy were dominated by Keynesian demand management on the macroeconomic side, and market failure theory on the microeconomic side. During the 1946–1980 period, the intellectual consensus was collectivist, and the policy practice was not lagging far behind. Government spending as a percentage of gross domestic product (GDP) in the United States expanded quickly as action chased after thought. There was no intellectual resistance to the growth of government. Ideas and interests aligned to transform Western societies and also to build a policy consensus in the West's efforts abroad to address underdevelopment that was decidedly anti-market.[9] The voices of economists born in the 19th century, such as Mises and Hayek, that were raised to caution against this trend were dismissed. But a growing counterrevolution that emphasized the institutional infrastructure and economic processes started to emerge within the profession to challenge the Keynesian and market failure hegemony.

The property rights economics of Armen Alchian, Ronald Coase, and Harold Demsetz; the public choice economics of James Buchanan and Gordon Tullock; the new learning in industrial organization associated with George Stigler and Yale Brozen; the theory of the entrepreneurial market process associated with Israel Kirzner; the new economic history associated with Douglass North; and the monetarist critique of Keynesianism associated with Milton Friedman—all emerged in the 1960s as a formidable opponent to the policy consensus from 1950 to 1970. By the mid-1970s, the presumption in thought had swung back decidedly in the direction of the classical political economy as the New Classical revolution of Robert Lucas challenged the Keynesian hegemony in macroeconomic research. Policy would lag behind and, unlike in the move from laissez-faire to statism, interest groups and politicians would block moves for policy to catch up to the new thinking.

If the period between 1945 and 1975 was one of "galloping socialism" in Western democracies, such as the United States and United Kingdom, as big government was called on to serve as a corrective to economic ills (justified by market failure theory and Keynesianism), the period between 1975 and 2005 was one of "creeping liberalism" in Western democracies, as the justification for the previous policies was soundly defeated on the intellectual level. However, the actual behavior of government—in terms of spending, taxation, and regulation—changed at a slower rate than would have followed from the intellectual victory.

Milton Friedman has argued that we have seen a victory in the realm of ideas, but a failure of implementation. In the move from rhetoric to thought, and from thought to action, the classical liberal movement has been tripped up at the second stage. The stumbling blocks have mainly been a consequence of the forces of inertia—the political resistance to change. Friedman explained this tyranny of the status quo as the alignment of intellectuals, interest groups, and politicians (an "iron triangle") who benefited from the existing array of policies and who would block any proposed change (see Friedman and Friedman 1984). Still, it is important to recognize that a counterrevolution in economic thought had been successful and that the Keynesian and market failure dominance in economic education was defeated to a considerable extent by 1980 and thereafter.[10] The justification for activist government in economic life needed to be grounded in an alternative microeconomic framework—at least at an intellectual level. The inertia in public policy, however, prevented the counterrevolution in economic theorizing from realizing the public policy consensus in economic policy to the same extent that the Keynesian consensus experienced between 1950 and 1980. Laissez-faire in rhetoric and dirigisme in practice is perhaps the more accurate description of the public policy consensus since 1980.

Path Dependency in Policy

During the Keynesian hegemony, various statistical metrics were developed for the task of social control. National income statistics were collected, and policy models of fine-tuning the macroeconomic system were developed. The two would serve each other—the macroeconomic models dictated what data should be collected, and the data collected would then be employed in the models to transform the analytical model into a tool for policy. Economics so conceived ceased to be a way of thinking about exchange relationships and the institutions within which exchange takes place, and, instead, became a tool for social control.[11] The analytical focus was on models postulating a relationship between macroeconomic variables, such as inflation and the rate of unemployment, and the empirical focus was on the statistical examination of these variables and the postulated relationships. Keynesian models raised

Keynesian questions that were examined with Keynesian data to produce Keynesian answers.

An excellent illustration of this can be found in the "Washington Consensus" of the 1990s. The Washington Consensus focused its rhetoric on privatization, deregulation, fiscal balance, monetary restraint, and free trade. But it still suffered from a one-size-fits-all approach to public policy, which paid little or no attention to the historical details of the institutions in the particular society under examination, and maintained a primacy on macroeconomic policy rather than a microeconomic analysis of the economic situation. In other words, while the Washington Consensus expressed a certain sympathy with aspects of the counterrevolution in economic theory, in practice, it did not represent a major departure in public policy but was, instead, merely "conservative Keynesianism" as opposed to the "liberal Keynesianism" of the earlier era. As another example, if you engage in a careful reading of Jeffrey Sachs's discussion of the policies required for postcommunism (shock therapy), it will reveal that Sachs was not offering a shift in the policy regime of Western democracies for Eastern and Central Europe and the former Soviet Union, but a desire to establish a market economy so that the necessary regulatory regime and tools of macroeconomic management could be institutionalized and implemented as tools for social control.[12] A new era of laissez-faire was not ushered in with the breakdown of the Keynesian consensus and the collapse of communism. The creeping liberalism of the 1975–2005 period began with the claim that government had grown too big when government spending represented 32 percent of GDP in the United States and ended with the claim that government had been drastically cut when government spending represented 31 percent of GDP. During that period, never once did that figure fall below 29 percent.

The creeping liberalism experience over the past 30 years is not limited to the United States. Consider the case of Russia after communism. In 1992, the ruble exchanged at Rub 180 to US$1.00, but in 1995 it exchanged at more than Rub 5,000 to US$1.00. This period was described by its critics as an era of "monetarism." During the 1990s, we heard repeatedly that Russia's citizens were subjected to the cruel consequences of market romanticism, yet a close reading of all media accounts reveals a growing "black market" during the 1990s. Underground markets are not associated with liberalism, but, instead, prohibitions. So again, Russia's problems in the 1990s were a consequence of too much government involvement in the economy, rather than too little.[13] The inertia in public policy that limited the pursuit of economic liberalism was true, even after a collapse of the previous policy regime. A similar story can be told of the so-called liberal reforms in Argentina in the 1990s, where market liberalism is blamed for failed policies, when a more subtle reading of the situation would reveal that the problems were caused by government distortions of the economic environment.

Liberal economic theory is not blameless in this confused intellectual and policy state of affairs. The academic defense of the liberal economic order has often portrayed the free-market system as requiring hyperrational individuals who interact in a mechanistic and impersonal system of ruthless efficiency. Demonstrations of deviations against the ideal of hyperrational action by individuals and static efficiency as realized by the system would demand government action to address social ills. Given the ridiculous benchmark of hyperrational individuals and ideal efficiency, the real world would, at every point, fall short and thus be in constant demand of, on the one hand, paternalistic intervention by government to save individuals from their alluring hopes and haunting fears (which produce "irrational" choices), and, on the other, government activism in the economic system to curtail problems of monopoly, externalities, public goods, and macroeconomic instability.

The inertia in public policy results in a recycling of the critique of laissez-faire and a tendency to ignore what was learned during the counterrevolution of the 1950–1975 period on the intellectual front because of the failure of implementation during the era of creeping liberalism between 1975 and 2005. It is inaccurate to claim that "big government has returned" for the simple reason that it never really left us in the democratic West. However, it is important that we recognize that the defense of "big government" now has new claims to our intellectual attention. The criticism of neoliberal policy associated with the anti-globalization movement (which focuses on inequality and questions of global justice), and the critique of economic growth and development connected with the "happiness" research (which focuses on how the preoccupation with per capita income does not address human well-being and thus serves as a poor guide for public policy), in combination, enhance the demand for government policy to move beyond questions of the institutional framework, and to play an active role within the economic process. In addition, the tension around the globe associated with the threat of terrorism is interpreted as evidence of the increased need for enhanced government powers to combat the current situation. Politics, in other words,

Figure 1.1. The Economist's Role in Society

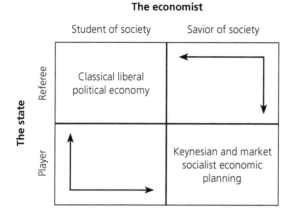

moves from setting the legal and political framework to having an active role within the economy.

Figure 1.1 tries to capture the economist's role in society and the tension with which the economist is confronted. As long as the economist is viewed as a student of society and the role of the state is limited to that of a referee, a classical liberal policy regime of laissez-faire can result and can be sustained. However, if the role of the state in the economic system is not limited, and, instead, is viewed as an important player in the economic game, then economists will gravitate toward viewing themselves (and demanding that others view them in the same light) as saviors of society via the tools of social control provided by economic theory and statistical analysis. Therefore, the two stable positions are the economist as student/state as referee and state as player/economist as savior (that is, the northwest and southeast quadrants). Outside of those stable relationships, the natural pull is toward either of these boxes because the other two situations are incentive incompatible.

Unfortunately, philosophical presumptions that envision economics as a tool for social engineering, rather than as a branch of moral philosophy, frame the debate in such a way as to bias the outcome in the direction of the state as player/economist as savior quadrant. There is a natural alliance between scientism and statism that is extremely hard to resist intellectually.[14] In addition, there are significant public-choice reasons why the natural pull in the policy world is toward the state as player/economist as savior quadrant. To agitate for the state as referee/economist as student quadrant is to forgo significant rents as an economist and to ask politicians to do the same.

Resistance of that natural tendency toward the state as player/economist as savior quadrant is the task of classical liberal political economists. The role of the economist in a free society from the perspective of classical liberalism is much humbler, yet still vitally important. The economist in a free society is charged with three tasks. The first is to be a teacher and to communicate to students and interested citizens the basic principles of the discipline of economics (the logic of choice, the economic forces at work in alternative systems, the principle of spontaneous order, and so on). The second is to be a student of society, to work hard as a scholar to understand the nature of economic processes through time. The third is to be a social critic, to analyze policies and economic ideas critically for their logical coherence and their vulnerability to opportunistic behavior. Through these roles, the economist can help fellow citizens become informed participants in the democratic process. And it is through pursuing these tasks competently that the economist can help break the policy inertia associated with the "iron triangle" of interest groups, bureaucratic structures, and politicians.[15]

Conclusion

The great classical economist John Stuart Mill pointed out:

> Ideas, unless outward circumstances conspire with them, have in general no very rapid or immediate efficacy in human affairs; and the most favorable outward circumstances may pass by, or remain inoperative, for want of ideas suitable to the conjuncture. But when the right circumstances and the right ideas meet, the effect is seldom slow in manifesting itself. ([1845] 2006, 370)

Ideas do ultimately rule the world, as John Maynard Keynes (1936, 383) taught us, but they must conspire with circumstances for their influence to be felt in the world of public policy. Sometimes, the changes that result from the conspiracy of economic ideas and political and historical circumstances can be for great good (e.g., the alliance of economists and abolitionists in the 19th century to eliminate slavery) and at others for great evil (e.g., the rise of communism and fascism in the first half of the 20th century).

Economic ideas play a vital role in the struggle to realize a better world. The hope for the 21st century—after the bloodshed of the 20th and the inauspicious beginning of this century in terrorism and militarism—resides in the liberal ideal of a free and prosperous cosmopolitan order. We need an ethic for strangers that transcends national borders, rather than an ethic of geopolitics that rewards allies and aggresses against perceived enemies. The civilizing role of commerce and trade, a role recognized by the classics, such as Voltaire, Montesquieu, Hume, and Smith, must be appreciated once again.

The economic advancement of countries, on the one hand, is a consequence of realizing the gains from trade (associated with the insights of Adam Smith on the division of labor) and the gains from innovation (associated with the insights of Joseph Schumpeter on entrepreneurship and creative destruction). The economic retardation of countries, on the other hand, is a consequence of foolish government policies that hamper exchange relations and curtail creative efforts of individuals. Therefore, the fate of humanity ultimately turns on the outcome of a "race" between Smithian gains from trade, Schumpeterian gains from innovation, and government folly in terms of policies that attempt to thwart exchange and curtail innovation. Rather than thwarting exchange and curtailing innovation, good rules of the game will thwart the predatory proclivities of rent-seeking actors and unleash the creative potential of mankind.

Notes

1. This chapter draws freely from chapter 3, which was originally published as "Liberty vs. Power in Economic Policy in the 20th and 21st Centuries" in the *Journal of Private Enterprise* 22, no.2 (Spring 2007): 7–36.
2. See, for example, McCloskey (2006) for a full discussion of the history of economic growth.
3. See R. J. Rummel's work *Death by Government* (1994). Rummel estimates the death toll as a result of direct government action against citizens in the 20th century to be 169,202,000 people.
4. See James Buchanan's insightful essay "The Potential and the Limits of Socially Organized Humankind" (1991). As Buchanan points out: "The great scientific discovery of the eighteenth century, out of which political economy (economics) emerged as an independent academic discipline, embodies the recognition that the complementary values of liberty, prosperity, and peace can be attained" (244). But while the historical experience provided empirical evidence of the ability of the classical liberal project to simultaneously achieve liberty, prosperity, and peace, the

project failed to capture the intellectual imaginations of leaders. "Why did social philosophers," Buchanan asks (245), "from the middle of the nineteenth century forward lose interest in the classical teachings? Why did the socialist century emerge, and with the active support of social philosophers?" Buchanan argues that the classical liberal vision proved vulnerable to claims about justice, and, in particular, claims about distributive justice. The fact that justice-driven moral purposes were exploited by interest-driven actors to produce undesirable outcomes in terms of liberty, prosperity, peace, and justice is beside the point for the critique of classical liberal political economy. The challenge today for political economists is to focus attention again on political structure (not political intervention) and to develop a concept of constitutional justice grounded in a realistic (not romantic) notion of politics that can resist the false claims of the welfare state and realize a social order that simultaneously achieves liberty, prosperity, peace, and justice.

5. Ludwig von Mises points out that once the state was attributed both benevolence and omniscience: "Then one could not help concluding that the infallible state was in a position to succeed in the conduct of production activities better than erring individuals. It would avoid all those errors that often frustrate the actions of entrepreneurs and capitalists. There would no longer be malinvestment or squandering of scarce factors of production; wealth would multiply. The 'anarchy' of production appears wasteful when contrasted with the planning of the *omniscient* state. The socialist mode of production then appears to be the only reasonable system, and the market economy seems the incarnation of unreason" ([1949] 1966, 692).

6. See Roy Weintraub (2002) where he discusses Alfred Marshall's role in the establishment of economics as a discipline at Cambridge. The classic critical reference on "scientism" is Hayek's *The Counter-Revolution of Science* (1952). Philip Mirowski's *More Heat than Light* (1989) and *Machine Dreams* (2002) explain how the formalistic aspirations of economists affected the development of economic thinking in the late 19th and early 20th centuries. See also Michael Bernstein's *A Perilous Progress* (2001) and Robert Nelson's *Economics as Religion* (2001) for a discussion of the discipline of economics and its relationship to public policy in the 20th century.

7. In his essay "Cost, Choice and Catallaxy," Buchanan (2005) provides an excellent discussion of how a slight revision to our understanding of the content of core theory can radically alter the framework for policy evaluation. In this instance, Buchanan is focusing on opportunity-cost reasoning and the idea of cost–benefit analysis in law and economics. In "High Priests and Lowly Philosophers: The Battle for the Soul of Economics" (Boettke, Coyne, and Leeson 2006), my coauthors and I argue that, when it is demanded of a discipline by the scientific establishment and public policy decision makers to provide results that it is constitutionally unable to achieve, the "soul" of the discipline and the intellectual integrity of its practitioners become at risk as those in the discipline strive to provide the results demanded. Science can quickly turn into nonsense, even if nobody wants to admit it.

8. In response to a criticism by William Baumol of his work, where Baumol defends the "impeccable logic" of the traditional Pigovian approach to welfare economics

with its calculation of taxes and subsidies to address the problems of externalities, Ronald Coase (1988, 185) states satirically: "My point was simply that such tax proposals are the stuff that dreams are made of. In my youth it was said that what was too silly to be said may be sung. In modern economics it may be put into mathematics."

9. For instance, consider the dismissive intellectual treatment that the work of P. T. Bauer on the economics of underdevelopment and the failure of foreign aid received in the 1960s and 1970s. My colleague Chris Coyne and I attended a conference in 2004 at Princeton University in honor of P. T. Bauer. In response to a question, Amartya Sen described the biggest difference between the intellectual state of play in 1964 and 2004 by stating that in 1964 the basic idea was that market economies were zero-sum games while politics represented opportunities for positive-sum games, whereas in 2004 politics were viewed as zero-sum games and markets as positive-sum games.

10. Consider the recognition by the Nobel Prize committee as weak evidence of this shift in thought: Friedman (1976), Stigler (1983), Buchanan (1987), Hayek ([1974] 1989), Coase (1992), Gary Becker (1993), North (1994), Lucas (1996), and Vernon Smith (2003). However, in the 1990s and the first decade of the 2000s, a resurgence of Keynesian-sympathetic political economy can be found in the works of Paul Krugman and Joseph Stiglitz, so there has been a counter-counterrevolution.

11. It should not be surprising that Abba Lerner's classic work was titled *The Economics of Control* (1944). However, see Milton Friedman's early critique (1953) of Lerner's work for a foreshadowing of the institutional emphasis that became a hallmark of the counterrevolution.

12. This is strikingly revealed in a comparative reading of *Poland's Jump to the Market Economy* (Sachs 1993) and *The End of Poverty* (Sachs 2005). Sachs's basic perspective of the "economist as savior" does not change, though the policy tools of salvation get different emphasis.

13. See my books *Why Perestroika Failed* (1993) for a discussion of the inconsistent reform efforts under Gorbachev and the difficulties in the policy changes initiated in the early Yeltsin years, and *Calculation and Coordination* (2001) for a further discussion of the general pattern of half measures and inconsistent policies through the 1990s in postcommunist Russia.

14. This was Hayek's theme in *The Counter-Revolution of Science* (1952), which constituted, in many ways, his most difficult intellectual challenge in trying to win acceptance of his ideas. For a discussion of the role of Hayek's "Abuse of Reason" project in his lifework, see Bruce Caldwell's *Hayek's Challenge* (2004, 232–60).

15. Henry Simons argued in his University of Chicago economics syllabus that the primary function of economic study was as a "prophylactic against popular fallacies" (1983, 3). Following this line of argument, the reader is encouraged to look at W. H. Hutt's *Politically Impossible . . . ?* (1971), which challenged economists to speak the truth about economic policy rather than worry about the pragmatic concern of "political feasibility."

References

Bastiat, Frédéric. 1996. *Economic Sophisms*. Edited and translated by Arthur Goddard. Irvington-on-Hudson, NY: Foundation for Economic Education.

Becker, Gary. 1993. "The Economic Way of Looking at Life." *Journal of Political Economy* 101 (3): 385–409.

Bernstein, Michael. 2001. *A Perilous Progress: Economists and Public Purpose in Twentieth-Century America*. Princeton, NJ: Princeton University Press.

Boettke, Peter J. 1993. *Why Perestroika Failed: The Politics and Economics of Socialist Transformation*. New York: Routledge.

———. 2001. *Calculation and Coordination: Essays on Socialism and Transitional Political Economy*. New York: Routledge.

Boettke, Peter J., Christopher J. Coyne, and Peter T. Leeson. 2006. "High Priests and Lowly Philosophers: The Battle for the Soul of Economics." *Case Western Reserve Law Review* 56 (3): 551–68.

Boulding, Kenneth E. 1948. "Samuelson's Foundations: The Role of Mathematics in Economics." *Journal of Political Economy* 56 (3): 187–99.

Buchanan, James M. 1987. "The Constitution of Economic Policy." *American Economic Review* 77 (3): 243–50.

———. 1991. "The Potential and the Limits of Socially Organized Humankind." In *The Economics and the Ethics of Constitutional Order*, edited by James Buchanan, 239–51. Ann Arbor: University of Michigan Press.

———. 2005. "Cost, Choice and Catallaxy." In *The Origins of Law and Economics*, edited by Charles Rowley and Francesco Parisi, 156–67. Cheltenham, UK: Edward Elgar.

Caldwell, Bruce. 2004. *Hayek's Challenge*. Chicago: University of Chicago Press.

Coase, Ronald. 1988. *The Firm, the Market, and the Law*. Chicago: University of Chicago Press.

———. 1992. "The Institutional Structure of Production." *American Economic Review* 82 (4): 713–19.

Friedman, Milton. 1953. "Lerner on the Economics of Control." In *Essays in Positive Economics*, edited by Milton Friedman, 301–19. Chicago: University of Chicago Press.

———. 1976. "Nobel Lecture: Inflation and Unemployment." *Journal of Political Economy* 85 (3): 451–72.

Friedman, Milton, and Rose Friedman. 1984. *Tyranny of the Status Quo*. London: Secker and Warburg.

Hayek, F. A. 1931. *Prices and Production*. London: Routledge and Kegan Paul.

———. 1948. *Individualism and Economic Order*. London: Routledge and Kegan Paul.

———. 1952. *The Counter-Revolution of Science: Studies on the Abuse of Reason*. Glencoe, IL: Free Press.

———. [1974] 1989. "The Pretence of Knowledge." *American Economic Review* 79 (6): 3–7.

Hutt, W. H. 1971. *Politically Impossible . . . ?* London: Institute of Economic Affairs.

Keynes, John Maynard. 1936. *The General Theory of Employment, Interest and Money.* New York: Harcourt, Brace and World.

Lerner, Abba. 1944. *The Economics of Control.* New York: Macmillan.

Lucas, Robert E. 1996. "Monetary Neutrality." *Journal of Political Economy* 104 (4): 661–82.

Madison, James. [1788] 1963. "Federalist No. 51." In *The Debate on the Constitution,* edited by Bernard Bailyn. New York: Library of America.

McCloskey, Deirdre N. 2006. *The Bourgeois Virtues: Ethics for an Age of Commerce.* Chicago: University of Chicago Press.

Mill, John Stuart. [1845] 2006. *The Claims of Labour: The Collected Works of John Stuart Mill, Volume 4: Essays on Economics and Society, 1824–1845.* Indianapolis: Liberty Fund.

———. [1848] 1967. *Principles of Political Economy, with Some of Their Applications to Social Philosophy.* New York: Augustus M. Kelley.

Mirowski, Philip. 1989. *More Heat than Light: Economics as Social Physics, Physics as Nature's Economics.* Cambridge: Cambridge University Press.

———. 2002. *Machine Dreams: Economics Becomes a Cyborg Science.* Cambridge: Cambridge University Press.

Mises, Ludwig von. [1949] 1966. *Human Action: A Treatise on Economics.* Chicago: Henry Regnery.

Nelson, Robert. 2001. *Economics as Religion: From Samuelson to Chicago and Beyond.* University Park: Pennsylvania State University Press.

North, Douglass C. 1994. "Economic Performance through Time." *American Economic Review* 84 (3): 359–68.

Rummel, R. J. 1994. *Death by Government.* New Brunswick, NJ: Transaction Publishers.

Sachs, Jeffrey. 1993. *Poland's Jump to the Market Economy.* Boston: MIT Press.

———. 2005. *The End of Poverty: Economic Possibilities for Our Time.* New York: Penguin Press.

Samuelson, Paul. 1947. *Foundations of Economic Analysis.* Cambridge, MA: Harvard University Press.

Say, Jean-Baptiste. [1820] 1971. *A Treatise on Political Economy.* New York: Augustus M. Kelley.

Simons, Henry C. 1983. *The Simons' Syllabus.* Edited by Gordon Tullock. Fairfax, VA: Center for the Study of Public Choice at George Mason University.

Smith, Adam. [1776] 1976. *An Inquiry into the Nature and Causes of the Wealth of Nations.* Chicago: University of Chicago Press.

Smith, Vernon L. 2003. "Constructivist and Ecological Rationality in Economics." *American Economic Review* 93 (3): 465–508.

Stigler, George. 1983. "The Process and Progress of Economics." *Journal of Political Economy* 91 (4): 529–45.

Weber, Max. 1927. *General Economic History.* New York: Greenberg.

Weintraub, Roy. 2002. *How Economics Became a Mathematical Science.* Durham, NC: Duke University Press.

Chapter 2
Economics and Public Administration

Little else is requisite to carry a state to the highest degree of opulence from the lowest barbarism, but peace, easy taxes, and a tolerable administration of justice, all the rest being brought about by the natural course of things.

—Adam Smith
Essays on Philosophical Subjects ([1755] 1982, 322)

Where the complex economic conditions of life necessitate social coordination and planning, there can sensible men of good will be expected to invoke the authority and creativity of government.

—Paul Samuelson
Economics (1948, 153)

What is the role of the state in economic development? This question has puzzled thinkers since before Adam Smith. And economists even to this day continue to puzzle this question, for what else is the contemporary discourse over state capacity in development other than a continuation of this centuries-long conversation?[1] What is needed in the effort to move the conversation along is to unpack Adam Smith's claim that all that is needed is a "tolerable administration of justice."

In order to do that, however, we need to revisit the analysis of public administration. There are, of course, several layers to that analysis. At one level, we must first and foremost determine what is the appropriate scale

Presidential address at the 86th meeting of the Southern Economic Association in Tampa, Florida, November 18, 2017. Published in *Southern Economic Journal* 84, no. 4 (2018): 938–59.

and scope of government action. This is not just a question of deciding on what the appropriate public policy would be, but also who will possess the appropriate decision-making authority entrusted with the implementation of public policy. Whether this occurs at the local, state, federal, or international level is just one question that must be addressed. We must also consider the particular content of policies, their implementation, and their management. My conjecture is that how the economics discipline answered these questions of public administration in the years between Adam Smith and Paul Samuelson dictated the character of the economic science that was practiced. And it continues to do so till today.

In a recent book, *Building State Capability*, Matt Andrews, Lant Pritchett, and Michael Woolcock (2017) examine what we have learned from the efforts to orchestrate economic development, to guide the transition process, and to draw the lessons learned on how to better conceptualize the task for the future efforts. In doing this, they are recognizing a point made by Douglass North in *Structure and Change in Economic History* (1981), where he said that the state, with its ability to define and enforce property rights, can provide the greatest impetus for economic development and human betterment, but can also be the biggest threat to development and betterment through its predatory capacity. James Buchanan, in *The Limits of Liberty* (1975), stated the dilemma that must be confronted as follows: the constitutional contract must be designed in such a way that empowers the protective state (law and order) and the productive state (public goods) while constraining the predatory state (redistribution and rent-seeking). If the constitutional contract cannot be so constructed, then economic development and human betterment will not follow. In other words, to realize productive specialization and peaceful social cooperation, an *institutional framework of governance* must be established, and absent that establishment, those great gains will be forgone.[2]

Institutions, as North (1990, 3; 1991, 97) has defined them, are the humanly devised rules of the social game, and their enforcement. These rules can be the by-product of evolutionary forces and can be the informal rules backed by social sanctions, or they can be the formal establishment of law and legislation backed by the apparatus of the state. As my colleague Peter Leeson (2017) likes to say, rules tell us what is permissible in any given society, but the existing constraints tell us what is feasible. Just as there is a production possibilities frontier, there is also an institutional possibilities frontier that is defined by technology and human capital at any given point in time (Boettke, Coyne, et al. 2005). Institutions cannot simply be transplanted as if it was costless to do so. And one of the most important constraints to the transplanting of formal institutions is the existing informal institutions, or what we have dubbed "institutional stickiness" (Boettke 2001, 248–65; Boettke, Coyne, and Leeson 2008).

The observational genius of the 20th century Yogi Berra once captured the essence of this argument while watching a rookie ball player attempting to imitate the batting stance of Frank Robinson, the recent triple crown winner, when he advised, "If you can't imitate him, don't copy him." Best practice in the realm of "tolerable administration of justice" seems to have a similar problem. The countries plagued by poverty cannot simply copy the government institutions of those that are not so plagued by poverty. They are constrained at any point in time by the existing institutional possibilities frontier, and thus must shift the institutional possibilities frontier as technology and human capital adjust to find the constitutional contract that can effectively empower the protective and productive state, while effectively constraining the predatory state (Leeson 2014, 155–210).

To put this in the language of Buchanan (see Brennan and Buchanan 1980) and Mancur Olson (2000) would be to translate the development puzzle into finding the institutional configuration of governance that ensures that the revenue-maximizing strategy for the state is also the wealth-maximizing strategy for the economy.[3] Such a configuration would align with the encompassing interests of those in positions of power and privilege, and would be within the constrained set of any given state of technology and human capital. This is a decidedly unromantic view of the political economy of development, but it does provide a way of thinking about state capacity in development that avoids the problems associated with viewing development and human betterment as merely technical problems to be addressed independent of institutional configurations and the costs and benefits of administering governance.

The problem of governance and administration is to be found in all economies—from the poorest of the poor to the most lavishly rich—and in all areas of applied economics, from public finance and monetary policy to antitrust to environmental regulation. And governance and administration are tricky areas of research because they constitute realms where the mechanisms identified within market settings that serve to coordinate activity are absent, yet we need to identify and analyze the alternative mechanisms at work (Boettke, Coyne, and Leeson 2011). Of course, this was the impetus behind public-choice analysis—or what Buchanan and Gordon Tullock originally called "Non-Market Decision Making."[4]

My argument is structured as follows. Section 2 will revisit the theory of economic policy in the classics and the moderns and their emphasis on the *institutional framework* within which economic activity takes place, as well as the positive program for laissez-faire that was evident in the work of the classical political economists and the early neoclassical economists. Section 3 will discuss the debate that took place in the 20th century over capabilities and capacities in public administration. Section 4 will address why this debate and how we understand it matter for the practice of political economy—teaching, research, and policy. Section 5 concludes.[5]

The Classical Political Economists and Public Administration

Lionel Robbins's *The Theory of Economic Policy in English Classical Political Economy* ([1952] 1965, 12) argues that the classical theory of economic policy must be seen not in juxtaposition to a positive theory of state action but "in combination with the theory of law and the functions of government which its authors also propounded; the idea of freedom *in vacuo* was entirely alien to their conceptions." Adam Smith and his contemporaries never argued that the individual pursuit of self-interest will always and everywhere result in the public interest, but rather that the individual pursuit of self-interest within a specific set of institutional arrangements—namely, well-defined and enforced private property rights—would produce such a result. Though as Robbins writes, "You cannot understand their attitude to any important concrete measure of policy unless you understand their belief with regard to the nature and effects of the system of spontaneous-cooperation" ([1952] 1965, 12). The system of spontaneous cooperation, or economic freedom, does not come about absent a "firm framework of law and order." The "invisible hand," according to the classical economists, "is not the hand of some god or some natural agency independent of human effort; it is the hand of the lawgiver, the hand which withdraws from the sphere of the pursuit of self-interest those possibilities which do not harmonize with the public good" (Robbins [1952] 1965, 56).

In other words, the market mechanism works as described in the theory of the "invisible hand" because an institutional configuration was provided for by a prior nonmarket decision-making process. The correct institutions of governance must be in place for economic life to take place (within those institutions).

Social life always exists inside an *institutional framework*. Whether social life exhibits Adam Smith's human propensity to "truck, barter, and exchange" or Thomas Hobbes's human capacity to "pillage and plunder" is a function of the *institutional framework* within which social life is played out. It is the *framework* that determines the marginal benefit/marginal cost calculus that individuals face in pursuing sociability. If the rewards for productive specialization and peaceful cooperation exceed those of predation and confiscation, then the Smithian expansion of commercial and civil society will follow. But if the calculus tends the other way, then the Hobbesian depiction of life as being "nasty, brutish, and short" will materialize.

Most of human history, in fact, is best characterized as Hobbesian. But starting with the historical period that triggered what Deirdre McCloskey has dubbed the "Great Enrichment,"[6] humanity took a different turn. McCloskey puts great emphasis on the ideas, and especially the societal "talk" about these ideas, in her explanation of this transformation. There was, in her historical narrative, a general shift in attitudes toward commercial life, and an attribution of dignity and respect to ordinary people "giving it a go" in the world of commerce that triggered the process of development. I agree with the primacy of ideas in economic, political, and social history, but for my purposes here the focus is on the *framework* that these ideas legitimated, and the practices that were engendered by that *framework*.[7]

As Ludwig von Mises put it:

> Saving, capital accumulation, is the agency that has transformed step-by-step the awkward search for food on the part of savage cave dwellers into the modern ways of industry. The pace-makers of this evolution were the ideas that created the *institutional framework* within which capital accumulation was rendered safe by the principle of private ownership of the means of production. Every step forward on the way toward prosperity is the effect of saving. The most ingenious technological inventions would be practically useless if the capital goods required for their utilization had not been accumulated by saving. ([1956] 2006, 24; emphasis added)

The pursuit of productive specialization and peaceful cooperation requires security and stability of possession, the keeping of promises, and the transference of property by consent (see Hume [1739] 2000, 311–31). Where property is insecure, promises are not kept, and violent taking characterizes the social situation, human sociability will be truncated and the Hobbesian propensities will prevail. On the other hand, when the social situation is characterized by property, contract, and consent, the Smithian propensities prevail and peace and prosperity prevail.

Smith's argument in *The Wealth of Nations* ([1776] 1976) must be understood in this two-stage manner. Yes, the greatest improvements in the material conditions of mankind are due to the refinement in the division of labor. But as Smith pointed out, the division of labor is limited by the extent of the market. The process of development follows from the expansion of the market, and thus the refinement of the division of labor. That fundamental cause of development—as mentioned already by Mises (and stressed by McCloskey)—is ideas that give rise to the *institutional framework* that in turn makes savings and capital accumulation safe. As Adam Smith put it:

> It is only under the shelter of the civil magistrate that the owner of that valuable property, which is acquired by the labour of many years, or perhaps of many successive generations, can sleep a single night in security. He is at all times surrounded by unknown enemies, whom, though he never provoked, he can never appease, and from whose injustice he can be protected only by the powerful arm of the civil magistrate continually held up to chastise it. The acquisition of valuable and extensive property, therefore, necessarily requires the establishment of civil government. ([1776] 1976, 232)

This is the foundation for Smith's "tolerable administration of justice."

The early neoclassical economists in the wake of the marginal revolution in value theory did not see their task as all that radically different from Smith's.[8] They simply had a new set of analytical tools to explain value, exchange, and productive activity *within* the market economy. Many of the early neoclassical theorists, such as Alfred Marshall and Frank Knight, possessed a deep appreciation of the *institutional framework* within which economic activity takes place. However, most theorists of this period simply began their analysis by assuming well-defined and strictly enforced property rights, and then proceeded from that starting point. In other words, the *institutional framework* was fixed and given for analysis, and not an object of analytical study.

This "given" aspect of the *institutional framework* is critical because it soon led to the *framework* being ignored in analysis altogether as economic thought evolved in the 20th century. This ignoring of institutions was most evident in the socialist calculation debate between Mises, F. A. Hayek, and Robbins on the one side and Oskar Lange, Abba Lerner, and Abram Bergson on the other. This debate has been a focus of my own research throughout my career, so I will not revisit it here, but will leverage the debate only to get to the point about public administration.[9]

The Mises-Hayek-Robbins side of the dispute stressed not merely the role of relative prices in the coordination of economic activity, but the *institutional framework* that made possible the configuration of the price system in the first place. As Hayek put it in the heat of the debate: "The fact is that it has never been denied by anybody, except socialists, that these formal principles [optimality conditions] *ought* to apply to a socialist society, and the question raised by Mises and others was not whether they ought to apply but whether they could in practice be applied in the absence of a market" (1948, 183).

In the analysis of the market system, prices have pride of place. Economic analysis flows from the recognition of scarcity and the fact that all choices are made within given constraints. For analytical tractability, the institutional context can be taken as part of the background conditions. Thus, during the first decades of the neoclassical refinements of economic theory, the analysis proceeded with a given institutional environment of fully defined and strictly enforced private property rights and freedom of contract embodied in the rule of law.

My point is simple: the classical political economists and the early heirs to that intellectual tradition saw economic activity as embedded within an institutional context and never as acontextual. Smith "derived" his famous "invisible hand" theorem from the self-interest postulate *via* institutional analysis.[10] The analytical devil was to be found in the institutional details.

It is relatively easy to see why, though, that as economic theory went through technical refinements in the early 20th century, historicist (e.g., Gustav Schmoller and Werner Sombart) and institutionalist (e.g., Thorstein Veblen and Clarence Edwin Ayers) critics tended to target the historical and institutional context as the source of denying the external validity of economics, and that defenders of economic theory would strive for an institutionally antiseptic theory. Math is math, after all. The relationship between averages and the marginal, to take one example, is true independent of whether we are talking about student test scores or the production costs within firms. That relationship also holds whether we are talking about students or firms in China or in the United States. And it is true independent of the motivations of the different actors.

The static optimality conditions of a competitive equilibrium possess this mathematical quality. Profit-maximization requires marginal revenue to equal marginal cost; cost-minimization requires production at the minimum point on the average cost curve; and so forth. All least-cost technologies must be deployed, and all opportunity costs in production and consumption must be taken into account if we are going to exhaust the gains from trade and from technology. If we do so, all the opportunities for mutually beneficial exchange that could be pursued will have been pursued, and all technological efficiencies will have been realized. As the terms imply, the pattern of resource utilization will be optimal. Logic conquers historical context, and economic theory is indeed a science on par ontologically with any of the hard sciences, including physics. This understanding of economic theory transformed the discipline from a branch of social philosophy to a new social physics, and the epistemological claims about economics transformed as well.

Let's cycle back for a moment to the feasibility of socialist economic planning and what this transformation of economic theory implied for the debate. Mises ([1920] 1975) had issued the challenge that, due to the inability to engage in rational economic calculation, socialist planning could not deliver on its stated goals of rationalizing production. Absent private ownership in the means of production, Mises argued, there would be no prices established on the market that could form the basis for rational economic calculation. Economic calculation enables *market* decision makers to sort out from an array of technologically feasible production projects those which are economically viable from those that are not. Economic calculation is a waste identifier and eliminator. By definition, the socialist aspiration of the rationalization of production requires that the waste of resources and errors in investment be eliminated. Mises's criticism was decisive and cut to the core of the promise of socialism.

This was also purely a point of positive economics. Mises did not question the socialists' ends. At the time of his original article, socialism meant something—the rationalization of production through the abolition of private property and commodity production. Mises simply asked if abolition of private property and commodity production was coherent with the rationalization of production, and he demonstrated it was not. Technological efficiency is not enough to answer the economic question of the efficiency of resource use. Prices without property rights are an illusion.

In an ironic twist of argument, Lange (1936, 55) actually accused Mises of being an institutionalist for making this point. But the fact that Lange said this should alert you to the changes that were taking place in the economic theorist's self-understanding from 1900 to 1930. Since math is math and institutions do not matter, if someone invokes institutional differences to explain comparative performance, then he has failed to appreciate the universal nature of economic theory. But to Mises, it was precisely the universality of economic theory that enabled him to understand why institutions matter for economic performance.[11]

Monetary economic calculation works by constantly revealing errors in decision-making, and the complex apparatus of market signals will continually prod and cajole participants to make less erroneous decisions than before. Adjustment and adaptation are unending in the market as the production plans of some must mesh with the consumption demands of others for the advanced coordination of economic activities through time.

But what happens when we move outside the realm of the market economy? Public administration begins where the realm of rational economic calculation ends. As Ludwig von Mises put it: "Where economic calculation is unfeasible, bureaucratic methods are indispensable" ([1949] 1966, 311). To put this in a concrete way, the rules of bureaucratic management are going to have to attempt to do for government services what property, prices, and profit and loss do within the market setting. And make no mistake, government decision makers are going to have to weigh tradeoffs, and they will face—however imperfectly—budget constraints. Again, as Mises (Mises [1949] 1966: 309) points out: "There is no doubt that the services rendered by the police department of the City of New York could be considerably improved by trebling the budgetary allocation. But the question is whether or not this improvement would be considerable enough to justify either the restriction of the services rendered by other departments—e.g., those of the department of sanitation—or the restriction of the private consumption of the taxpayers" ([1949] 1966, 309). But *how* are government decision makers going to accomplish this?

Debate over the Capabilities of Public Administration

The epigraph from Samuelson's *Economics* that I use at the beginning of this chapter reflects the shift in the expectations for public administration from the classics to the moderns. The moderns simply expected more from public administration than the classics. By the time of the writings of John Maynard Keynes and certainly by the time of Samuelson, the sort of Smithian concerns about "authority" and "arrogance" were secondary at best.[12] The Progressive Era transformed the expectations about public administration, and you cannot accurately understand the fate of economic thinking in the 20th century unless this transformation is taken into account.

In one of the most important books in the history of American political life—Herbert Croly's *The Promise of American Life* (1909)—a contrast is drawn between Thomas Jefferson and Alexander Hamilton, where Hamilton is taken to symbolize professional bureaucracy and a large and effective national government. As America shifted in the 19th and beginning of the 20th century from a predominately agrarian economy to an industrial one, Croly argues, the Jeffersonian vision of extreme individualism was no longer a viable model of government for America. In the industrial age, government could no longer be content with protecting negative rights; it needed to actively promote the general welfare.[13] To achieve this, Croly envisioned that we could not rely on the "invisible hand" of the market, but instead must rely on the very "visible hand" of modern public administration, including a three-pronged program that entailed the nationalization of large corporations, the strengthening of labor unions, and a strong central government.

This progressive vision of government has been in the public imagination of the elite ever since. It is what guided Keynes's turn to the administrative state to manage investment and maintain full employment levels of output; it is what guided Samuelson's neoclassical synthesis that would enlist the administrative state to correct for macroeconomic imbalances and microeconomic inefficiencies; it was the vision behind John Kenneth Galbraith's demand that the administrative state be structured to reinforce the countervailing force to manage the relationship between business, labor, and the public sector; and it is the vision that governs the contemporary recipes for the activist administrative state that one can read in Paul Krugman, Joseph Stiglitz, and Larry Summers.

The transformation of public administration from the democratic form of Jefferson to the bureaucratic form of Hamilton and Woodrow Wilson is laid out in detail in such work as Dwight Waldo's *The Administrative State* (1948). The romantic vision of democratic citizenry, Waldo explained, needed to be replaced by a more modern Wilsonian understanding of government efficiency. Citizens had to come to understand that there are two essential building blocks in governing a modern society: politics and public administration. In a telling passage, Waldo (1948, 132) explains how the older arguments about constraints on government no longer resonate with modernity as we now believe in the goodness and rationality of men, rather than in their moral weaknesses. Man does not suffer from original sin, and is therefore not "fallen" and in need of checks and balances. Instead, it is man's traditional institutions that are bad, and thus must give way to new institutions so that man's goodness and rationality will be enabled to grow. True democracy means popular enlightenment and control over society. This requires centralization and efficient management to achieve the good society. As Wilson put it: "Large powers and unhampered discretion seem to me the indispensable conditions of responsibility" (1887, 213). The danger isn't in concentrations of power, but in divided, disjointed, and decentralized government.

To cycle back to the socialist calculation debate, note how strange it must have been to confront the economists' doubts concerning the efficiency of administrative planning of economic life with this Progressive Era intellectual background. It is no exaggeration to say that Hayek's arguments such as those developed in *The Road to Serfdom* ([1944] 2007, 94–96) ran the exact opposite from the emerging consensus methodologically, analytically, and practically. His claim that "if we had to rely on conscious central planning for the growth of our industrial system, it would never have reached the degree of differentiation, complexity, and flexibility it has attained" (96) would have to be viewed as anathema to the Progressive mind as Tocquevillian concerns about democratic despotism.

One way to interpret the evolution of property rights economics, law and economics, public-choice economics, and market process economics in the second half of the 20th century is as part of a long intellectual march to reclaim the classical political economy and early neoclassical research program on how alternative institutional arrangements enable individuals to pursue productive specialization and realize the gains from social cooperation. Hayek, of course, was not alone in offering a challenge to the *positive analysis* of the administrative state and public policy (see Buchanan [1979] 2015). In the 1940s, Hayek was in many ways merely pursuing a line of argument long developed by Frank Knight and Ludwig von Mises but would later be joined by other voices.

Milton Friedman pointed out, in his *Journal of Political Economy* review (1947) of Lerner's *The Economics of Control* (1946), that while Lerner's technical analysis was logically unassailable, the work was nevertheless not very helpful for the subject at hand because it failed to address the administrative costs of public policy. Friedman's essay is worth a very careful reading to get a good sense of the extent of the problem. "The institutional problems," Friedman points out, "are largely neglected and, where introduced, treated by assertion rather than analysis" (1947, 405). Friedman provides a nice summary of what would later be known as his argument about the long and variable lag in public policy, and arguments on how rules will outperform discretion in government policy. And Friedman suggests that the technically competent and certainly capable economic thinker Lerner is misled in his analysis because his focus is on how society ought to work rather than how it does work, and thus on optimality conditions rather than how those might be reasonably achieved in any real-world setting. As Friedman points out, in order for Lerner's system to work, not only must the economic managers possess intentions to pursue the public good, but also they must be able to translate those intentions into practice costlessly and flawlessly. So despite the fact that Lerner engages, as Friedman describes it, a brilliant exercise in logic, the analysis falls short of the author's considerable gifts as a thinker because Lerner's intellectual talents "have been employed in a vacuum and have not been combined with a realistic appraisal of the administrative problems of economic institutions or of their social and political implications" (Friedman 1947, 416).

The debate over the capabilities of public administration follows a pattern that Peter Leeson and I identify in *The Economic Role of the State* (2015)—that the basic presumptions in political economy oscillate between optimism and pessimism about private and public ordering. In the Samuelsonian consensus, there was a pessimism about private ordering due to monopoly power, externalities, and macroeconomic instability, and optimism about antitrust legislation, regulation of industry, fiscal authority to tax or subsidize, and the use of monetary and fiscal policy to provide aggregate demand management. The classical political economists, and the post–World War II challengers to the hegemony of neoclassical synthesis, on the other hand, were more optimistic about the self-regulating capacity of the market economy, and more pessimistic about the idea of government as a corrective.

We cannot solve this debate, but we can insist that there are argumentative targets that must be met. Those who favor public administration over the market mechanism must at least acknowledge the questions raised earlier: How is government going to accomplish the task of economic management? What alternative mechanisms in public administration will serve the role that property, prices, and profit and loss serve within the market setting?

Let us consider the following example—a vacant piece of land in a downtown area of a growing city. The plot of land could be used as a garage, which would complement efforts to develop commercial life downtown. Or, it could be used to build a park, encouraging city residents to enjoy green space and outdoor activities. Alternatively, it could be used to locate a school, which would help stimulate investment in human capital. All three potential uses are worthy endeavors. If this was to be determined by the market, then the problem would be solved via the price mechanism and the willingness and the ability to pay. But if led by government, the use of this land will need to be determined by public deliberation and voting. We cannot just assume that the "right" decision on the use of this public space will be made in the public arena. In fact, due to a variety of problems associated with preference aggregation mechanisms, we might have serious doubts as to any claim of "efficiency" in such deliberations.

In *The Politics of Bureaucracy*, Tullock (1965, 161ff) asked his readers to consider the example of management of spare parts of the United States Army's fleet of motor vehicles. The army has attempted to standardize in an effort to streamline maintenance. Yet as Tullock points out, despite these efforts, the Army throughout the post–World War II era was plagued with a spare parts problem. On the other hand, there appears to be little to no difficulty during this same period with the United States trucking industry with nonstandardized vehicles. Tullock's suggestion is simple: the dynamic adjustments to changing conditions guided by prices, enticed by profit, and penalized by loss in the market work, while the bureaucratic management is too inflexible to make the necessary adaptations.

More recently, Richard Wagner, in *Politics as a Peculiar Business* (2016, 146ff), uses the example of a marina surrounded by shops, hotels, and restaurants—think of Tampa, Florida. The marina, shops, hotels, and restaurants operate on market principles, but the maintenance of the roads and waterways are objects of collective decision-making. Road maintenance and waterway dredging, for example, will be provided by government bureaus, but how well those decisions are made will affect the operation of the commercial enterprises, and the viability of the commercial enterprises will no doubt influence the urgency and care of these bureaucratic efforts.

Buchanan's (1949) great innovation in the theory of public finance was to challenge the conventional wisdom that in discussions of government expenditures we could assume, for the sake of analytical tractability, a unified state with a God's-eye view of the situation—what he called the "fisc." If instead, we reject the "fisc" and open ourselves to the study of how public choices are in fact made within a democratic system of governance, we will have to study the bumping and bargaining that constitutes politics. We will need to postulate some form of "invisible hand" theorizing with regard to collective decision-making that provides the coherence to the complexity of the entangled political economy of modernity. Consider the example Buchanan (1964) used in his Southern Economic Association presidential address of mosquito abatement programs and the political bargaining required between those located near the swamp and those located downtown far from the swamp. How do such bargains get negotiated, and how coherent are the outcomes in a means/ends sense?

Remember that property, prices, and profit and loss are absent in government activity, so other mechanisms operate to serve as proxies for the functions of incentivizing, guiding, luring, and disciplining decisions. Public administration begins where the realm of rational economic calculation ceases to be applicable. Socialism sought to make all decisions via public administration, but even Smith's night watchman state must engage in a "tolerable administration," so how is that accomplished if we do not permit the God's-eye view assumption?[14]

In *Free to Choose*, Milton and Rose Friedman ([1980] 1990) argue that there is indeed an "invisible hand" in operation in politics analogous to that which operates in the market, but with the opposite effect. Whereas Smith's "invisible hand" squared the pursuit of self-interest with the achievement of the public interest due to the institutional environment of private property, prices, and profit and loss, public-sector decision-making engenders a process where "an individual who intends only to serve the public interest by fostering government intervention is led by an invisible hand to promote private interests, which was no part of his intention" (5–6).

This is how the Friedmans explain the frustrating outcomes that arise from the expansion of government policies. Government intervention in the economy grew throughout the 20th century both in scale and, perhaps more importantly, in scope. Government grew because it failed, and it continued to fail because it grew. It was also this recognition of the frustration with government failure in matters both big (such as military interventions) and small (such as garbage collection) that led Elinor and Vincent Ostrom (1971) to publish their article in the *Public Administration Review*, introducing public-choice analysis to the discipline of public administration.[15] In *The Intellectual Crisis in American Public Administration*, Vincent Ostrom wrote: "If the methods of studying, teaching, and practicing the subject matter of public administration have become problematical then the profession cannot have much confidence in what it professes. The practice of a profession rests upon the validity of the knowledge it professes. When the confidence of a profession in the essential validity of its knowledge has been shattered, that profession should be extraordinarily modest about the professional advice it renders while keeping up its appearances" ([1973] 2008, 10).

The social pathologies that continue to plague Western democratic societies (let alone less developed countries and failed and weak states) have seemed to defy solution with the conventional approach to public administration. A new paradigm is required, the Ostroms argued, that would once again be grounded in fallible but capable human actors and capture the self-governing capacity of citizens within collective entities. As Vincent Ostrom put it: "The major task in the next generation will be to lay new foundations for the study of public administration. If these foundations are well laid, we should see a new political science join a new economics and a new sociology in establishing the basis for a major new advance upon the frontiers of public administration" ([1973] 2008, 5).

We are still in the process of laying those foundations, and breaking out of the "iron cage" of bureaucratic public administration mindset has proved more difficult than simply identifying the social pathologies that the model has not only failed to ameliorate but has actually arguably exacerbated.

Why Does All This Matter?

If Smith is right, then answering the question of what the "tolerable administration of justice" is determines the economic fate of millions, perhaps billions of souls. Getting this answer right matters because the overadministration of economic life has significant costs, yet the underadministration also leaves "big bills" on the sidewalk due to ill-defined and weakly enforced property rights and general ambiguity in the economic environment.

To escape the habits of thought that follow from the bureaucratic public administration mindset, we must open ourselves to the possibility and study of alternative governance providers rather than continuing to focus exclusively on questions of the state's capacity to govern. Elinor Ostrom's (1990) work on communal governance systems that enable covenants without swords is but one example. Her choice of studying common-pool resource problems is particularly telling because her case selection was in areas where we would least expect bottom-up solutions to emerge through institutional craftsmanship within the community. We economists too often stack the deck intellectually with our model choices, and thus stifle our imaginations with respect to the amazing array of ways and means that human beings can enter into mutually beneficial relationships with one another. As Elinor Ostrom (9) points out, the centrality of the prisoners' dilemma model in our thinking about social cooperation is a case in point. The prisoners in the dilemma, she reminds us, are prisoners who are incapable of changing the constraints. "I would rather," Ostrom states, "address the question of how to enhance the capabilities of those involved to change the constraining rules of the games to lead to outcomes other than remorseless tragedies" (7).

Ostrom's *Governing the Commons* demonstrates that acts of public entrepreneurship and constitutional craftsmanship occur across time and place and among diverse populations. She unearthed a diversity of institutional forms which exhibit general traits of social rules that transform situations of conflict into opportunities for social cooperation through limiting access, assigning accountability, and introducing graduated penalties. Self-governing democratic societies, her work demonstrates, are grounded in mediating conflicts and finding rules that enable individuals to live better together than they ever could in isolation. Traditional public administration, with its top-down and expert rule, does not fit with this vision of democratic self-governance.

More recent work by Edward Stringham (2015), David Skarbek (2014), and Peter Leeson (2014) also challenges the conventional wisdom of bureaucratic public administration. Stringham studies several profit-driven entities—both historical and contemporary—that offer governance services and enable individuals to realize productive specialization and peaceful social cooperation in a variety of difficult situations. Skarbek's work on prison gangs shows how even those who are seemingly trapped in a remorseless tragedy and prone to devolve into conflict will find ways to establish binding rules that minimize conflict and permit cooperation. Leeson shows through a variety of historical cases how mechanisms of self-governance emerge and work to realize social cooperation among diverse populations better than what could reasonably be expected in these environments from formal governmental arrangements.

These examples show that a variety of entities can serve in the capacity of providing "public" administration. We are not limited only to a monopoly provider. It must be admitted that this subtle change from talking about government to discussing governance is actually quite a radical shift in perspective in the field of public administration. But this is what is needed I would argue, and economics as a discipline will need to adjust accordingly as well, if we want to enhance our understanding of the institutional foundations of human sociability.

Bruno Frey (2001) presented a vision of government without territorial monopoly. His idea of overlapping competing jurisdiction is one such idea of how to cultivate the sort of public learning the Ostroms advocated for with the idea of polycentricity.[16] In his book *Doing Bad by Doing Good* (2013), Christopher Coyne demonstrates repeatedly the dysfunction of even well-meaning efforts of public administration pursuing the top-down logic. On the other hand, Virgil Storr, Stefanie Haeffele, and Laura Grube (2015) demonstrate how, even in the wake of disasters, the local and nimble entrepreneurial solutions in the private and nonprofit sectors provide the vibrancy and creativity that enable successful recovery. Also see the work done on the Katrina project organized by our team of researchers at the Mercatus Center at George Mason University for a multidisciplinary and multiple-methods approach to the study of community revival in the wake of a natural disaster (Boettke, Chamlee-Wright, et al. 2007).[17]

In this emerging vision of public administration, the idea of a unitary state populated by omniscient and benevolent expert bureaucrats is rejected. Instead, government is studied as an entity of our collective decision-making populated by ordinary people who have limited knowledge and respond to basic incentives in their pursuits. Elinor Ostrom explains why this intellectual discipline is so vital to the political economists:

As an institutionalist studying empirical phenomena, I presume that individuals try to solve problems as effectively as they can. That assumption imposes a discipline on me. Instead of presuming that some individuals are incompetent, evil, or irrational, and others are omniscient, I presume that individuals have very similar limited capabilities to reason and figure out the structure of complex environments. It is my responsibility as a scientist to ascertain what problems individuals are trying to solve and what factors help or hinder them in these efforts. When the problems that I observe involve lack of predictability, information, and trust, as well as high levels of complexity and transactional difficulties, then my efforts to explain must take these problems overtly into account rather than assuming them away. (1990, 25–26)

Traditional public administration lacked this discipline, and assumed instead that the bureaucratic experts lived outside the ordinary lives of the citizens and could design optimal solutions. These experts govern *over*, not *with*, other citizens. This belief is what was behind the establishment of independent regulatory agencies in the United States throughout the 20th century, and the phenomenon in general of what James Scott has described as "seeing like a state" as opposed to "seeing like a citizen."[18]

But this discussion of public administration matters for another reason. It is my contention that, at least in part, economics as a discipline is evaluated as an intellectual input into public administration. In this sense, economic research and teaching does not have an intrinsic demand for its output, but a derived demand instead. Economists are hired not only to be academics, but also to work in the public and private sectors. In fact, if we study the supply and demand of economists, as Robert Tollison (1986) suggested we must in his Southern Economic Association (SEA) presidential address, these alternative avenues of employment have been very important in terms of attracting talented individuals into the field as well as driving up wages. Rather than pursue Tollison's line of reasoning on this, however, I want to stress a different point.

The shift in public administration from democratic to bureaucratic administration transformed the discipline of economics. Since the value of economics is derived from the value attributed to public administration, when what is expected from public administration shifts, economics adjusts to service that shift (otherwise it will be left by the wayside). In previously published articles, I have used a table similar to figure 2.1 to capture the essence of the issue.[19]

Figure 2.1. Effect of a Shift in Public Administration on the Discipline of Economics

	State as referee in economic game	State as active player in economic game
Economist as citizen and student	Democratic public administration	
Economist as trained expert		Bureaucratic administration

Only the diagonals are stable. As we saw in the time of Smith, an economist or statesman who claimed to know better than private citizens how to manage their affairs was ridiculed for arrogance, while by the time of Samuelson, an economist who refused to wear the mantle of science as a trained expert to aid the state in managing economic affairs would be dismissed as a relic of a bygone era.

The rise of independent regulatory agencies in the 20th century and the growth of doctoral programs in the social sciences (and economics in particular), as well as programs specifically designed for public administration, are correlated with one another. But what if the transformation of public administration led to a transformation of economic science that was counterproductive for the scientific progress of the discipline?

This is the position that Hayek maintained in his 1974 Nobel Prize lecture, "The Pretense of Knowledge" (see Hayek [1974] 2016). Hayek issued an indictment of modern economic policy and economic science as practiced between the end of World War II and the mid-1970s in the United States and United Kingdom. At the start of Hayek's lecture, he implores his audience to fess up to the fact that those in the economics profession had nothing to be very proud of, as they have made a mess of things. Hayek goes on to argue that the cause of the mess was the misconstruing of what economics can, and cannot, achieve as a science. Economics is a science of complex phenomena, yet the modern administrative state demanded an economics of simple phenomena to accomplish the policy tasks so conceived. The problem is that such an approach must confront the strange situation that the approaches that superficially look the most scientific to outside observers are often in reality the least scientific, while the approaches that superficially look the least scientific are actually the most scientific because they understand the limits to our knowledge in the science of complex phenomena. And Hayek ended his lecture with a warning that unless we learn these limits, the economist will run the risk of not only becoming a tyrant over his fellow citizens, but also becoming the destroyer of civilization.

Hayek firmly thought the state should be limited in the role of the referee, or Smith's night watchman state, and thus the economist should be a student of society and never assume the mantle of scientific expert in the administrative state. Hayek, like Smith or Buchanan, argued for a liberal political economy that would effectively solve, to invoke Buchanan's language, the puzzle of empowering the protective and productive state while restraining the predatory state and thus achieve freedom in the constitutional contract.

As already mentioned, Hayek was not alone in his concern with how the transformation of public administration affected economic science. Knight's American Economic Association (AEA) presidential address (1951) and his last book, *Intelligence and Democratic Action* (1960), highlight how this transformation was fundamentally undemocratic. This is a theme one can see in Buchanan's work as well. The expert-driven public finance of, say, Richard Musgrave is simply anathema to an economist trained as he was under Knight.[20] David Levy and Sandra Peart, in their book *Escape from Democracy* (2016), detail this criticism of the economist as expert who transcends the process, rather than the economist as being firmly placed in the model of policy design and implementation, as well as science and the organization of inquiry itself. And Roger Koppl (2018) demonstrates the significant problems that emerge when monopoly status is granted to the "expert."

So while Hayek's concerns were not widely shared, they were also not completely alien to other leading thinkers in economic thought. Though Hayek may have been harsher in his judgment that this transformation results in placing the economist on the path toward intellectual charlatanism, his agitation against scientism would be shared by such scholars as Knight and Mises before him, and Buchanan, Coase, and the Ostroms after him.

A classic illustration of the dispute over rule by experts in economic policy is to consider the case of development economists such as P. T. Bauer and William Easterly. The post–World War II era of development economics was dominated by international agencies that sought to engineer development through orchestrated state action with respect to infrastructure investment, population control, human capital investment, and poverty alleviation. Bauer, however, argued that the process of development was more a Smithian one laid out in my epigraph, and as such he emphasized that we were all once poor, and that the move from subsistence to exchange follows a path where small-scale trading and small-scale capital accumulation transition to medium-scale trading and capital accumulation and then finally to large-scale trading and capital accumulation. The explanation of the wealth and poverty of nations is found in the institutional environment that triggers this shift in the path from subsistence to exchange.[21]

Bauer was heard during his career at Cambridge and the London School of Economics, but he was not listened to, and his views were largely dismissed by those who were pessimistic about private ordering and optimistic about public administration. But the failure of development planning to achieve its stated goals[22] led to a reassessment. In the late 1990s and the 2000s, the work of William Easterly (2001, 2006, 2014) would once again raise concerns not just about the incentive compatibilities of development planning, but also the knowledge problems and political problems that international development agencies were ignoring at the peril of the populations that they were entrusted to assist.

But like Bauer, Easterly is more heard than listened to, especially with the rise of so-called evidence-based policy and randomized controlled trials in the field of development economics. This is not the time to engage that debate, but it does reflect that the dispute from the 20th century continues in the 21st century over what constitutes "tolerable administration" and what that means for the practice of economic science. Development economics in theory and practice continues to be guided by the bureaucratic vision of public administration, and not the democratic vision of public administration. Elinor Ostrom and her colleagues attempted to offer an alternative vision in *Aid, Incentives, and Sustainability* (2002), but like Bauer and Easterly their message might have been heard, but not listened to. We have to listen to those on the ground; we have to understand the different games they are playing, and the nested nature of these games, and the meanings and symbolism they attach to the games they are playing to understand the incentives as they understand them, and the expectations they have which guide their actions. Economics is a *social science*, and any habits of thought which de-emphasize the social will cause problems with the science.

When Buchanan gave his SEA presidential address "What Should Economists Do?" (1964), he argued that instead of assuming a unitary state that could choose optimal policies, we should as economists direct our analytical attention toward exchange relationships and the institutions within which these relationships are formed and transactions are conducted. This is what Buchanan meant when he argued that economists should be "market economists"—that we should study market behavior and nothing more, and where the market is defined in the broadest possible sense to include commercial and noncommercial exchange and the institutions within which these relationships are formed, are transacted, and are either sustained or disappear. I read Buchanan's essay as a first-year graduate student, and it has shaped everything I have done as an economist ever since.

Conclusion

It is my contention that if we take seriously the points raised by Hayek, Friedman, Buchanan, and the Ostroms about the costs of public administration, then our judgment of what we can reasonably expect from bureaucratic public administration will need to adjust. And that we must rethink our practice of economic science in order to fully account for and analyze these costs. In short, my message is that we must expect far less from economics as a tool of social control and rethink the very task of public administration.

In Charles Plott's SEA presidential address (1991), he raised his fundamental equation, which is summarized in figure 2.2. In this simple rendering, we can explain the variation in outcomes by varying preferences and fixing institutions, or by fixing preferences and varying institutions. Because public-choice scholars wanted to focus on how alternative institutional arrangements affect the ability of individuals to pursue productive specialization and realize the gains from social cooperation, they generally eschewed explanations based on preference variation. Instead, their mantra became "Same players, under different rules, produce different outcomes." Change the institutional context, and the incentives, information, and feedback provided change, and thus behavior changes. Same players, different rules, different outcomes. Buchanan hammers this point home in *Cost and Choice* (1969) and his discussion of the contrast between the opportunity costs faced by decision makers in the market versus in other contexts.

Figure 2.2. The Role Preferences and Institutions Play in Determining Outcomes

Preferences   +   Institutions   →   Outcomes

Plott was making a very straightforward scientific point about experimental design and controls, whereas his teacher Buchanan was making a broader philosophical point about agency and structure and the political economy of the good society. In either case, any version of economics that does not allow us to put institutions and institutional variation at the center of our explanations is doing something wrong and will run the risk of missing some very basic points in the economic way of thinking. As Elinor Ostrom (1990, 22) argued, we simply cannot make progress with "institution-free" analysis, regardless of whether we are talking about idealized government regulation or idealized markets, because the explanation is to be found in the "institutional details." Our theoretical *framework* and our empirical strategies for research must capture the effect of institutional variation on economic performance and human well-being.

We cannot assume omniscient and benevolent bureaucrats occupying places of public administration and thus costlessly and flawlessly delivering the answer to Smith's question about how to execute a "tolerable administration of justice." As Friedman (1947) pointed out in his discussion of Lerner's *The Economics of Control*, economic analysis that assumes omniscience and benevolence is irrelevant to the real problems that must be addressed. James Buchanan begins his 1986 Nobel lecture with a summary of the main lesson he learned from the Swedish economist Knut Wicksell, a message Buchanan insisted was "clear, elementary and self-evident." The message was: "Economists should cease proffering policy advice as if they were employed by a benevolent despot, and they should look to the structure within which political decisions are made" (Buchanan [1986] 2016, 44). Elinor Ostrom concludes her 2009 Nobel lecture by summarizing the main lessons learned in her intellectual journey: we must "move away from the presumption that the government must" solve our problems; "humans have a more complex motivational structure and more capability to solve social dilemmas" than traditional theory suggests; and "a core goal of public policy should be to facilitate the development of institutions that bring out the best in humans" ([2009] 2016, 237–38).

Self-governing democratic societies are fragile entities that require continual reaffirmation by fallible but capable human beings.[23] "We need to ask," Elinor Ostrom continued, "how diverse polycentric institutions help or hinder the innovativeness, learning, adapting, trustworthiness, levels of cooperation of participants, and the achievement of more effective, equitable, and sustainable outcomes at multiple scales" (237–38). This polycentric vision of governance stands in stark contrast with one that sees the necessity of a single hierarchical government that must induce compliance from its citizens.

Such a program in political economy and public administration would require that we address the essential complexity of human societies, instead of assuming it away. We are imperfect beings living in an imperfect world bumping into each other and bargaining with one another in the hope of finding rules that will enable us to live better together. We strive to turn situations of potential conflict into situations of cooperation so we can realize mutual benefits. Smith's "tolerable administration of justice" emerges when the rules of the game are those that enable individuals to pursue productive specialization and realize the gains from peaceful social cooperation.

Drawing on the insights of F. A. Hayek and James Buchanan, Karen Vaughn, in her SEA presidential address (1996), argued for reinvigorating classical political economy. The discipline of political economy will advance, she argues, when we reject postulated perfection in our modeling and the corresponding view that government is the only corrective to any imperfections in our policy practice, and instead cultivate an understanding of the complexity of the social world that is more appropriate for an economic policy for an imperfect world. Such a perspective will put explanatory focus on how alternative institutional arrangements affect the learning that human actors experience in both the private and public sectors.

Hayek once remarked, "The curious task of economics is to demonstrate to men how little they really know about what they imagine they can design" (1988, 76). Economics, in this sense, teaches us humility. From Adam Smith to Vernon Smith, the evolution of economic thought taught us not only what economics as a science can tell us about the workings of an economic system, but perhaps more importantly what economics as a science *cannot* tell us. There are real limits to economic analysis, and with that economic systems design and control. I have argued that the transformation of public administration in the 20th century from democratic administration to bureaucratic administration nudged economics off track by failing to recognize those limits, and the confusion of the policy sciences with the engineering sciences. Economics, I contend, is too important an intellectual endeavor to be rendered irrelevant by a false view of science and the demands from a false picture of public administration.

Notes

1. See Douglas Irwin's (2014) discussion of Smith's thesis concerning "tolerable administration" and the wealth of nations and its general support in the contemporary empirical literature in economic development.

2. Raghuram Rajan (2004) argued that standard economic models that assumed the *institutional framework* as given were not particularly helpful to the analysis of developing and transitioning economies. That is precisely because countries that are failed and weak states in the first place are lacking the critical institutional framework. So it is better to "Assume Anarchy" and focus analytical attention on endogenous rule formation and institution building in these situations. On the political economy of failed and weak states, see Coyne (2008).

3. F. A. Hayek (1948), in his essay "Individualism: True and False," tackled this question from the other side. He argued that Adam Smith and his contemporaries sought to find that set of institutions that would ensure that bad men would do the least harm if they should rise to power. This is a system of constraints—of restrictions on the exercising of power—such that anyone could be entrusted with power because the institutions would work to bind the behavior of the rulers. He contrasts this with the French Enlightenment, which he argued sought a system that would entrust only to the best and the brightest the power to rule unconstrained institutionally but imbued with expert knowledge. This dichotomy is critical to keep in mind for the narrative of economics and public administration that I am constructing.

4. It is always important, I believe, to remember that the Public Choice Society was originally called the Committee on Non-Market Decision Making, and the journal *Public Choice* was initially published as *Papers in Non-Market Decision Making*. The first four presidents of the society included James Buchanan, Gordon Tullock, William Riker, and Vincent Ostrom. Mancur Olson, Elinor Ostrom, Charles Plott, and Vernon Smith also served as presidents of the Public Choice Society.

5. In writing this chapter, I have drawn upon my teachers who have been previous presidents of the Southern Economic Association: James Buchanan (1964), Gordon Tullock (1981), Robert Tollison (1986), and Karen Vaughn (1996), as well as some others who were students of those professors, such as Charles Plott (1991). I will also draw on the independent and joint research of myself and colleagues over the past two decades that directly relates to this topic of economics and public administration.

6. The Great Enrichment refers here to an increase in income per capita by a factor of 40 to 100 that began first in northwestern Europe around 1800. See McCloskey's *The*

Bourgeois Virtues (2006), *Bourgeois Dignity* (2010), and *Bourgeois Equality* (2016). Also see McCloskey (2015) on the primacy of ideas in the explanation of modern economic growth.

7. As discussed earlier, ideas (a part of human capital) along with technology help establish the institutional possibilities frontier. If the institutions sought for good governance are so divorced from the prevailing attitudes and beliefs of the people, then the enforcement costs will be too high for those institutions to be in the feasible set. Remember the Leeson (2017) point—rules define what is permissible; constraints inform us on what is feasible.

8. It is important to remember that the original founders of the American Economic Association were neither classical political economists nor neoclassical economists, but historical and institutional economists with a strong reformer zeal consistent with the Progressive Era. See the work of A. W. Coats (1993) and also Thomas Leonard's *Illiberal Reformers* (2016).

9. See my book *Calculation and Coordination* (Boettke 2001), and also the nine-volume reference work I edited, *Socialism and the Market: The Socialist Calculation Debate Revisited* (Boettke 2000). Also see Don Lavoie's *Rivalry and Central Planning* (1985).

10. See *Living Economics* (Boettke 2012), where I make the distinction between "mainline" economics and "mainstream" economics. Also see Boettke, Haeffele, and Storr (2016) and Mitchell and Boettke (2017).

11. Also see Lange's (1937: 127) theory that incentive arguments belong to the field of sociology and not economy theory.

12. "The statesman who should attempt to direct private people in what manner they ought to employ their capitals," Smith warned, "would not only load himself with a most unnecessary attention, but assume an authority which could safely be trusted, not only to no single person, but to no council or senate what-ever, and which would no-where be so dangerous as in the hands of a man who had folly and presumption enough to fancy himself fit to exercise it" ([1776] 1976, 478). "The man of system," Smith argued in *The Theory of Moral Sentiments* ". . . is apt to be very wise in his own conceit. . . . He seems to imagine that he can arrange the different members of a great society with as much ease as the hand arranges the different pieces upon a chess-board. He does not consider that the pieces upon the chess-board have no other principle of motion besides that which the hand impresses upon them" ([1759] 1976, 233–34).

13. This same sentiment is evident in Samuelson (1948, 152), where he argues that "no longer is modern man able to believe that government governs best which governs least." Samuelson goes on to argue that in the modern interdependent society, individualism can no longer serve as a guiding principle in the affairs of men.

14. The rejection of the assumptions of omniscience and benevolence in political economy is critical to understanding not just the approach of Mises and Hayek, but also of Buchanan and Tullock and Vincent and Elinor Ostrom. One of the most challenging areas in this regard is to consider collective decision-making concerning national defense. Christopher Coyne (2015) argues that just as Buchanan argued

it was inappropriate to work with the assumption of a "fiscal brain" or what he called "fisc," it is also inappropriate to work in the field of defense economics with the assumption of a "defense brain." Once the assumption of an omniscient and benevolent "defense brain" is rejected, the analysis of even such critical issues as military strategy is more analogous to the bargaining one finds in the swamp concerning mosquito abatement than some ideal public interest deliberation.

15. See Aligica and Boettke (2009, 7–29); Boettke, Coyne, and Leeson (2011); and Boettke, Lemke, and Palagashvili (2013, 2016) for a discussion of the Ostroms' contribution to the municipalities debate in public administration.

16. See Aligica and Boettke (2009) for an overview of the Ostroms' intellectual system, including social philosophy.

17. Also see Boettke (2015).

18. See Scott's *Seeing Like a State* (1998). As for seeing like a citizen, see the work of the Ostroms as discussed in Aligica and Boettke (2009) and Aligica (2013). Elinor and Vincent Ostrom saw their work as contributing to the "science and art of the association" that made possible a democratic self-governing society. They were working on an alternative way of looking at governance and institutional order of a society of free people. "Seeing like a citizen" is one possible name for it; "seeing like a self-governing human being" would be another. This endeavor is built on two foundational convictions: (a) one cannot build a self-governing society of free individuals when the prevalent, elite mode of thinking about institutional order and governance thinks like a state and strives for monocentrism; and (b) the ideal of a society of self-governing, fallible, but capable human beings who are able to master the "art and science of the association" is worth pursuing because self-governing democratic societies are always fragile and vulnerable and thus maintenance, renewal, and sustainability depend on disseminating as much as possible the knowledge of this unique and fragile but vital "art and science."

19. See, for example, Boettke and Horwitz (2005) and Boettke and Coyne (2006). The Boettke and Coyne article addresses the role of the economist in development economics, and I think this field of inquiry is a perfect example of the rise and fall of different economic approaches and the confidence one has with respect to the administrative state.

20. See Buchanan and Musgrave (1999, 17) where Buchanan argues that the economist trained at Chicago "does not project an image of becoming an advisor to government" and that they "learn how economies work rather than how economies might be controlled." Buchanan conjectures that this contrast in professional attitude might explain differences in both research and career paths.

21. See Bauer (2000) for a selection of his essays on the topic of economic development.

22. See Boettke (1994).

23. In my book with Paul Aligica on the Ostroms (see Aligica and Boettke 2009, 159), we include an interview with Elinor where she states: "One of our greatest priorities at the Workshop has been to ensure that our research contributes to the education of future citizens. . . . Self-governing, democratic systems are always fragile enterprises.

Future citizens need to understand that they participate in the constitution and reconstitution of rule-governed polities. And they need to learn the art and science of association. If we fail in this, all of our investigations and theoretical efforts are useless."

References

Aligica, Paul Dragos. 2013. *Institutional Diversity and Political Economy: The Ostroms and Beyond*. New York: Oxford University Press.

Aligica, Paul Dragos, and Peter J. Boettke. 2009. *Challenging Institutional Analysis and Development*. London: Routledge.

Andrews, Matt, Lant Pritchett, and Michael Woolcock. 2017. *Building State Capability: Evidence, Analysis, Action*. New York: Oxford University Press.

Bauer, Peter T. 2000. *From Subsistence to Exchange*. Princeton, NJ: Princeton University Press.

Boettke, Peter J., ed. 1994. *The Collapse of Development Planning*. New York: New York University Press.

———, ed. 2000. *Socialism and the Market: The Socialist Calculation Debate Revisited*. Vol. 9. New York: Routledge.

———. 2001. *Calculation and Coordination: Essays on Socialism and Transitional Political Economy*. New York: Routledge.

———. 2012. *Living Economics: Yesterday, Today, and Tomorrow*. Oakland, CA: The Independent Institute.

———. 2015. "Katrina 10 Years Later: Disaster Recovery and the Political Economy of Everyday Life." Mercatus Center at George Mason University, August 23.

Boettke, Peter J., Emily Chamlee-Wright, Peter Gordon, Sanford Ikeda, Peter T. Leeson, and Russell S. Sobel. 2007. "The Political, Economic, and Social Aspects of Katrina." *Southern Economic Journal* 74 (2): 363–76.

Boettke, Peter J., and Christopher J. Coyne. 2006. "The Role of the Economist in Economic Development." *Quarterly Journal of Austrian Economics* 19 (2): 47–68.

Boettke, Peter J., Christopher J. Coyne, and Peter T. Leeson. 2008. "Institutional Stickiness and the New Development Economics." *American Journal of Economics and Sociology* 67 (2): 331–58.

———. 2011. "Quasimarket Failure." *Public Choice* 149 (1/2): 209–24.

Boettke, Peter J., Christopher J. Coyne, Peter T. Leeson, and Frederic Sautet. 2005. "The New Comparative Political Economy." *Review of Austrian Economics* 8 (3/4): 281–304.

Boettke, Peter J., Stefanie Haeffele, and Virgil Henry Storr, eds. 2016. *Mainline Economics: Six Nobel Lectures in the Tradition of Adam Smith*. Arlington, VA: Mercatus Center at George Mason University.

Boettke, Peter J., and Steven Horwitz. 2005. "The Limits of Economic Expertise: Prophets, Engineers, and the State in the History of Development Economics." *History of Political Economy* 37 (1): 10–39.

Boettke, Peter J., and Peter T. Leeson, eds. 2015. *The Economic Role of the State*. Cheltenham, UK: Edward Elgar.

Boettke, Peter J., Jayme S. Lemke, and Liya Palagashvili. 2013. "Riding in Cars with Boys: Elinor Ostrom's Adventures with the Police." *Journal of Institutional Economics* 9 (4): 407–25.

———. 2016. "Re-Evaluating Community Policing in a Polycentric System." *Journal of Institutional Economics* 12 (2): 305–25.

Brennan, Geoffrey, and James M. Buchanan. 1980. *The Power to Tax: Analytical Foundations of a Fiscal Constitution*. New York: Cambridge University Press.

Buchanan, James M. 1949. "The Pure Theory of Government Finance: A Suggested Approach." *Journal of Political Economy* 57 (6): 496–505.

———. 1964. "What Should Economists Do?" *Southern Economic Journal* 30 (3): 213–22.

———. 1969. *Cost and Choice: An Inquiry in Economic Theory*. Chicago: Markham.

———. 1975. *The Limits of Liberty: Between Anarchy and Leviathan*. Chicago: University of Chicago Press.

———. [1979] 2015. "Notes on Hayek." *Review of Austrian Economics* 27 (4): 257–60.

———. [1986] 2016. "The Constitution of Economic Policy." Reprinted in *Mainline Economics: Six Nobel Lectures in the Tradition of Adam Smith*, edited by Peter J. Boettke, Stefanie Haeffele, and Virgil Henry Storr, 43–59. Arlington, VA: Mercatus Center at George Mason University.

Buchanan, James M., and Richard A. Musgrave. 1999. *Public Finance and Public Choice: Two Contrasting Visions of the State*. Cambridge, MA: MIT Press.

Coats, A. W. 1993. *The Sociology and Professionalization of Economics*. New York: Routledge.

Coyne, Christopher J. 2008. *After War: The Political Economy of Exporting Democracy*. Stanford, CA: Stanford University Press.

———. 2013. *Doing Bad by Doing Good: Why Humanitarian Action Fails*. Stanford, CA: Stanford University Press.

———. 2015. "Lobotomizing the Defense Brain." *Review of Austrian Economics* 28 (4): 371–96.

Croly, Herbert. 1909. *The Promise of American Life*. New York: Macmillan.

Easterly, William. 2001. *The Elusive Quest for Growth: Economists' Adventures and Misadventures in the Tropics*. Cambridge, MA: MIT Press.

———. 2006. *The White Man's Burden: Why the West's Efforts to Aid the Rest Have Done So Much Ill and So Little Good*. New York: Penguin Books.

———. 2014. *The Tyranny of Experts: Economists, Dictators, and the Forgotten Rights of the Poor*. New York: Basic Books.

Frey, Bruno S. 2001. "A Utopia? Government without Territorial Monopoly." *Journal of Institutional and Theoretical Economics* 157 (1): 162–75.

Friedman, Milton. 1947. "Lerner on the Economics of Control." *Journal of Political Economy* 55 (5): 405–16.

Friedman, Milton, and Rose Friedman. [1980] 1990. *Free to Choose: A Personal Statement.* New York: Harcourt Brace Jovanovich.

Hayek, F. A. [1944] 2007. *The Road to Serfdom.* Chicago: University of Chicago Press.

———. 1948. *Individualism and Economic Order.* Chicago: University of Chicago Press.

———. [1974] 2016. "The Pretense of Knowledge." Reprinted in *Mainline Economics: Six Nobel Lectures in the Tradition of Adam Smith,* edited by Peter J. Boettke, Stefanie Haeffele, and Virgil Henry Storr, 25–39. Arlington, VA: Mercatus Center at George Mason University.

———. 1988. *The Fatal Conceit: The Errors of Socialism.* Chicago: University of Chicago Press.

Hume, David. [1739] 2000. *A Treatise on Human Nature.* Edited by David Fate Norton and Mary J. Norton. New York: Oxford University Press.

Irwin, Douglas A. 2014. "Adam Smith's Tolerable Administration of Justice and the Wealth of Nations." NBER Working Paper 20636, National Bureau of Economic Research, Cambridge, MA.

Knight, Frank H. 1951. "The Role of Principles in Economics and Politics." *American Economic Review* 41 (1): 1–29.

———. 1960. *Intelligence and Democratic Action.* Cambridge, MA: Harvard University Press.

Koppl, Roger. 2018. *Expert Failure.* New York: Cambridge University Press.

Lange, Oskar. 1936. "On the Economic Theory of Socialism: Part One." *Review of Economic Studies* 4 (1): 53–71.

———. 1937. "On the Economic Theory of Socialism: Part Two." *Review of Economic Studies,* 4 (2): 123–42.

Lavoie, Don. 1985. *Rivalry and Central Planning: The Socialist Calculation Debate Reconsidered.* New York: Cambridge University Press.

Leeson, Peter T. 2014. *Anarchy Unbound: Why Self-Government Works Better than You Think.* New York: Cambridge University Press.

———. 2017. *WTF?! An Economic Tour of the Weird.* Stanford, CA: Stanford University Press.

Leonard, Thomas C. 2016. *Illiberal Reformers: Race, Eugenics, and American Economics in the Progressive Era.* Princeton, NJ: Princeton University Press.

Lerner, Abba P. 1946. *The Economics of Control.* New York: Macmillan.

Levy, David M., and Sandra J. Peart. 2016. *Escape from Democracy: The Role of Experts and the Public in Economic Policy.* New York: Cambridge University Press.

McCloskey, Deirdre N. 2006. *The Bourgeois Virtues: Ethics for an Age of Commerce*. Chicago: University of Chicago Press.

———. 2010. *Bourgeois Dignity: Why Economics Can't Explain the Modern World*. Chicago: University of Chicago Press.

———. 2015. "Ideas, Not Interests or Institutions, Caused the Great Enrichment." *Man and the Economy* 2 (1): 7–24.

———. 2016. *Bourgeois Equality: How Ideas, Not Capital or Institutions, Enriched the World*. Chicago: University of Chicago Press.

Mises, Ludwig von. [1920] 1975. "Economic Calculation in the Socialist Commonwealth." In *Collectivist Economic Planning*, edited by F. A. Hayek, 87–130. Clifton, NJ: August M. Kelley.

———. [1949] 1966. *Human Action: A Treatise on Economics*. 3rd ed. Chicago: Henry Regnery.

———. [1956] 2006. *The Anti-Capitalist Mentality*. Indianapolis: Liberty Fund.

Mitchell, Matthew D., and Peter J. Boettke. 2017. *Applied Mainline Economics: Bridging the Gap between Theory and Public Policy*. Arlington, VA: Mercatus Center at George Mason University.

North, Douglass C. 1981. *Structure and Change in Economic History*. New York: W. W. Norton.

———. 1990. *Institutions, Institutional Change, and Economic Performance*. New York: Cambridge University Press.

———. 1991. "Institutions." *Journal of Economic Perspectives* 5 (1): 97–112.

Olson, Mancur. 2000. *Power and Prosperity: Outgrowing Communist and Capitalist Dictatorships*. New York: Basic Books.

Ostrom, Elinor. 1990. *Governing the Commons: The Evolution of Institutions for Collective Action*. New York: Cambridge University Press.

———. [2009] 2016. "Beyond Markets and States." In *Mainline Economics: Six Nobel Lectures in the Tradition of Adam Smith*, edited by Peter J. Boettke, Stefanie Haeffele, and Virgil Henry Storr, 191–250. Arlington, VA: Mercatus Center at George Mason University.

Ostrom, Elinor, Clark Gibson, Sujai Shivakumar, and Krister Andersson. 2002. *Aid, Incentives, and Sustainability*. Stockholm: Swedish International Development Cooperation Agency.

Ostrom, Vincent. [1973] 2008. *The Intellectual Crisis in American Public Administration*. 3rd ed. Tuscaloosa: University of Alabama Press.

Ostrom, Vincent, and Elinor Ostrom. 1971. "Public Choice: A Different Approach to the Study of Public Administration." *Public Administration Review* 31 (2): 203–16.

Plott, Charles R. 1991. "Will Economics Become an Experimental Science?" *Southern Economic Journal* 57 (4): 901–19.

Rajan, Raghuram. 2004. "Assume Anarchy." *Finance and Development* 41 (3): 56–57.

Robbins, Lionel. [1952] 1965. *The Theory of Economic Policy in English Classical Political Economy*. London: Macmillan.

Samuelson, Paul A. 1948. *Economics*. New York: McGraw-Hill.

Scott, James C. 1998. *Seeing Like a State: How Certain Schemes to Improve the Human Condition Have Failed*. New Haven, CT: Yale University Press.

Skarbek, David. 2014. *The Social Order of the Underworld*. Oxford: Oxford University Press.

Smith, Adam. [1755] 1982. *Essays on Philosophical Subjects*. Indianapolis: Liberty Fund.

———. [1759] 1976. *The Theory of Moral Sentiments*. Chicago: University of Chicago Press.

———. [1776] 1976. *An Inquiry into the Nature and Causes of the Wealth of Nations*. Chicago: University of Chicago Press.

Storr, Virgil Henry, Stefanie Haeffele, and Laura E. Grube. 2015. *Community Revival in the Wake of Disaster*. New York: Palgrave Macmillan.

Stringham, Edward Peter. 2015. *Private Governance: Creating Order in Economic and Social Life*. New York: Oxford University Press.

Tollison, Robert D. 1986. "Economists as the Subject of Economic Inquiry." *Southern Economic Journal* 52 (4): 909–22.

Tullock, Gordon. 1965. *The Politics of Bureaucracy*. Washington, DC: Public Affairs Press.

———. 1981. "The Rhetoric and Reality of Redistribution." *Southern Economic Journal* 47 (4): 895–907.

Vaughn, Karen I. 1996. "Economic Policy for an Imperfect World." *Southern Economic Journal* 62 (4): 833–44.

Wagner, Richard E. 2016. *Politics as a Peculiar Business: Insights from a Theory of Entangled Political Economy*. Cheltenham, UK: Edward Elgar.

Waldo, Dwight. 1948. *The Administrative State: A Study of the Political Theory of American Public Administration*. New York: Ronald Press.

Wilson, Woodrow. 1887. "The Study of Administration." *Political Science Quarterly* 2 (2): 197–222.

Chapter 3

Liberty vs. Power in Economic Policy in the 20th and 21st Centuries

E very semester, students throughout the world are introduced to the teachings of economics and political economy. What are the first things students learn as they enter the world of the economic way of thinking? Obviously, the answer to that question varies from instructor to instructor.[1] Some will emphasize behavioral assumptions and the logic of choice; others will emphasize institutional structure and economic performance as captured in notions of efficiency; some will emphasize the harmony of interests that are reconciled through the market system, while others will highlight the conflict of interests that result from market imperfections. The intellectual battle lines in public policy between liberty and power are often drawn based on these points of emphasis in economic teaching.

I believe that in studying the development of the history of ideas in political economy it is useful to distinguish between the mainline of argument and the mainstream in the currently fashionable practice of the science. The mainline of argument emphasizes the core propositions that have been argued throughout the history of the discipline. Mainstream, on the other hand, defines whatever is currently fashionable within the discipline. Economics is whatever current economists do. To be a mainstream economist does not necessarily mean that one is comfortable with the mainline of argument from Adam Smith onward. The mainline of argument stresses the harmony of interests that emerges through the competitive market process. David Hume and Adam Smith emphasized this reconciliation power of the market economy in the 18th century; Jean-Baptiste Say and Frédéric Bastiat did so in the 19th century; and F. A. Hayek and James

Published in the *Journal of Private Enterprise* 22, no. 2 (Spring 2007): 7–36. This speech was first delivered as a Plenary Lecture at the 2006 Association of Private Enterprise Education meetings in Las Vegas, Nevada.

Buchanan represent perhaps the most articulate defenders of spontaneous order in the 20th century. But throughout the history of political economy, there were always individuals who sought to juxtapose their own position with this harmony of interest doctrine: from those who argued against free trade such as Friedrich List to those who emphasized the possibility of a general glut in economic activities such as Thomas Malthus; from those who emphasized class conflict such as Karl Marx to those who emphasized the instability of financial markets such as John Maynard Keynes. Modern mainstream economists such as Joseph Stiglitz, who emphasize the imperfections in market structure and imperfect information, are more in line with List, Malthus, Marx, and Keynes than they are with Hume, Smith, Say, Bastiat, Hayek, and Buchanan.

The contemporary discipline of economics has often lost sight of the core propositions that emerge in the mainline of political economy. My contention is that economics as a discipline should be defined by the propositions it advances about the real world, and not the form in which economic statements are presented. Mathematical models and techniques of statistical significance are useful tools in examining certain economic propositions, but we must never forget that it is the propositions that must be assessed rather than the formal tools utilized in examining them. The crisis in modern economics is that theorists as divergent on substance as Stiglitz and Robert Lucas are accounted as mainstream, while figures such as Hayek and Buchanan are often described as nonmainstream. But one would be hard-pressed to deny mainline status to Hayek and Buchanan, and would be hard-pressed to force fit Stiglitz or Jeffrey Sachs or Paul Krugman into the mainline of argument in political economy from Hume and Smith to Hayek and Buchanan. Lord Acton perhaps stated the position best: "But it is not the popular movement, but the traveling of the minds of men who sit in the seat of Adam Smith that is really serious and worthy of all attention" (1904, 212).

So let's go back to our erstwhile principles of economics students being exposed to the economic way of thinking for the first time. They learn about incentives and choice on the margin, the productive gains from the division of labor, and the mutually beneficial aspect of trade. Even those teachers who want to emphasize the currently fashionable critique of the mainline must first teach students the mainline claim about how competing interests are reconciled through the market system to produce social cooperation and harmony, if only to criticize it.

I've stressed this distinction between mainline and mainstream because my contention is that the intellectual oscillations around the mainline proposition concerning the harmony of interest define the policy ethos of any historical era. The choice is between liberty and power. For much of the 20th century, mainstream opinion in economics and political economy deviated considerably from the mainline of political economy. The consequences of this deviation were not trivial. Grand social experiments—with government power substituting for the voluntary choices of individuals within the market process—were undertaken through the world. The most extreme versions led to totalitarianism and economic deprivation; the tamer versions led to economic stagnation and the "nanny state." Since the 19th century, the intellectual moments when the mainline and the mainstream were aligned have been fleeting.

In my narrative of modern political economy, I argue that the 20th and 21st centuries have seen three critical historical moments when the oscillation around the mainline was particularly volatile. The first was the End of Laissez-Faire that described the intellectual discourse between 1900 and 1930. The second was the End of Socialism that defined the 1980–1995 period, when the mainline seemed to push back against the mainstream. The third is the Rise of Leviathan that has emerged since September 11, 2001.

To make sense of these historical moments, I rely on three propositions. The first proposition is that political and economic ideas can and do have consequences in the world of public policy. In short, we must pay attention to ideas if we want to make sense of the policy choices that are ultimately made. Interest-group machinations are always present, but they take place within a climate of public opinion that is shaped by ideas. The second proposition is that there must be an alignment of ideas and circumstances for rapid change based on ideas to be manifested in public policy. And the third proposition is that whenever ideas that argue that liberty must give way to power in human affairs become dominant, the consequences are dire to the social progress of humanity. Reliance on power makes us worse off, not better off. And this last proposition brings us back to the core teachings of political economy from Adam Smith to F. A. Hayek. Material progress, social cooperation, and harmony result not from judicious government planning but through the free choices of individuals within a system of private property, freedom of contract, and consent.

The Presumption toward Liberty and against Power

Among the first lessons one learns in economics is the positive-sum nature of voluntary exchange. Both parties expect to benefit from exchange; otherwise, they would not have engaged in the act of exchange. The essence of wealth creation in a market economy is to be found in the act of mutually beneficial exchange. Of course, errors can be made in making the decision to trade, but not ex ante. Regret is an ex post phenomenon. Moreover, because economic decision makers must bear the costs of their decisions, they have a strong incentive to be alert to those opportunities in their interest to be alert to. Individuals may err, but they will learn of those errors quickly in their exchange behavior and adjust to avoid economic losses in the future.

That individuals should be regarded as the best judge of their situation has been a building block in economics since the writings of Adam Smith. In *The Wealth of Nations*, Smith ([1776] 1976) argued that a virtuous circle led to greater prosperity. The source of economic growth and development was the gains from specialization and trade realized through the greater division of labor and the expansion of the market. The division of labor was indeed limited by the extent of the market. But as the market expands, the division of labor is refined even further and the gains from specialization increase productivity even more. There are, in other words, increasing returns to the expansion of the market arena. This Smithian virtuous circle counteracts any tendency toward being caught in the Malthusian trap of subsistence levels of production and represents instead the progressive march of modernity.

In the lectures and notebooks used in writing his great treatise, Smith summarized his position in the following manner: "Little else is requisite to carry a state to the highest degree of opulence from the lowest form of barbarism, but peace, easy taxes and a tolerable administration of justice: all the rest being brought about by the natural course of things" ([1776] 1976, xl). Smith goes further and argues, "All governments which thwart this natural course, which force things into another channel or which endeavor to arrest the progress of society at a particular point, are unnatural, and to support themselves are obliged to be oppressive and tyrannical" ([1776] 1976, xl). Evidence from the history of economic development supports Smith—in terms of both the path to successful development and the consequences of steering off that path. But one must unpack the basic institutional infrastructure that serves as the background to Smith's policy prescription. Smith's system of natural liberty, or Hume's system of property, contract, and consent, consists of a network of complementary institutions that all serve to minimize the threat of predation from both public and private actors.

Once stated in this manner, the "paradox of government" becomes apparent. Government is called on to ward off the threat of private predation, but in so empowering government the problem of public predation is created. As James Madison put it:

> If men were angels, no government would be necessary. If angels were to govern men, neither external nor internal controls on government would be necessary. In framing a government which is to be administered by men over men, the great difficulty lies in this: You must first enable the government to control the governed; and in the next place, oblige it to control itself. ([1788] 1993, 164)

Neither appeals to the wisdom of nobility nor romantic dreams of the perfectibility of mankind address this paradox. Instead, institutional arrangements must be forged that will check ambition against ambition to ward off predation by private and public actors.

The system that Smith and Hume built to understand the political economy of growth and development did not rely on behavioral assumptions to generate the conclusions concerning the beneficial consequences of the "invisible hand." Self-interest is postulated as a universal aspect of man's nature, but the pursuit of self-interest is not the causal factor relied on to explain how beneficial social order can emerge. In Smith's comparative political economy, the self-interest of businessmen (reflected in their special-interest pleading), the self-interest of the clergy and academics (reflected in the laziness demonstrated when in protected positions), and the self-interest of politicians (reflected in their arrogance and grabs for power) are all contrasted with situations where the self-interest of buyers and sellers in a system of property, contract, and consent produces a social order that is both unintended and desirable. To put it another way, both the "invisible hand" and the "tragedy of the commons" explanations of social phenomena utilize the self-interested motivational assumption, but the driving force in the analysis is the institutional context not the behavioral assumption.

The intellectual project of Hume and Smith was to discover through analytical inquiry and historical investigation the institutional environment that could produce peace and prosperity despite the foibles of man. F. A. Hayek summed up the Smith project as follows:

> The main point about which there can be little doubt is that Smith's chief concern was not so much with what man might occasionally achieve when he was at his best but that he should have as little opportunity as possible to do harm when he was at his worst. It would scarcely be too much to claim that the main merit of the individualism which he and his contemporaries advocated is that it is a system under which bad men can do least harm. It is a social system which does not depend for its functioning on our finding good men for running it, or on all men becoming better than they now are, but which makes use of men in all their given variety and complexity, sometimes good and sometimes bad, sometimes intelligent and more often stupid. . . . The chief concern of the great individualist writers was indeed to find a set of institutions by which man could be induced, by his own choice and from the motives which determined his ordinary conduct, to contribute as much as possible to the need of all others; and their discovery was that the system of private property did provide such inducements to a much greater extent than had yet been understood. (1948, 11–13)

In the reading that Hayek provides, the classical political economy of Smith was grounded in comparative institutional analysis. The subject matter of economics in this conception of the discipline is exchange and the institutions within which exchange takes place. Human beings are in possession of two competing natural proclivities: to pillage and plunder, on the one hand, and to truck, barter, and exchange, on the other. Which proclivity is stimulated and encouraged is a function of the institutional context within which man finds himself interacting with others. Institutions are defined as the "rules of the game" that are in operation and their enforcement in any given specific historical situation.

The presumption toward liberty that existed in classical political economy was predicated on two subsidiary arguments. First, that individuals, not government officials, are the best judge of their situation and thus should be free to choose. Second, that the specific institutional context that is consistent with the freedom of the individual will steer individuals in the direction of truck, barter, and exchange rather than the violent path of pillage and plunder. The social order will not be predatory, but cooperative.

On the issue of who is in the best position to pass judgment on economic decisions, Smith stated clearly:

The statesman who should attempt to direct private people in what manner they ought to employ their capitals would not only load himself with a most unnecessary attention, but assume an authority which could safely be trusted, not only to no single person, but to no council or senate whatever, and which would no-where be so dangerous as in the hands of a man who had folly and presumption enough to fancy himself fit to exercise it. ([1776] 1976, 478)

The teachings of political economy, Smith argued, were disregarded by an alliance of the sophistry of the businessman engaged in special-interest pleading, and power-wielding preferences of politicians. In short, the disregard for the first argument led directly to the second argument concerning government arrogance and power.

The great French political economist Frédéric Bastiat chose satire to expose the sophistry of special-interest protection by government when he penned his petition of the candlestick makers for protection against the unfair competition from the sun ([1845] 1964). Bastiat's countryman Jean-Baptiste Say didn't choose ridicule but instead soberly discussed the problem of political power and economic efficiency that results from government-sanctioned monopolies in his *Treatise on Political Economy* ([1821] 1971, 146–47). As Say put it: "The public interest is their plea, but self-interest is evidently their object" (161). The system of government privileges that sought to control trade was "pregnant with injustice" (164) and created serious mischief throughout the economy, according to Say.

John Stuart Mill wrote perhaps some of the most elegant passages on the presumption for voluntarism. He argued in his *Principles of Political Economy* ([1848] 1967, 881–83) that the first principle of social order is the protection of persons and property. Without this protection, the social order breaks down into uncertainty and violence. Mill was quick to point out that government was not the only source of this protection, though a government that habitually violated these protections would destroy society. The prosperity experienced by the free cities of Italy, Flanders, and the Hanseatic League in an age of "lawlessness" demonstrates that a certain level of insecurity can be managed through means of self-protection.

Insecurity paralyzes only when it is such in nature and in degree that no energy of which mankind in general are capable affords any tolerable means of self-protection. And this is a main reason why oppression by the government, whose power is generally irresistible by any efforts that can be made by individuals, has so much more baneful an effect on the springs of national prosperity, than almost any degree of lawlessness and turbulence under free institutions. Nations have acquired some wealth, and made some progress in improvement in states of social union so imperfect as to border on anarchy; but no countries in which the people were exposed without limit to arbitrary exactions from the officers of government ever yet continued to have industry and wealth. A few generations of such a government never fail to extinguish both. Some of the fairest, and once the most prosperous, regions of the earth have, under the Romans and afterwards under the Turkish dominion, been reduced to a desert, solely by that cause. (Mill [1848] 1967, 882–83)

As a general rule, a progressive social order is built on a foundation of individual liberty and the system of property, contract, and consent. Even though John Stuart Mill would eventually make the case for an expanded role for government interference, he argued, "Whatever theory we adopt respecting the foundation of the social union, and under whatever political institutions we live, there is a circle around every human being which no government, be it that of one, of a few, or of the many, ought to be permitted to overstep" ([1848] 1967, 943). Violating this principle ran the risk of the loss of human freedom and dignity. As such, Mill argued that "the onus of making out a case always lies on the defenders of legal prohibitions" (943). He even argued more forcefully when he stated later in this chapter, "Laissez-faire, in short, should be the general practice: every departure from it, unless required for some great good, is a certain evil" (950).

The German sociologist and economic historian Max Weber made similar arguments to explain why capitalism had developed in the West but not in China. In his *General Economic History* (1927), Weber enumerated the defining characteristics of modern capitalism. Though there is no doubt that the value system in a society was a significant contributing factor, it was not just the existence of, or lack of, the Protestant work ethic that provided the explanation as to why there was no capitalism in China, according to Weber as so many have concluded. Weber, instead, put great emphasis on the arbitrariness in the law and in the tax system that was practiced in China and that was inconsistent with the development of a modern economy.

Modern capitalism was instead characterized by rational accounting, freedom of the market, modern scientific technology, rule of law, free labor, a rationalization of the conduct of life consistent with market activity, and the commercialization of economic life. These factors all worked to provide a rational ethic for enterprise, and a political and legal environment that was predictable and that guaranteed market participants a semiautonomous area in society. In short, the basic lesson was once again that whenever peace, easy taxes, and a reasonable administration of justice prevail, economic development follows in the natural course of things, and efforts by governments to thwart the natural development lead instead toward poverty and tyranny.

When one reads these different arguments from a Scotsman, two Frenchmen, a Brit, and finally a German, the consensus on the fundamental question of the causes of the wealth and poverty of nations is striking. But this consensus proved to be extremely fragile. Classical political economy proved to be quite vulnerable to critiques that focused on (a) instability, (b) monopoly, and (c) inequality. Karl Marx was the most thorough critic along these lines, but several others contributed along the way by pecking holes in the classical system of political economy. The presumption was being reversed.

Obviously, as with all living bodies of thought, there were weak spots in the classical presentation of laissez-faire, but eventually these would be addressed to a considerable extent by the neoclassical theory of value and price (Boettke 2006).[2] For example, the neoclassical theory of factor pricing challenged theories of exploitation. But as Hayek has pointed out, by the time those theoretical revisions were made, the public mind had already been swayed to the other side:

> It takes a long time to rebuild the structure of a science if one starts by revising the fundamental concepts. And the modern revision of theoretical economics has occupied sufficient time to allow what was at first the heretical view of a number of radical economists—who had to fight what was then the conservatism of the practical men who were still under the influence of economic liberalism—to pervade the thought of the public and to establish itself as the dominating doctrine, not only among advanced social reformers, but even among the most conservative businessmen. The public mind in all leading countries of the world is now completely under the domination of the views which spring from the revolt against the classical economics of seventy years ago. ([1931] 2009, 24)

After examining their refinements to the core of economic theory, the early neoclassical economists increasingly came to the consensus that classical economists had arrived at essentially the correct conclusions with cruder instruments. Despite this fact, the classical presumption toward freedom of choice gave way to a popular demand for government action, and concern with the abuse of political power was dismissed as the groundless fear of a predemocratic era.

Theory and experience sided with the general thrust of the classical political economists, but the public mind and the political elite resisted that conclusion and were instead under the sway of interventionism guided by democratic consensus.[3] By the first decades of the 20th century, the classical presumption against interventionism was reversed, and now those who argued for laissez-faire were on the defensive.

The End of Laissez-Faire

In the United States in 1900, the government expenditures at the local, state, and federal levels added up to only 6 percent of gross domestic product (GDP), but by 1944 that figure was 48 percent. The policy changes of the Progressive Era that were initiated to address the supposed problems of private market monopoly, worker exploitation, and consumer ignorance were pushing against an "open door." The economists' presumption was gone as a constraint, and the intellectuals, politicians, and special interests were able to form a coalition that would not be denied. As government grew with World War I and in response to the Great Depression and then World War II, the problems of instability and injustice were said to be finally addressed by democratic governments in the West. The intellectual consensus was that capitalism was plagued by microeconomic inefficiencies in the form of monopoly and external effects in production and exchange, as well as macroeconomic instability that manifested itself in the form of business cycles and unemployment. Laissez-faire as a policy rule was unable to meet the challenge of the modern age. Instead, government was called on to serve as a corrective to the social ills through microeconomic regulation and macroeconomic fine-tuning and economic management. The discipline of economics was transformed to provide these policy tools of economic planning and social control, and various policy institutions were established with the purpose of carrying out the mission of economic policy so defined. As a consequence, government grew in both scope and scale.[4]

The main generation of economists and public policy intellectuals of the 20th century came of political consciousness during the Great Depression, finished their graduate education either during or after World War II, rose to professional prominence in the 1950s and 1960s, and became elder statesmen of the profession in the 1970s and 1980s. This was a generation that had lost faith in unbridled capitalism; believed deeply in the ability of democratic governments to address the social ills of poverty, racism, sexism, and other forms of social injustice; and took great pride in the new science of economics they had helped create, which could serve as a tool for social control to meet those challenges. This was a generation that defeated Hitler in their youth, and put a man on the moon by middle age. Only the most cynical and superstitious of that generation, it was believed, could doubt the progressive thrust of the new science of economics and democratically elected government, and instead demand a return to the older teachings of classical political economy that emphasized the institution of private property, freedom of contract, and constitutional constraints on the power of government.

By 1950, economic thought and policy were dominated by Keynesian demand management on the macroeconomic side, and market failure theory on the microeconomic side. During the 1946–1980 period the intellectual consensus was collectivist, but the policy practice was lagging behind. Government spending as a percentage of GDP in the United States expanded quickly as action chased after thought—while government spending declined immediately after World War II to 17 percent of GDP by 1948, it climbed to 32 percent by 1975. There was no serious intellectual resistance, save Milton Friedman, to the growth of government. Ideas and interests aligned to transform Western societies and also to build a policy consensus in the West's efforts abroad to address underdevelopment that was decidedly anti-market.[5] The voices of economists born in the 19th century, such as Mises and Hayek, that were raised to caution this trend, were dismissed. But a growing counterrevolution that emphasized the institutional infrastructure and economic processes started to emerge within the profession to challenge the Keynesian and market failure hegemony.

The property rights economics of Armen Alchian, Ronald Coase, and Harold Demsetz; the public choice economics of James Buchanan and Gordon Tullock; the new learning in industrial organization associated with George Stigler and Yale Brozen; the theory of the entrepreneurial market process associated with Israel Kirzner; the new economic history associated with Douglass North; and the monetarist critique of Keynesianism associated with Milton Friedman all emerged in the 1960s as a formidable opponent to the policy consensus from 1950 to 1970. By the mid-1970s, the presumption in thought had swung back decidedly in the direction of classical liberal political economy.

The reason for the counterrevolution was not exclusively intellectual. The fact that the Keynesian system was flawed due to its lack of a choice theoretic foundation was only part of the problem with the policy consensus. The real problem was that empirically the policy recipe did not deliver in either the United States or the United Kingdom. These economies stagnated, and they did so while also experiencing inflation. Unions were granted too much legal power and thus ossified labor markets; regulations and taxes strangled businesses and stifled innovation; permanent deficits and the distortions caused by inflation could all be accounted as a consequence of Lord Keynes. Even the Scandinavian welfare states had to confront the reality of fiscal imbalance, bloated bureaucracies, and the inverted pyramid as more and more citizens were public employees or on public support rather than in the private sector generating the wealth that in this system was taxed. Absent wealth generation, there just wasn't enough to tax to finance the extensive state that was created. Government could no longer be viewed as the corrective, since it was now evident that government was in fact the problem.

Policy would lag behind this intellectual recognition and unlike in the move from laissez-faire to statism, interest groups and politicians would block moves for policy to catch up to the new thinking. If the period between 1945 and 1975 was one of "galloping socialism" in Western democracies such as the United States and United Kingdom as big government was called on to serve as a corrective to economic ills (justified by market failure theory and Keynesianism), the period between 1975 and 2005 was one of "creeping liberalism" in the Western democracies as the justification for the previous policies were soundly defeated on the intellectual level, but the actual behavior of government in terms of spending, taxation, and regulation changed at a slower rate than should have followed from the intellectual victory.

Milton Friedman has argued that we have seen a victory in the realm of ideas, but a failure of implementation.[6] In the move from rhetoric to thought, and from thought to action, the classical liberal movement has been tripped up at the second stage. The stumbling blocks have mainly been a consequence of forces of inertia—the political resistance to change. Friedman explained this tyranny of the status quo as the alignment of intellectuals, interest groups, and politicians (an "iron triangle") who benefited from the existing array of policies and who would block any proposed change. Still, it is important to recognize that a counterrevolution in economic thought had been successful, and that the Keynesian and market failure dominance was defeated to a considerable extent by 1980 and thereafter.[7]

The End of Socialism

The collapse of socialism in the late 1980s represented what many thought would be a final blow against government planning and interventionism. The resurgent classical liberal political economy that represented the counter-revolution was firmly established in the academic world. Its basic rhetorical message was creeping into the intellectual culture and general climate of public opinion: socialism does not work. However, the general sentiment in the dominant intellectual culture—that humanity failed to live up to the ideals of socialism—got the message completely backward. Socialism did not fail because humanity could not live up to its lofty ideals, but the other way around: socialism failed to live up to the demands of humanity. To go back to the two natural proclivities mentioned earlier, socialism by suppressing our proclivity to engage in truck, barter, and exchange unleashed our proclivity for pillage and plunder. Instead of an egalitarian paradise, we had a reality of perverse incentives, economic inefficiency, political corruption, and regimes of ruthless brutality.

As socialism collapsed and the transition to capitalism was undertaken, it became evident fairly quickly that this would not be a smooth process. The triple transition of politics, economics, and national psychology was going to be more difficult than the promises of "500-day plans" or "shock therapy" seemed to offer.

The lesson to be learned from the experience in Eastern and Central Europe and the former Soviet Union is not that "shock therapy" is wrong. It is (a) that the introduction of market forces are only the first step in the process of transition, (b) that implementation via half measures more often than not will result in unintended and undesirable consequences that will undermine the long-term legitimacy of the policy change, and (c) that economic reforms do not exist within a vacuum but instead take place within a context of political/legal systems and social/cultural belief systems.[8] But the lesson that most policy observers come to is different. Instead, the difficulties of the transition were attributed to the so-called callousness of "neo-liberalism." We are told monetarism failed in Russia, when in fact we saw wild inflation in the 1990s as the Russian central bank printed rubles with reckless abandon. The result was that while in 1992 the ruble exchanged at roughly Rub 180 to US$1; in 1995, the ruble exchanged at over Rub 5,000 to US$1. Monetarism, if it means anything, should mean something about price level stability and the monetary rule. Obviously, Russia did not follow monetarism. Privatization also gets criticized, as does trade liberalization.

By the late 1990s, intellectual and policy patience with laissez-faire had worn off. Instead, questions such as "Who lost Russia?" or "What should be done about African underdevelopment and the AIDS epidemic?"' or "How is globalization adversely affecting the lives of the least-advantaged members of underdeveloped countries?" moved to the center stage in intellectual and policy discussions. We knew from economics and political economy that foreign aid was not particularly effective at addressing the systemic problems in underdeveloped countries, but the intellectual culture refused to follow the implication that it was trade and not aid that would lift the economic conditions (Easterly 2001, 2006).

Similarly, we learned from economics that trade harmonizes conflicting interests through market reconciliation over the terms of exchange, but our intellectual culture instead emphasized the clash of civilizations and the disillusion with globalization. Most of these critiques come from sources unenlightened by the economic way of thinking, but not always as some of the more vociferous criticisms and calls for government solutions come from the likes of Joseph Stiglitz, Jeffrey Sachs, and Paul Krugman.

Stiglitz (2003) basically argues that globalization has gone astray mainly because the world's governments have not listened to him. Sachs (2005) argues that Africa is trapped in a geographic situation that it cannot lift itself out of; it requires saviors, and he has volunteered. Krugman (2004) has decided that since he is so very smart, it is perfectly reasonable to use the op-ed page of the *New York Times* to discredit himself and his profession by becoming a political hack instead of practicing the sober analysis of the dismal science. In all three cases, we have economists who wish to return to the days of the Keynesian consensus when economists were in control of the instruments of social control and economic management (Krugman 2000). The lessons of the counterrevolution are alien to them. And as with Keynes before them, they ushered in a shift in the presumption in economic affairs.

The current presumption is that liberty must cede space to government power to do those things which liberty alone cannot accomplish. Fearfulness of the arrogance of power, on the one hand, and bureaucratic ineptitude, on the other, are disregarded. Instead, the mistaken belief is that if the right people are in power, and listen to the right ideas, then government can be the most significant source of positive change in the world, and that economists can provide the vital information required for efficient and just social control.[9] We can eliminate underdevelopment and poverty within a generation and establish an era of global justice, but only if we act in concert with one another and utilize the great power evident in good government.

The Rise of Leviathan

On the morning of September 11, 2001, the emerging intellectual consensus that challenged laissez-faire at the end of the 20th century was cemented into the cultural and policy zeitgeist of our times. Socialism may have failed. Interventionism may have proved unstable and fiscally unsound. But the belief was that the market had indeed met its match in the difficult transitions in the postcommunist countries of Eastern and Central Europe and the former Soviet Union, and the lingering underdevelopment in Africa, Asia, Latin America, and the failed and weak states of war-torn Middle East. Moreover, none of the thriving capitalist countries followed strict laissez-faire despite the instability and fiscal imbalance that interventionism wrought. Instead, the philosophy of "best practice" seemed to suggest that some form of mixed economy, which encourages technological innovation and wealth creation and yet redistributes income to care for the least advantaged, was the system to be emulated. The secret of success was not to be found in the power of the market, but in "good governance."

After the terrorist attacks on US soil, the argument about markets versus government seemed to be completely off the mark. Certainly, laissez-faire could not provide an answer to questions of national security against the terrorists' attacks. Liberty had to cede space to government power not only to realize global social justice, but also to provide security and safety at home.

Benjamin Franklin once wisely remarked that a people who would be willing to give up their liberty in the name of security deserve neither. Franklin understood something that our contemporary policy culture fails to appreciate—namely, that the sicknesses in government can generate a sickness in the people. The human character can atrophy under government domination, and a culture of dependency replaces a culture of self-reliance and initiative. Classical thinkers from Montesquieu to Tocqueville understood this point about human faculties, as did Hume, Smith, Hayek, and Buchanan (see Buchanan 2005).

Despite these warnings from our forebearers, big government has returned in the name of providing security to protect our way of life—which was presumably grounded in individual liberty. Total government spending as a percentage of GDP was 32 percent in 1976, prior to the so-called "age of Milton Friedman," and 31 percent in 2005. The counterrevolution in economic thought has not produced the same change in actual government behavior that was evident in the wake of the Keynesian and market failure revolutions in thought. Whereas those earlier shifts in ideas pushed against an "open door" of government's natural proclivity to spend and cater to special-interest groups, the counterrevolution of privatization, deregulation, fiscal restraint, monetary responsibility, and free trade pushes against a "closed door."

To put it another way, the expansion of government promises direct benefits to well-organized and well-informed interest groups with costs being spread to the unorganized and ill-informed mass of voters. However, when that process is reversed, we confront a situation where we are attempting to concentrate costs on the organized and well-informed (who will lose their special privileges) and disperse the benefits on the unorganized and ill-informed (who will experience these benefits). As a result, while the Keynesian and market failure revolutions produced "galloping socialism" in the United States, the counterrevolution in political economy has produced only a "creeping liberalism."

We were poised for more change in the direction of liberty and against power, but the disillusionment with market reforms in the former Soviet Bloc and in Latin America (in particular Argentina)[10] and then the terrorist threat effectively eliminated the momentum for real substantive changes. Ironically, the intellectual battle was so decisively won by the counterrevolution that the champions of big government often use the language of the market and voluntarism to defend the expansion of powers by the state.

Those in power see the great creative responsiveness of the voluntary nonprofit sector in responding to those in need, and so they establish government programs to support the voluntary sector (and in the process co-opt the voluntary sector into the coercive sector of the state). Those in power see the great innovativeness of the entrepreneurial market economy, and so they establish government programs to encourage entrepreneurship and seek to orchestrate clusters of scientists, businesspeople, and intellectuals in would-be economic growth areas (and in the process undermining the natural development of mutually reinforcing bonds of inquiry, innovation, and profit seeking). We have President George W. Bush preaching fiscal conservatism, while increasing spending more than any other president, including Lyndon Johnson during his "Great Society" programs.[11]

Consider the spending of the Department of Homeland Security alone: in fiscal year 2001, it was a little over $10 billion, but in fiscal year 2005 that figure was over $25 billion. Also consider the organizational logic of that department. Faced with a crisis, the government vertically integrated and established a hierarchical bureaucracy. The United States centralized to fight an enemy that is decidedly decentralized. A bureaucratic behemoth was created to defeat a nimble entrepreneurial enemy. If the lessons of the mainline of argument in political economy had been learned, then perhaps we would think about this differently.[12]

The push toward centralization and the expansion of powers was set in motion well before the domestic crisis that hit the Gulf Coast in August/September 2005. Katrina was in many ways a first test case of the ability of this new bureaucracy to respond quickly and effectively to a crisis that threatened domestic tranquility, and it failed miserably. Government ineptitude and callousness stood out in stark contrast to the individual initiative and heroic compassion of the voluntary-sector first responders. If the heroes of 9/11 were the New York City firefighters that risked their lives to save others, the heroes of Katrina were the religious leaders and others in the voluntary sector who worked around the government system to get into the impacted areas to get people out before the storm, and to recover and rescue individuals who were stranded after the storm. And in the rebuilding effort after the storm, we can see the power of individual initiative in the voluntary sector as neighborhoods, commerce, and lives are rebounding, and the ineptitude of government that slows the recovery with unnecessary regulations and restrictions and often devolves into opportunities for corruption.[13]

If Katrina is any sort of "test" of the system in a post-9/11 world, then we should be concerned that the increased centralization of the response to crisis fails to address the basic economic problems of incentives and information. The "mainstream" response from mechanism design theory—which says that duplication and delays in response to crisis can be avoided through centralization—has confused the issue. The "mainline" wisdom about who is in the best situation to judge the use of local knowledge and the arrogance and abuse-of-power problem associated with state centralization is directly on point (Sobel and Leeson 2006).[14] Indeed, how can anyone schooled in the teachings of political economy from Smith to Hayek expect a behemoth bureaucracy, competing with a nimble entrepreneurial enemy, to secure domestic safety and leave room for the freedom that we are supposedly fighting for?

A century after we started our narrative, we are back to the critical question of whether laissez-faire or government control should be the basis for the political economy of the future. The argument and evidence weight on the side of laissez-faire. Moral intuitions about the zero-sum nature of exchange and the lust for power by those in politics cut against the teachings of political economy. Ludwig von Mises perhaps summed up the state of intellectual affairs best:

> The issue has been obfuscated by the endeavors of governments and powerful pressure groups to disparage economics and to defame the economists. Despots and democratic majorities are drunk with power. They must reluctantly admit that they are subject to the laws of nature. But they reject the very notion of economic law. Are they not the supreme legislators? Don't they have the power to crush every opponent? No war lord is prone to acknowledge any limits other than those imposed on him by a superior armed force. Servile scribblers are always ready to foster such complacency by expounding the appropriate doctrines. In fact, economic history is a long record of government policies that failed because they were designed with a bold disregard for the laws of economics.
>
> It is impossible to understand the history of economic thought if one does not pay attention to the fact that economics as such is a challenge to the conceit of those in power. An economist can never be a favorite of autocrats and demagogues. With them he is always the mischief-maker, and the more they are inwardly convinced that his objections are well-founded, the more they hate him. ([1949] 1966, 66–67)

The intellectual battleground that Mises so clearly envisioned is the very battleground we must be ready to engage today. We are at a critical juncture in the history of political economy and public policy. If, as in the past, the dominant historical interpretation comes to be that power is the only appropriate response to crisis, then the gains that classical liberal political economy earned (however fleeting) with the defeat of Keynes and the collapse of socialism will be lost on the new generation. Just as the interventionist interpretation of the Progressive Era, the Great Depression, and the New Deal were countered with impeccable historical scholarship informed by the teachings of the mainline of political economy, a whole new set of arguments must be countered. The idea that market reforms in Eastern and Central Europe have failed, the idea that big government initiatives generate development in the underdeveloped world, and the idea that big government must protect us from foreign invasion in our homeland must be countered with careful reasoning and close attention to the historical facts.

The greatest accomplishment of the discipline of political economy demonstrates how peaceful social cooperation can emerge through voluntary choices and mutually beneficial exchange. Conflicting interests are reconciled in the market and social harmony is produced—as stated in the classical tradition, the Jew, the Gentile, and the Muslim may be at war with one another but can find peace through their transactions in the market. It is a great intellectual shame that "mainstream" economics has often lost the ability to understand the civilizing function of trade and commerce.

Conclusion

The role of the economist in a free society is that of a teacher, scholar, and critic, but never that of a social engineer and planner. The political economists in the tradition of the mainline reject the role of expert for state-directed economic planning. But if government is viewed as a corrective to social ills, someone must be there to supply the arguments and tools to aid the government in this task. Economists—as they have come to be defined in the mainstream of economics throughout much of the 20th and into the 21st century—are precisely those who pretend to be able to provide the arguments and tools for government policy to fine-tune, manage, or plan the economy.

I have argued that the distinction between mainline and mainstream helps us understand the critical points in policy history and the role that economic ideas played in them. These historical turning points turned on who won the debate over the relative merits of liberty versus power. Unfortunately, in the historical sample we considered the policy world turned in favor of power over liberty with the consequence of economic deprivation and political tyranny in the worst cases, and economic stagnation and the nanny state in the best cases.

The unfortunate consequences of ceding liberty to power should give us pause. The intellectual argument for liberty has had only fleeting success in the 20th century, but hope remains for the 21st century. My sincere hope is that groups like the Association for Private Enterprise Education will serve as a catalyst for a new generation of political economists who want to walk in the mainline path of Adam Smith, Frédéric Bastiat, and F. A. Hayek.

Notes

1. For my own approach to teaching the economic way of thinking, see *The Economic Way of Thinking* by Paul Heyne, Peter J. Boettke, and David L. Prychitko (2005).
2. The tension evident in the classical liberal position between the presumption toward voluntarism but the claimed necessity for government coercion to provide the framework within which voluntary action can be relied on to produce social order will not be discussed here, but is addressed in my paper "Anarchism as a Progressive Research Program in Political Economy" (2006).
3. Ludwig von Mises points out that once the state was attributed both benevolence and omniscience, "then one could not help concluding that the infallible state was in a position to succeed in the conduct of production activities better than erring individuals. It would avoid all those errors that often frustrate the actions of entrepreneurs and capitalists. There would no longer be malinvestment or squandering of scarce factors of production; wealth would multiply. The 'anarchy' of production appears wasteful when contrasted with the planning of the omniscient state. The socialist mode of production then appears to be the only reasonable system, and the market economy seems the incarnation of unreason" ([1949] 1966, 692).
4. The best work on the growth of government in the United States during the 20th century is Robert Higgs's *Crisis and Leviathan* (1987). Also see his most recent work *Depression, War, and the Cold War* (2006) for an examination of the critical decades dealing with the Great Depression and World War II.
5. Consider the dismissive intellectual treatment that the work of P. T. Bauer on the economics of underdevelopment and the failure of foreign aid received in the 1960s and 1970s. A conference honoring Bauer was held at Princeton University in May 2004. During the question-and-answer period, Amartya Sen was asked what the biggest difference was in development economics from 1964 to 2004. He responded that in 1964 everyone viewed the market system as a zero-sum game and thus politics had to provide the answer, while in 2004 it is the other way around.
6. Friedman being interviewed on *The Charlie Rose Show*, December 26. 2005.

7. Consider the recognition by the Nobel Prize committee as weak evidence of this shift in thought: Hayek (in 1974), Friedman (in 1976), Buchanan (in 1986), Coase (in 1991), and North (in 1993).

8. It's not my purpose here to detail the politics and economics of socialist transformation, but I have presented my position elsewhere (see Boettke, *Why Perestroika Failed* [1993] and *Calculation and Coordination* [2001]). For a quick summary of the basics of what we have learned from our experience with economics in transition, see Boettke (2004).

9. For a critique of this idea of economists as saviors, see Boettke and Coyne (2006b).

10. See the critiques of the "Washington Consensus" that emerged in the late 1990s and early 2000s. Stiglitz (2003) is the most recognized critic, but also see Amsden, Kochanowicz, and Taylor (1995).

11. The annualized real growth in discretionary spending by Bush is 8 percent and Johnson is 4.6 percent.

12. Obviously, there are many issues associated with the post-9/11 world we live in. On why the war on terror is not being carried out in an effective manner from an economic point of view, see Boettke and Coyne (2006a). Christopher Coyne's book *After War: The Political Economy of Exporting Democracy* (2008) is the most comprehensive examination of the difficulties associated with constructivist attempts to impose sustainable democracies and market economies in these war-torn regions.

13. See the working papers released by the Mercatus Center at George Mason University by Emily Chamlee-Wright (2006) and Peter Leeson and Russell Sobel (2006).

14. A story from World War II by George Stigler when he worked at the Office of Price Administration is right on this point. Stigler was amazed at how unprepared and ridiculous the procedures for military procurement were. He was later asked by Tjalling Koopmans whether or not it was true that he (Stigler) had advocated the use of the price system to evacuate Manhattan in the case of a bombing. Stigler responded that he did not make the proposal, and that in the case of a bombing of Manhattan, he expected any system of evacuation to be confused and inefficient. But then he added, "If the bombings became repetitive, however, I thought the price system could handle the problem well. . . . I believe now even more than I did then in the market system's flexibility, adaptability, and resourcefulness in finding new ways to make money" (1988, 61).

References

Acton, Lord. 1904. *Letters of Lord Acton to Mary Gladstone*. Edited by Herbert Paul. London: Macmillan.

Amsden, Alice H., Jacek Kochanowicz, and Lance Taylor. 1995. *The Market Meets Its Match: Restructuring the Economies of Eastern Europe*. Cambridge, MA: Harvard University Press.

Bastiat, Frédéric. [1845] 1964. "A Petition." Reprinted in *Economic Sophisms*. New York: Foundation for Economic Education.

Boettke, Peter J. 1993. *Why Perestroika Failed: The Politics and Economics of Socialist Transformation*. New York: Routledge.

———. 2001. *Calculation and Coordination: Essays on Socialism and Transitional Political Economy*. New York: Routledge.

———. 2004. "An 'Austrian' Perspective on Transitional Political Economy." *Ama-Gi: Journal of the Hayek Society at the London School of Economics* 6 (2): 12–14.

———. 2006. "Anarchism as a Progressive Research Program in Political Economy." In *Anarchy, State and Public Choice*, edited by Edward Stringham, 51–66. Cheltenham, UK: Edward Elgar.

Boettke, Peter J., and Christopher J. Coyne. 2006a. "Liberalism in a Post-9/11 World." *Journal of Private Enterprise* 22 (2): 7–36.

———. 2006b. "The Role of the Economist in Economic Development." *Quarterly Journal of Austrian Economics* 19 (1): 47–68.

Buchanan, James M. 2005. "Afraid to Be Free: Dependency on Desideratum." *Public Choice* 124 (1): 19–31.

Chamlee-Wright, Emily. 2006. "After the Storm." Working paper, Mercatus Center at George Mason University, Arlington, VA.

Coyne, Christopher J. 2008. *After War: The Political Economy of Exporting Democracy*. Stanford, CA: Stanford University Press.

Easterly, William. 2001. *The Elusive Quest for Growth: Economists' Adventures and Misadventures in the Tropics*. Cambridge, MA: MIT Press.

———. 2006. *The White Man's Burden: Why the West's Efforts to Aid the Rest Have Done So Much Ill and So Little Good*. New York: Penguin Books.

Hayek, F. A. [1931] 2009. *The Trend of Economic Thinking: Essays on Political Economists and Economic History*. Edited by W. W. Bartley III and Stephen Kresge. Indianapolis: Liberty Fund.

———. 1948. *Individualism and Economic Order*. Chicago: University of Chicago Press.

Heyne, Paul, Peter J. Boettke, and David L. Prychitko. 2005. *The Economic Way of Thinking*. 11th ed. Upper Saddle River, NJ: Prentice Hall.

Higgs, Robert. 1987. *Crisis and Leviathan*. New York: Oxford University Press.

———. 2006. *Depression, War, and Cold War*. New York: Oxford University Press.

Krugman, Paul R. 2000. *The Return of Depression Economics*. New York: W. W. Norton.

———. 2004. *The Great Unraveling: Losing Our Way in the New Century*. New York: W. W. Norton.

Leeson, Peter T., and Russell S. Sobel. 2006. "Weathering Corruption." Working paper, Mercatus Center at George Mason University, Arlington, VA.

Madison, James. [1788] 1993. "The Federalist LI." *Independent Journal*, February 6. Reprinted in *The Debate on the Constitution, Part Two*. New York: Library of America.

Mill, John Stuart. [1848] 1967. *Principles of Political Economy, with Some of Their Applications to Social Philosophy*. New York: Augustus M. Kelley.

Mises, Ludwig von. [1949] 1966. *Human Action: A Treatise on Economics*. Chicago: Henry Regnery.

Sachs, Jeffrey. 2005. *The End of Poverty: Economic Possibilities for Our Time*. New York: Penguin Press.

Say, Jean-Baptiste. [1821] 1971. *A Treatise on Political Economy*. New York: Augustus M. Kelley.

Smith, Adam. [1776] 1976. *An Inquiry into the Nature and Causes of the Wealth of Nations*. Chicago: University of Chicago Press.

Sobel, Russell S., and Peter T. Leeson. 2006. "The Use of Knowledge in Natural Disaster Relief Management." Working paper, Mercatus Center at George Mason University, Arlington, VA.

Stigler, George J. 1988. *Memoirs of an Unregulated Economist*. New York: Basic Books.

Stiglitz, Joseph E. 2003. *Globalization and Its Discontent*. New York: W. W. Norton.

Weber, Max. 1927. *General Economic History*. New York: Greenberg.

Chapter 4
What Happened to "Efficient Markets"?

The financial crisis of 2008 has challenged the reputation of the free-market economy in the public imagination in a way that it has not been challenged since the Great Depression. The intellectual consensus after World War II was that markets are unstable and exploitive and thus in need of government action on a variety of fronts to counteract these undesirable characteristics. In the United States, this intellectual consensus did not result in nationalization of industry, but in detailed regulation and heavy government involvement in economic life.

The stagnation of the 1970s reversed this trend of public policy, at least in regard to the related rhetoric. A new sense of reliance on the market's capabilities and a fear of the government's overreaching took hold of the public imagination. By the end of the 1980s, communism's collapse throughout Eastern and Central Europe and in the former Soviet Union reinforced a sense of intellectual triumph for market-oriented thinking over the demands for government regulation and control. The consensus in favor of the free-market economy proved fleeting, however, as the difficulties of transition, the plight of underdeveloped countries, and the tensions of globalization all came to represent, in the eyes of several pivotal intellectuals, the failings of the free-market system.

With the stock market losing 50 percent of its value over the past year, major banks failing, real estate values collapsing, and unemployment creeping toward double digits, claims about the superiority of the market economy over government intervention are difficult for many to view with credibility. But this situation arises from previous intellectual failings in the discourse concerning the nature of the market economy, the failings of socialism, the costs of government intervention, and the role of public policy. Simply put,

Presentation at the Mont Pelerin Society special meeting "The End of Globalizing Capitalism? Classical Liberal Responses to the Global Financial Crisis," New York, March 5–7, 2009. Published in *The Independent Review* 14, no. 3 (Winter 2010): 363–75.

we must always remember that bad economic ideas result in bad public policies, which in turn produce bad economic outcomes. The economist's role must be to counter the first step and defeat the promulgation of bad economic ideas. Doing so is no easy task given the counterintuitive nature of economic reasoning and the role of vested interests in the development of public policy in democratic systems. But if the economist does not do the job, market corrections may be transformed into economic crises by the implementation of ill-fated government policies. And economic crisis may be transformed into political and economic catastrophe as bad ideas are joined with opportunistic politicians who, in the name of meeting the challenge of the crisis, persuade the public to trade their liberties for the promise of security.

In a time of extreme economic adjustment, it is important to remind everyone how markets in fact work. Falling asset prices, business failures, and reallocations of resources (including workers) evince efficient-market adjustments to changing circumstances as much as the exploitation of profit opportunities and the exhaustion of mutual gains from exchange do. In fact, they are the flip side of one another, just as maximizing profits and mini-mizing costs are. The market process is a profit-and-loss system. Prudent economic decisions are rewarded, and imprudent decisions are penalized. The market economy in this regard is indeed a ruthless, unrelenting, and ceaseless process of economic change.

Viewed in this light, "efficient" markets are evident every day on Wall Street, as well as on Main Street, whether we are living through "good times" or "bad times." Resources are continually being shuffled and reshuffled in attempts to realize their greatest return. This version of the claim of efficient-market adjustment through time follows simply from the basic economic insight that incentives matter and from the proposition that individuals will discover what they have an interest in discovering. As Adam Smith put it, the neces-sary adjustments are not accomplished by "accurate measure, but by the hig-gling and bargaining of the market," and although the result is not exact, it is "sufficient for carrying on the business of common life" ([1776] 1976, 36).

Ludwig von Mises makes a similar point about economic calculation's not being "perfect," yet nevertheless necessary and sufficient for the practical demands of commercial life. The deficiencies of monetary calculation that critics of economics often highlight are real, but their criticism is misplaced because within the specified limits (and Mises argues that within practical life, these limits are never overstepped) "monetary calculation does all that we are entitled to ask of it. It provides a guide amid the bewildering throng of economic possibilities" ([1922] 1981, 100).

The classical economists' market theory did not provide a point prediction of exchange ratios except in the simplest of examples (e.g., Smith's deer-and-beaver model). Instead, the theory traced out tendencies and the direction of change in response to shifting conditions in supply and demand. The price system was depicted as one of adjustment to and accommodation of constantly changing tastes and technology. The classical theory did not maintain that producers and consumers never make errors in judgment, but that persistent errors are weeded out as producers confront resource constraints and consumers are presented with alternatives.

Consumers' buying and abstaining from buying as they seek greater satisfaction ultimately direct resource use, and the striving for profit ensures that producers employ least-cost methods in their attempts to meet consumer demand. Any position short of this end point will mean that both consumers and producers can become better off by changing their behavior and realizing the mutual gains. The classical theory of the market economy is a theory of *economic activity*, not of a state of affairs, and it relies not only on the individuals currently populating the market to correct previous errors, but also on perceptive entrepreneurs who may enter the market to eradicate error. Property, prices, and profit or loss cajole and discipline market participants to act so as to realize gains from trade and create wealth.

The depiction of economic activity is less analytically precise than the depiction of a settled state of affairs. As the scientific demands on economic theory shifted from a theory of price formation to a theory of price determination in the late 19th century, the analytical focus centered on the settled state of affairs rather than on the economic activity. This state of affairs was previously described using simple examples and was intended only to highlight the central tendencies of the market-exchange process. The classical economists' value theory and cost theory could not explain several paradoxes that demanded resolution for scientific refinement. It must be stressed, however, that although in a fundamental sense the classical economists of the 18th and 19th centuries were correct in their understanding of market theory and the price system—the big picture—they were wrong about the particulars of value and cost. In their turn, the emerging neoclassical economists—in resolving the paradoxes in value theory and cost theory—at times unfortunately lost sight of the big-picture understanding of the market system as the active process of "higgling and bargaining" that was evident in the work of David Hume, Adam Smith, Jean-Baptiste Say, David Ricardo, and John Stuart Mill.

This is not to say that classical economics needed no adjustment—it certainly did. But the great discovery of the self-regulating properties of a market economy and the central importance of private property, free pricing, and the lure of pure profit and the penalty of loss in explaining the market's self-regulation needed not so much repair as refinement in explanation.

In striving to provide a formally rigorous explanation of self-regulation, neoclassical models have tended to focus not on the adjustments to changing conditions, but on the settled state of affairs that results when all changes have ceased. The equilibrium condition occupies center stage, and the idea of an "efficient market" has come to mean something entirely different. It took decades for this transformation to fully take hold of the imagination of economists, but the analytical roots are found in the effort to depict the economic system as a set of simultaneous equations with unique price and quantity vectors that will clear the market.

For mathematical tractability, the model relies on a prereconciliation of economic plans prior to the posting of bids and asks. Because no "false trades" are allowed in the market, the precision of the mathematical solution to a system of simultaneous equations means that the "higgling and bargaining" process that Smith described as the core of the market economy is formally suppressed in the neoclassical model of the market: the current market price not only clears the market, but also fully reflects opportunity costs. Firms produce the quantities of outputs that minimize average costs of production; in other words, they employ in production the least-cost technology. With proof of the existence of unique price and quantity vectors, not only will quantities supplied and demanded be equated and the market clear, but also such a state of economic affairs will possess simultaneously the desirable welfare properties of achieving exchange efficiency, production efficiency, and product-mix efficiency. In other words, such a world cannot be improved because all gains from trade are being realized—and realized in the most efficient way.

This quick detour through 250 years of intellectual history in economics provides background for the three competing hypotheses about "efficient markets" that exist to this day in economic discourse:

1. H_1 (neoclassical perfect competition perspective): Markets are efficient, and there are no unexploited opportunities for mutual gain.
2. H_2 (neo-Keynesian synthesis, market failure perspective): Markets are imperfect and inefficient, and government intervention is a necessary corrective.
3. H_3 (classical and new institutional market process perspective): Markets at any point in time have many unexploited opportunities for mutual gain, but this fact drives the market system to mobilize individual initiative effectively and to use the dispersed knowledge in the system to realize gains from trade and gains from innovation, and in so doing to make systemic adjustments that promote wealth creation and produce generalized prosperity.

The intellectual problem that economists face, especially in our current context of economic woe, is that H_3 is too subtle to capture in a formally precise model, and therefore scientific debate, not to speak of public debate, tends to focus on the clash of H_1 and H_2, often leaving unexamined the proposition that government can serve effectively as a corrective agency.[1]

As a result, we simultaneously fail to understand how markets actually work to coordinate economic life and underestimate the cost of government intervention in economic affairs. The consequence of this sad dual state of intellectual affairs is that economics as a discipline loses its ability to ward off public fallacies, and therefore public policies that undermine long-term wealth creation (and in the extreme limit the nation's economic viability) are more likely to be adopted.[2]

This situation obviously has relevance for current policy debates over the role of the market economy in generating long-term prosperity. In the scientific and public imagination, efficient markets came to mean that at any point in time the current market arrangement is the best of all possible worlds. Even the most ardent defenders of the efficient-market hypothesis were usually more subtle in their verbal presentations, but this nuance was glossed over owing to the primacy placed on the formal model for assessment. In *Foundations of Finance*, Eugene Fama argues: "An efficient capital market is a market that is efficient in processing information. . . . In an efficient market, prices 'fully reflect' available information" (1976, 132). In *The Theory of Finance*, Fama and coauthor Merton Miller explain:

Such a market has a very desirable feature. In particular, at any point in time market prices of securities provide accurate signals for resource allocation; that is, firms can make production-investment decisions, and consumers can choose among the securities that represent ownership of firms' activities under the presumption that security prices at any time 'fully reflect' all available information. A market in which prices fully reflect available information is called efficient. (1972, 335)

As noted earlier, such a market simultaneously achieves exchange efficiency, production efficiency, and product-mix efficiency. The proofs are elegant, and the implications are astonishing in that under such market conditions there is no need for government action beyond establishment of the framework—law and order, a monetary system, and international peace. In the public imagination, this depiction is the modern rendition of Adam Smith's "invisible hand" and thus provides the technical argument for laissez-faire economic policy.

The market economy would truly be self-correcting in this scenario because no errors would be made. No $20 bills would be left lying on the sidewalk except when the cost of picking them up exceeded $20. The only change to the system would be exogenous changes in tastes or technology, but the market would adapt to those changes instantaneously, and the prices in the economy would fully reflect the relevant information.

In contrast to Fama and Miller (and others), theorists such as Joseph Stiglitz (developing earlier ideas of market failure found in the writings of Samuelson, Francis Bator, and Kenneth Arrow) set out to offer an alternative to the efficient-market hypothesis. Stiglitz built his career on demonstrating the fragility of the neoclassical model of market efficiency, given slight deviations from its restrictive assumptions. Stiglitz stresses imperfections in the information that actors possess and deviations from perfectly competitive market conditions. Given asymmetric information and a monopolistically competitive environment, Stiglitz argues, market perversities rather than market perfection are likely to result. Summarizing his contribution to the literature on market efficiency in *Whither Socialism?* Stiglitz writes:

One of the claims frequently made of the price system is its informational efficiency. . . . To be sure, there is great informational efficiency. Under the idealized conditions of the Arrow-Debreu model, prices do convey information efficiently from producers to consumers, and vice versa. Yet this is an extremely limited information problem. When a heavier informational burden is placed on markets—when it must sort among workers of different ability or securities of different qualities, when it must provide incentives to workers in the presence of imperfect monitoring, when it must obtain and process new information about an ever changing environment—markets do not perform so well, even in terms of our limited welfare criterion of constrained Pareto efficiency. (1994, 43–44)

Between Fama and Stiglitz, Stiglitz would seem to have the upper hand in the debate in our current context. The reason for this verdict is simple: the informational burden of the investment market during the 2000s obviously appeared to be greater than what the efficient-market hypothesis can bear. But this conclusion is only an artifact of the model fetishism of 20th-century economics.

First, even the strictest model of competitive equilibrium does not contend that government policy cannot derail the market economy. To use an analogy, if Michael Phelps were thrown into a pool of water with his hands tied and his legs shackled with a weighted ball, he would still be the world's best swimmer, even if he sank. He simply would be prevented from swimming. The problem is not swimmer failure, but the rope and shackle with weighted ball that prevent him from making the very movements required to swim effectively. If government interventions distort information and provide perverse incentives, and in this situation economic actors make mistakes, the market is not leading them astray; the government interventions have discouraged the market's participants from weeding out error.

Second, the market failure criticism fails to appreciate how, from Adam Smith to F. A. Hayek, the historical argument in favor of markets does not focus on the equilibrium properties of the market, but on its adjustment properties. Today's inefficiency represents tomorrow's profit for the entrepreneur who recognizes and grasps the opportunity. The market economy's strength is its dynamic adjustment to constantly changing circumstances. Entrepreneurs react to the existing array of prices to realize gains from trade through arbitrage, and the lure of pure profits spurs entrepreneurs to realize the gains from innovation through the introduction of new products or the discovery of better ways to produce or deliver existing products.

In the 1940s, Hayek warned his fellow economists of the misleading standards of perfect competition and static efficiency in assessing the market economy. As he wrote in *Individualism and Economic Order*:

These adjustments are probably never 'perfect' in the sense which the economist conceives them in his equilibrium analysis. But I fear that our theoretical habits of approaching the problem with the assumption of more or less perfect knowledge on the part of almost everyone has made us somewhat blind to the true function of the price mechanism and led us to apply rather misleading standards in judging its efficiency. (1948, 87)

The efficient-market hypothesis theoretically represents a misplaced concreteness as the formal model becomes confused with the reality of the market process. The price system's "true function" is to guide entrepreneurial discovery and adjustment. Hayek also recognized the market's robustness in the face of numerous interventions. In *The Constitution of Liberty*, he points out:

A free system can adapt itself to almost any set of data, almost any general prohibition or regulation, so long as the adjusting mechanism itself is kept functioning. And it is mainly changes in prices that bring about the necessary adjustments. This means that, for it to function properly, it is not sufficient that the rules of law under which it operates be general rules, but their content must be such that the market will work tolerably well. (1960, 228)

Making a similar point almost two centuries earlier, Adam Smith argued:

The natural effort of every individual to better his own condition, when suffered to exert itself with freedom and security, is so powerful a principle, that it is alone, and without any assistance, not only capable of carrying on the society to wealth and prosperity, but of surmounting a hundred impertinent obstructions with which the folly of human laws too often incumbers its operations. ([1776] 1976, 49–50)

To use my earlier analogy, Michael Phelps certainly might still swim with hands tied and feet shackled (he did win the gold medal in the butterfly, so he could do some sort of kick to get across the pool), but if a weighted ball were added to drag him down, the restraint of his movement and the burden of the weight would probably prove to be insuperable. Government policies can likewise reach a point at which they obstruct the market from working effectively to make the necessary adjustments. This situation does not evince the inefficiency of the market economy, but only the destructive power of sufficiently burdensome government intervention.[3]

The critical question we must ask is, what government policies represent the tipping point at which market forces cannot overcome the obstruction?

I suggest three: inflation, price controls, and regime (or rule) uncertainty. Each of these government policies undermines the market economy's basic functions. Inflation threatens to destroy the meaningfulness of the capital and cost accounting that provides the basis for commercial decisions. Price controls block the market's ability to adjust to changing conditions of supply and demand. And regime uncertainty (not a policy itself, but a condition that results from the kind of policies adopted and the frequency with which they are altered)—by shifting the ground on which economic actors make decisions about saving, investment, and consumption—clouds an already murky economic landscape and thus distorts choices and shortens time horizons. All three conditions curtail the market's ability to muddle through the trials and tribulations of ordinary politics.

The case for laissez-faire is often difficult to communicate when, if the government obstructions are overcome, the economy muddles through, and the society materially progresses because the case ultimately relies on a counterfactual claim: economy X had a 10-year period of growth with government interventions a, b, c, and d, but had no such interventions occurred, more rapid growth would have occurred. How much greater growth there would have been nobody knows, because the counterfactual world was not experienced.

This problem is, of course, not new to economic reasoning. Frédéric Bastiat described it as a comparison between "what is seen" and "what is unseen," and he warned that bad economic reasoning results from focusing only on "what is seen." Hayek similarly argued that owing to the intellectual prejudices of scientism, expediency always defeats principle in public policy because the benefits for specific parties are identifiable, whereas when principle guides the government's actions, the benefits are dispersed and not identified by any specific party, but enjoyed by all. In fact, economic reasoning may be so counterintuitive that ignoring its teachings leads policy intellectuals to conclude that the government interventions *caused* the good economic performance (rather than *hindering* the economic performance) simply because the growth was experienced after the interventions were instituted—*post hoc ergo propter hoc*, a logical fallacy that rears its ugly head all too often in economic policy discussions.

We find ourselves in this situation today. The debate over the merits of the market intellectually misses the main merit of the price system and the market economy—their dynamic adjustment ability as prices, profits, and losses continuously signal, adapt to, and accommodate the ceaseless changes that occur in tastes and technology. Public policy debate assumes that the "efficient-market" theory has been found wanting and that government must be the only viable corrective. Both "right" and "left" call for activist government to stem the economic crisis; they just differ only on the details. The cost of government intervention is either unexamined or understated throughout the debate.[4] In short, the current intellectual consensus on economic policy fails to understand how markets work and why they are the source of prosperity and social harmony, and it underestimates how political control of economic life distorts incentives and information and gives rise to social conflict.

The public policy reality is that laissez-faire economics was *not* the policy norm in the United States over the past 25 years. Keynesian economics might have been intellectually defeated in the 1970s among academic economists, but in practice Keynesianism was the core intellectual framework for public policy and the guiding light for macroeconomic data collection and analysis. The main shift in "paradigm" spearheaded in the 1970s was actually an oscillation between "conservative" and "liberal" Keynesianism, *not* between laissez-faire and Keynesianism. Ronald Reagan's supply-side policies were "conservative" Keynesianism, whereas Barack Obama's fiscal stimulus is "liberal" Keynesianism. Both, however, are fundamentally Keynesian policies and therefore suffer from the same fundamental problems that plague all Keynesian policies, as pointed out more than 50 years ago by economists such as W. H. Hutt, F. A. Hayek, and James Buchanan. In fact, if I could choose a quick and easy set of mandatory readings for all politicians and policy advisers to offer them reasons for caution concerning our current path, it would comprise Hayek's *A Tiger by the Tail: The Keynesian Legacy of Inflation* (1979) and Buchanan and Richard Wagner's *Democracy in Deficit: The Political Legacy of Lord Keynes* ([1977] 2000). Both of these books explain how, once all restrictions (formal and informal) on government interference in economic life have been removed, the natural policy outcomes of democratic governments are government budget deficits, public debt, and monetary debasement.

Hayek argues that attempting to control inflation in our current monetary system is analogous to holding a tiger by the tail: if we let it go, it will eat us; if instead the tiger runs faster and faster, and yet we attempt desperately to hold on, we are still going to be eaten in the end (1979, 110). Buchanan and Wagner sum up the dire situation on the fiscal side less colorfully, but every bit as desperately: "Sober assessment suggests that, politically, Keynesianism may represent a substantial disease, one that can, over the long run, prove fatal for a functioning democracy" ([1977] 2000, 57).

Democratic government's natural proclivity is to concentrate benefits on the well-organized and well-informed interest groups in the short run and to disperse the costs across the ill-organized and ill-informed mass of voters and consumers in the long run. Fiscal responsibility is relaxed not only during a war or an economic crisis, but permanently as part of ordinary politics. Budgetary deficits finance the concentration of government benefits and steadily enlarge the public debt, which, in turn, is paid down through monetization. Thus, Keynesianism unleashes the natural proclivities of electoral politics, and debt, deficits, and debasement follow. Only through institutional innovations that minimize the role of government in the economy and through the introduction of binding restrictions on the natural proclivities of electoral politics will fiscal responsibility and monetary stability have a chance of being established.[5] But we are not heading in this policy direction.

As I am writing (in March 2009), the Obama administration is simultaneously continuing the Bush administration's activist agenda and distancing itself from that administration—quite a political balancing act. We are told that only bold and decisive government action can stave off catastrophe. When pushed during a House Ways and Means Committee hearing (US Congress 2009), Treasury Secretary Timothy Geithner claimed that the government's drastic actions during the fall of 2008 were essential to stop a complete collapse of all financial institutions in the United States and that the aggressive steps now being taken are fiscally responsible given the magnitude of the economic challenges the administration faces. He defended not only the fiscal stimulus, but also the Troubled Asset Relief Program and the various bailouts—indeed, the entire set of policies implemented since September. He clearly blamed the policymakers of the previous eight years, whom he claimed had engaged in reckless fiscal policy and gutted regulations, thereby letting loose Wall Street greed. And he repeated the standard line that all of the income growth over the past eight years was experienced by the top 2 percent of the income recipients, whereas the middle class enjoyed little to no income growth. Such rhetoric fosters class warfare, reckless spending, and credit expansion, and the consequences are disincentives to work and invest, unsustainable public debt, and long-term inflation. Repeat: deficits, debt, debasement.

The Bush administration certainly may be faulted, but the roots of our current crisis go much deeper in US history. The housing bubble, for example, owes much to policy initiatives introduced in the 1990s. The 1977 Community Reinvestment Act effectively lowered banks' lending standards so as to encourage home ownership, and in 1996 regulations issued under this act were extended from small to large banks. At the same time, the Clinton administration put pressure on the government-sponsored agencies Fannie Mae and Freddie Mac to expand mortgage lending to low-income borrowers. These policies perverted incentives and distorted the economic signals that individuals faced in making choices.

In addition, although the practice of central banking seemed to have become "perfected" during the post–World War II era and settled on a Milton Friedman–inspired "inflation-targeting" policy rule, Friedman's explanation of the Great Depression as the result of a series of policy errors, most notably monetary contraction and deflation, appeared to have been taken to heart by the central bankers. In 2002, at a celebration of Milton Friedman's 90th birthday, Ben Bernanke said the following: "Let me end my talk by abusing slightly my status as an official representative of the Federal Reserve. I would like to say to Milton and Anna: regarding the Great Depression, you're right, we did it. We're very sorry. But thanks to you, we won't do it again."

Little did Bernanke know that he would be the Federal Reserve chair when the bank confronted an economic crisis some are describing as the greatest challenge to the US economy since the Great Depression. Bernanke has definitely not allowed a "great contraction" during this period. Instead, he has done everything in his power to respond to the credit crunch with expansionary monetary policy.

To my mind, this situation illustrates Hayek's "tiger by the tail." Because of Friedman's concern with deflation, postwar monetary policy fought inflation in theory, but feared deflation in practice. The result was that Paul Volcker, Alan Greenspan, and now Bernanke have spoken about controlling inflation, but their monetary policy has been highly expansionary whenever economic times turn bad. The monetary base expanded tremendously under Greenspan in response to the dot-com, Y2K, and 9/11 scares, and again during the housing bubble. Market corrections take the form of price reductions, businesses failures, and resource (including labor) reallocations to higher-valued uses. But if each time a market correction takes place, the monetary authorities ease credit in an attempt to minimize the market correction's pain, they further distort the pattern of economic activity and delay the needed market adjustments.

Let us sum up the current US policy situation. A future of microeconomic distortions awaits us owing to the bank nationalizations, proposed restrictions on compensation, talk of financial reregulation, and changes in the tax structure. Ill-designed and ill-thought-out macroeconomic policies are being implemented, justified by the analogy that policymakers are throwing water to stop a burning fire, when, to stay within the analogy, they are actually throwing gasoline on the fire. Expansionary monetary policy to deal with the credit crunch is inflationary, and expansionary fiscal policy is not facing up to the microeconomic reality of the necessary market corrections to the previous resource misallocations.

A fundamental semantic issue also clouds current policy making because many of the proposed policies confuse credit with capital. Capital formation requires savings, not credit expansion. Recapitalization of the banks cannot be accomplished through easy credit, but only through increased saving. Credit expansion distorts rather than aids the relationship between saving and investment. If fiscal stimulus further distorts the process of market correction to the previous misallocation of resources, then the public spending will likewise be counterproductive. To repeat, policies that unleash the government habit, rather than constraining it, do not foster the creation of wealth. Deficits, debts, and debasement do not promote long-term economic prosperity. Yet the policy choices under the Bush administration and now under the Obama administration have moved us farther in this ill-fated direction.

To return to my opening question, "What happened to efficient markets?," I conclude that they are alive and kicking to survive. The "bad news" we often hear actually evinces market participants' working to correct for previous errors in the pattern of exchange, production, and distribution. However, if whenever the market attempts to adapt to changing circumstances and correct for previous errors, the government implements policies to stop the adjustments and corrections, the unfortunate outcome signifies not a failure of "efficient markets," but rather a government failure. Some of the propositions that follow from this perspective are difficult to swallow. Unemployment, for example, attests that the market is working to reallocate scarce labor resources to more productive uses. Idle resources may very well be idle because they are no longer of sufficient value in their previous uses. Resources must be reallocated in the process of economic-value creation. Wage rigidities, unemployment compensation, and so forth prevent labor from being reallocated as quickly as normal market pressures would bring about its reallocation.

So, if by "efficient market" we mean the sort of dynamic adjustment to changing conditions that I identified with the classical and new institutional/market process schools of economics, the workings of an efficient market are evident throughout the economy. Markets work through a process of entrepreneurial discovery and competitive selection. If, however, an "efficient market" entails that no errors are ever made and that adjustments occur instantaneously so that a Pareto-optimal pattern of resource allocation exists at any point in time, then we have to reject this standard.

This conception of market efficiency is not what thinkers from Smith to Hayek ever embraced in arguing for the market economy's superiority to alternative economic systems. Instead, their claim for the market was more dynamic in nature and humble in policy prescription. They argued that the advocates of government intervention displayed a "pretense of knowledge" and an "arrogance of power." Perhaps the most timely passage on this point in classical political economy belongs to Adam Smith, and it is fitting that I conclude this article by quoting it:

> What is the species of domestic industry which his capital can employ, and of which the produce is likely to be of the greatest value, every individual, it is evident, can, in his local situation, judge much better than any statesman or lawgiver can do for him. The statesman who should attempt to direct private people in what manner they ought to employ their capitals would not only load himself with a most unnecessary attention, but assume an authority which could safely be trusted, not only to no single person, but to no council or senate whatever, and which would nowhere be so dangerous as in the hands of a man who had folly and presumption enough to fancy himself fit to exercise it. ([1776] 1976, 478)

Notes

1. It is for this reason that I have argued that economics during the 20th century for the most part engaged in an intellectual detour where economists became increasingly precise about irrelevant points—precisely irrelevant (Boettke 1997). This was the fate of the discipline that Kenneth Boulding (1948) predicted in his review of Paul Samuelson's *Foundations of Economic Analysis* (1947). The flawless precision of mathematical economics, Boulding argued, may prove incapable of matching the insights of the literary vagueness of classical political economy and sociology.

2. Henry Simons taught a generation of students in the 1930s and 1940s at the University of Chicago that "academic economics is primarily useful, both to the student and to the political leader, as a prophylactic against popular fallacy" (1983, 3).

3. To illustrate both the robustness of markets and yet the vulnerability of economies to sabotage by obtrusive government, I often use the metaphor of a horse race between Adam Smith (who is realizing the gains from trade), Joseph Schumpeter (who is realizing the gains from innovation), and Stupidity (who is pursuing government power). As long as Smith and Schumpeter stay slightly ahead of Stupidity, tomorrow's trough will be higher than today's peak in terms of economic performance. But if Stupidity starts to get ahead of Smith and Schumpeter, the trend will be reversed, and economic performance will not improve through time. In other words, we can, economically speaking, put up with a great deal of government stupidity provided freedom of price fluctuations remains so that arbitrage opportunities can be pursued and also provided freedom of entry remains so that entrepreneurial discovery and innovation can continue.

4. A classic example is the discussion of nationalization of financial institutions and the idea that they can be nationalized, restructured, and then sold off at a profit so as to minimize the nationalization's cost. No serious effort is made to account for the vested interests that will form around the nationalized entity. It is as if public policy were made in a vacuum and the actors were all economic eunuchs.

5. Hayek argued for the denationalization of money to keep countries from feeding their government habit through inflation; Buchanan has argued in favor of a constitutional amendment to require a balanced budget; and both Hayek and Buchanan argued for a constitutional rule to force democratic policy to pass a generality test to curb the interest-group politics that drives the government habit of deficits, debts, and debasement.

References

Bernanke, Ben S. 2002. "Remarks by Governor Ben S. Bernanke on Milton Friedman's Ninetieth Birthday." Speech at the Conference to Honor Milton Friedman, University of Chicago, November 8.

Boettke, Peter J. 1997. "Where Did Economics Go Wrong? Modern Economics as a Flight from Reality." *Critical Review* 11 (1): 11–64.

Boulding, Kenneth E. 1948. "Samuelson's Foundations: The Role of Mathematics in Economics." *Journal of Political Economy* 56 (3): 187–99.

Buchanan, James M., and Richard E. Wagner. [1977] 2000. *Democracy in Deficit: The Political Legacy of Lord Keynes.* Vol. 8 of *The Collected Works of James M. Buchanan.* Indianapolis: Liberty Fund.

Fama, Eugene F. 1976. *Foundations of Finance.* New York: Basic Books.

Fama, Eugene F., and Merton H. Miller. 1972. *The Theory of Finance.* New York: Holt, Rinehart and Winston.

Hayek, F. A. 1948. *Individualism and Economic Order*. Chicago: University of Chicago Press.

———. 1960. *The Constitution of Liberty*. Chicago: University of Chicago Press.

———. 1979. *A Tiger by the Tail: The Keynesian Legacy of Inflation*. Washington, DC: Cato Institute.

Mises, Ludwig von. [1922] 1981. *Socialism: An Economic and Sociological Analysis*. Indianapolis: Liberty Fund.

Samuelson, Paul A. 1947. *Foundations of Economic Analysis*. Cambridge, MA: Harvard University Press.

Simons, Henry C. 1983. *The Simons' Syllabus*. Edited by Gordon Tullock. Fairfax, VA: Center for the Study of Public Choice at George Mason University.

Smith, Adam. [1776] 1976. *An Inquiry into the Nature and Causes of the Wealth of Nations*. Chicago: University of Chicago Press.

Stiglitz, Joseph E. 1994. *Whither Socialism?* Cambridge, MA: MIT Press.

US Congress, House Committee on Ways and Means. 2009. *The President's Fiscal Year 2010 Budget Overview: Hearing before the Committee on the Budget House of Representatives*. Washington, DC: US Government Printing Office.

Chapter 5

Is State Intervention in the Economy Inevitable?

G iven the prevailing ideology of our age, and the alignment of incentives within modern democratic governance, the *intervention* of the state in the economy (and in all walks of life) *is not inevitable* but *highly probable*. And that is unfortunate.

In this essay, state intervention refers to *discretionary* acts by government to intervene in the market economy. Such intervention violates the general operating rules of social interaction that were agreed upon in establishing the framework of governance. The good society is one where the framework of governance enables individuals to realize the gains from social cooperation under the division of labor, and therefore to experience the benefits of material progress, individual freedom, and peace—a society of free and responsible individuals who participate and have the opportunity to prosper in a market economy based on profit and loss, and who live in and are actively engaged in caring communities.

The great expansion of trade and technology in the 20th and 21st centuries has produced a level of material wealth that enabled the cost of government intervention to be offset, and remain largely hidden to many observers. This possibility is not a new phenomenon. Adam Smith pointed out long ago that the power of self-interest exercised in the market economy is so strong that it can overcome a "hundred impertinent obstructions with which the folly of human laws too often encumbers its operations" ([1776] 1981, 540). But it is important to stress that the great material progress realized over the past 100 years was not caused by the expansion of state intervention in the economy but in spite of those interventions. And the tipping point is when the number of "impertinent obstructions" grow from

Based on the paper presented at the 2011 Mont Pelerin Society meeting in Istanbul. Published in *Policy: A Journal of Public Policy and Ideas* 28, no. 2 (2012): 38–42.

hundreds to thousands so that the market economy can no longer hide the costs of the folly of human laws.

These follies are a consequence of ideas and interests. We need to first address the ideas that demand state intervention and then the institutional environment that structures incentives in the policy-making process. Mario Rizzo (2011) listed three big threats to the argument for a free market unencumbered by government intervention: (a) externality environmentalism, (b) the resurgence of Keynesianism, and (c) behavioral economics. But these are just the most recent manifestation of arguments that strive to undermine the laissez-faire principle. As these arguments gain in strength, the probability of state intervention into the economy will also rise. The task of the economist committed to the laissez-faire principle is to lower that probability.

Government's growth in terms of both scale (expenditures as a percentage of gross domestic product [GDP]) and scope (increasing responsibilities of the state) in the 20th century has been astronomical. In the 21st century, this growth has accelerated as the Western democracies have had to deal with perception of tensions due to globalization and the widening income gap between the "West and the rest." But as the fiscal situation in Europe and the United States has demonstrated so clearly over the past few years, the current scale and scope of government are unsustainable.

Government spending in Western democracies as a percentage of GDP has grown from about 12.7 percent in 1914 to 47.7 percent in 2009 (Micklethwait 2011). Spending has increased even more since 2009 in the effort to boost aggregate demand in the wake of the global financial crisis. Government spends because the economy is weak, and the economy continues to perform poorly because government spending is crowding out productive private investment. It is a vicious cycle that has to be broken by reevaluating the role and scope of government in a society of free and responsible individuals. The important political/intellectual activity of our age is not to starve the state of resources but to build the intellectual case that we can starve the state of responsibility. Society can in fact provide the necessary framework and acts of compassion to render state actions needless. But before that, it is necessary to demonstrate that the justificatory arguments for the state are not as airtight as imagined and that the supply and demand for state action actually has its sources elsewhere.

Moral Intuitions and the Moral Demands of the Extended Order

One of the greatest challenges to the unhampered market economy is the belief that the wealth discrepancies as a result of ill-gotten gains are destructive to social order. Class war breeds real war, as the downtrodden rebel against the injustice. Analytical egalitarianism (striving for a politics characterized by neither discrimination nor dominion) becomes a political demand for resource egalitarianism, and the step from one to the other is taken without much thought.

This claim of injustice is deeply rooted in our evolutionary past. As James Buchanan put it, the great contribution of the classical political economists was the demonstration that autonomy, prosperity, and peace could be simultaneously achieved by the private property market economy ([1988] 1991). But it was precisely at the high point of the empirical confirmation that the private property market economy was criticized as an illegitimate form of social organization because of the injustice it permitted. The development of the marginal productivity theory of wages did not stop the spread of the moral belief that capitalism was unjust. The cold logic of economics clashed against the hot emotions of moral injustice.

Why does this tension exist? Economics is a scientific discipline that offers conjectures about how the world works, while moral theory passes judgment and suggests how the world ought to be. But what if our moral intuitions are at odds with the institutional demands that must be met so individuals can flourish? F. A. Hayek postulated that this tension between our moral intuitions and the moral demands of the extended order was a product of our evolutionary past ([1988] 1991). Culturally, human beings were conditioned by social norms that were appropriate for small-group living. But with specialization and exchange, the norms of the intimate order must give way to norms more appropriate for the interactions with anonymous others.

Our dilemma is not how to ensure a fair division of a fixed amount of income but deciding what rules we can live by that will allow strangers to live better together by realizing the gains from trade with one another. Small-group morality must be replaced by large-group morality. Instead of moral sympathy, we need general rules that are equally applicable—rules for anonymous interactions. Deirdre McCloskey (2006) argues that this shift from the morality of the ancients to the ascendancy of the bourgeois virtues resulted in the miracle of modern economic growth and improved the lives of billions in Europe, the United States, and eventually through-out the world.

The state is not required to intervene to rid injustice with respect to income discrepancies that result in a truly free-market economy. Individuals earn profits by satisfying the demands of consumers—the lure of profit not only alerts the entrepreneur to opportunities for beneficial exchange but also gains from technological innovation. Competition drives costs down while improving product quality, so businesses can earn higher profits only by better meeting the demands of their consumers. Ultimately, consumers decide the profitability of commercial venture by buying or abstaining from buying. There is nothing unjust about such a distribution. Yes, Bill Gates has greater wealth than I do, but only because he better met the demands of a far greater multitude of individuals.

Curbing Private Predation, Creating Public Predation

The idea of curbing private predation is used to justify the very existence of the state: without a sovereign to define and enforce property rights, the state would devolve quickly into a war of all against all, and life would be "nasty, brutish, and short." Everyone would be better off if they cooperated with one another, but the opportunists would be even better off if everyone else cooperated and they could confiscate the wealth created from everyone's cooperation. The only way out of this predation equilibrium is to establish a strong third-party enforcer.

But such entities are also capable of far greater and more menacing public predation than private predators. Research conducted in the past 25 years shows that communities can curb private predation by making rules that (a) limit access, (b) assign accountability, and (c) institute graduated penalties for violators. In small-group settings, this is mainly done through reputation and ostracism, but in larger-group environments, where the actor is not clear, deterrence and effective punishment must be instituted without recourse to a government entity, or at least without expanding the role of government.

Although humans have historically exhibited a propensity for violence (pillage and plunder), we have also found ways to overcome that propensity and realize the benefits of peaceful social cooperation (truck, barter, and exchange). The worlds that cater to our cooperative propensity grow rich and create healthy and wealthy people, whereas worlds that cater to our violent propensity subject their people to a life of ignorance, poverty, and squalor.

The state as the geographic monopoly on the legitimate means of coercion is put in the advantaged position to predate and violate the human rights of its citizens and impoverish the population. Empowering the state to curb private predation creates the possibility of public predation. As David Hume stressed, when designing government institutions we must assume that all men are knaves, and that the appropriate constraints are built in to ward off knavish behavior even if knaves are in power ([1754] 1907). A robust political economy—similar to what the classical political economists wanted to establish—is one that builds in constraints on the predatory ability of government such that bad men, if they somehow got in power, could do least harm.

Market Failure Becomes Justification for Impediments to Market Adjustment

Market failure theory provides the economic justification for government intervention in the unhampered market economy. The four basic market failures are (a) monopoly, (b) externalities, (c) public goods, and (d) macroeconomic instability. To classical economists, monopoly power was a creation of state intervention, not of market forces. This definition gave way in the late 19th century and early 20th century to the theory that monopoly power was an outgrowth of competitive capitalism. Despite empirical evidence and theoretical developments proving that the definition of classical political economists is the more coherent explanation of monopoly power, the idea that monopoly power is an outgrowth of unbridled capitalism dominates.

Classical economists argued that public goods did result in a demand for increased state intervention in the economy. Roads and bridges, for example, would not be provided by the market economy because individuals could benefit from them and simultaneously avoid payment for that benefit. The "free rider" problem would impede the ability of firms to profitably provide that service. This intuition developed into a pure theory of public goods. But there are technological solutions to the "free rider" problem and numerous examples of Coasean bargains that enabled private solutions to public-good problems throughout history.

According to the theory of external effects, the market economy will often overproduce economic "bads" and underproduce economic "goods" because the social costs and private costs in decision-making are not aligned. The "invisible hand" fails to reconcile the differences. But the primary reason for the breakdown is the inability to define, assign, and enforce property rights. Pollution is one example, where because of the confused defining and poor enforcing of property rights, individuals will overproduce. But if we could clarify the rights, then the internalization of the externality would reduce pollution to its optimal level. Today's inefficiency represents tomorrow's profit opportunity for the entrepreneur who can address the inefficiency effectively. State intervention, on the other hand, thwarts that process of discovery and market adjustment by individuals and instead offers a political solution.

The most significant claims for state intervention in the economy in modern times come from the argument about macroeconomic instability. The unhampered market economy is unstable and suffers from periodic crises; it brings uncertainty about the future and unemployment and thus poverty. The Great Depression destroyed an entire generation's faith in the market economy in Western democracies. The global financial crisis has once again challenged it. But in both instances, government policy was responsible for the economic distortions that led to the current economic crisis. The length and severity of the recovery are due to failed monetary and fiscal policies, and increased regulations and restrictions that inhibit the market adjustment process.

Public-Choice Problems Rather than Market Failure Are the Reason for Intervention

Even if the counterarguments and evidence for nonintervention are persuasive, standard public-choice arguments will lead to state interventions in the market economy because of the erosion of constraints on democratic action.

Independent of any intellectual argument demanding state intervention, the political process is governed by the vote motive (on the demand side) and vote-seeking behavior (on the supply side). Policymakers will favor policies that have immediate and easily identifiable consequences over policies that have only long-term consequences even if those are wealth enhancing. But as multiple studies of the conservation of natural resources within a setting of well-defined and enforced property rights have demonstrated, the market economy will effectively allocate investment funds over time.

Government by definition holds a geographic monopoly on the legitimate use of coercion, and as such there is a strong incentive for interest groups to capture this powerful entity to benefit themselves at the expense of others. Government can be, and will be, used by interest groups to benefit themselves at the expense of others unless effectively constrained from doing so.

A Politics without Discrimination or Dominion

James Buchanan ([1975] 1999) divides the economic role of government into three distinct categories: (a) the protective state, (b) the productive state, and (c) the redistributive state. A wealth-creating society will empower the protective state (law and order) and the productive state (public goods such as infrastructure), and will constrain the redistributive state. The churning state will unleash the redistributive state (rent-seeking) and thwart the wealth-creating capacity of the protective and productive state. The puzzle of modern political economy, according to Buchanan, is to find constitutional rules that will enable a wealth-creating society.

Adam Smith argued long ago that governments ancient as well as modern had a strong proclivity to endlessly engage in the "juggling trick" of running deficits, accumulating public debt, and debasing the currency to monetize the debt ([1776] 1981, 908–47). Bankruptcy, on the other hand, Smith argued, was the least dishonorable and least harmful policy but was rarely followed. In the current crisis, this endless cycle of deficit, debt, and debasement continues to plague European and US economies.

Faced with "juggling tricks," the only way to constrain the state is to tie the decision maker's hands or take away the juggler's balls. So we need to establish binding rules for monetary and fiscal policy or take away the responsibility from the state. We cannot talk about fiscal policy outside the sphere of state action, but we can do something about monetary policy, which can and has historically been outside the domain of state action for certain periods and in certain countries. So some combination of binding constitutional constraints, fiscal decentralization, and denationalization of money may empower the policy regime and constrain it effectively.

Without such drastic restraining steps, the demand for state intervention in the economy will be constant. Not inevitable but probable. We need a rejuvenated defense of the classical liberal argument for binding rules on government. Only then can we reduce the probability of state intervention and unleash the wealth-creating power and creative energy of the free market.

References

Buchanan, James M. [1975] 1999. *The Limits of Liberty: Between Anarchy and Leviathan.* Indianapolis: Liberty Fund.

———. [1988] 1991. "The Potential and Limit of Socially Organized Humankind." In *The Economics and Ethics of Constitutional Order.* Ann Arbor: University of Michigan, 239–51.

Hayek, F. A. [1988] 1991. *The Fatal Conceit: The Errors of Socialism.* Chicago: University of Chicago Press.

Hume, David. [1754] 1907. *Essays: Moral, Political, and Literary.* Vol. 1. London: Longmans, Green, and Co.

McCloskey, Deirdre N. 2006. *The Bourgeois Virtues: Ethics for an Age of Commerce.* Chicago: University of Chicago Press.

Micklethwait, John. 2011. "Taming Leviathan." *The Economist*, March 19.

Rizzo, Mario. 2011. "What Is Economics Today?" *ThinkMarkets* (blog), September 1. https://thinkmarkets.wordpress.com/2011/09/01/what-is-economics-today/.

Smith, Adam. [1776] 1981. *An Inquiry into the Nature and Causes of the Wealth of Nations.* Vol. 2 of *The Glasgow Edition of the Works and Correspondence of Adam Smith*, edited by R. H. Campbell, A. S. Skinner, and W. B. Todd. Oxford: Oxford University Press.

Chapter 6
Why Does Government Overspend? Because It Has Too Much Power

J ohn Maynard Keynes is credited with once remarking about fiscal policy: "You cannot make a fat man skinny by tightening his belt." Such a dilemma is precisely what confronts Europe and the United States at the moment. Government obligations have simply outstripped the fiscal ability of the economies to generate the revenue to pay them. That is, indeed, not a problem of belt-tightening. The problem is not so much that the scale of government has gotten out of control, but rather its scope. Yes, government spending is bloated, but that is the symptom, not the cause. The cause is the expansion of the scope of government controls in the economy. Obligations that were once left to private citizens and their local communities (including churches and other institutions of civic association) have been assumed by the government authorities. No squeezing and tightening of the belt will make this fat man skinny. The only way to do that, to push Keynes's analogy, would be for the fat man to become lean through exercise and diet and then the belt will tighten as a natural consequence. The debate over austerity—budgetary political tricks aside—misses the essential point that must be discussed: the challenge is not starving the state of resources, as much as starving the state of responsibility.

But such a reassessment of the state is at odds with the breakdown of the constraints on government spending. Adam Smith pointed out that governments—ancient as well as modern—had consistently engaged in a "juggling trick" of running deficits, accumulating public debt, and then attempting to pay off those debts through debasement of money ([1776] 1976, 466–68). The cycle of deficits, debt, and debasement is a governmental habit as old as the exercise of political power itself. Only if the ruler's hands are effectively

Adapted from a talk delivered at a meeting of the Mont Pelerin Society in September 2012 in Prague, Czech Republic. Published by *The Insider*, Summer 2013, pp. 5–11.

tied will this endless juggling cease. Constitutionally constrained government emerges as a result of the effort to limit the scope of government power. The effort to constrain the power of the state can be traced from antiquity to today, but the historical records provide only fleeting examples of success.

Unless the state is effectively constrained, fiscal irresponsibility will destroy the long-run viability of the political and economic order. If we take the desire to spend at will as a government habit that exists across time and place, as Adam Smith so urgently warned his readers about, and combine that with both the electoral logic of democratic politics and the vote motive faced by citizens within a modern democracy, then the necessity of effective constraints on the fiscal behavior of government is as true for democracies as it is for kingdoms or even dictatorships. It doesn't matter if citizens have the right to voice their opinion on fiscal irresponsibility. The bias in democratic decision-making is to concentrate benefits in the short run on the well-informed and organized interest groups, and to disperse the costs in the long run on the unorganized and ill-informed. In this way, good politics is not necessarily good economics. Or to think about it another way, fiscal irresponsibility may be extremely popular, political and fiscal responsibility may be extremely unpopular, but that doesn't change the reality that fiscal irresponsibility is irresponsible.

As economist Richard Wagner has so aptly put it, responsible budgeting may very well be a casualty of rational politics. It is a staple of political and economic thought that the persistence of a pattern in human affairs over time reflects some systemic incentive in the institutional framework. "During the first 150 or so years of the American republic," Wagner writes, "that pattern conformed largely to the budgetary principles of sound finance" (2013, 13). Following Adam Smith's wisdom that "what is prudence in the conduct of every private family, can scarce be folly in that of a great kingdom," the American republic ran deficits during times of war and depression, and surpluses recorded during normal times were used to reduce the debt ([1776] 1976, 478). This pattern changed in the past 60 years. The principle of responsible budgeting was replaced with functional finance, according to which "the condition of the budget, whether in deficit or surplus, should be whatever is necessary to promote full employment, however this might be defined" (Wagner 2013, 13).

Keynesian fiscal policy supplanted the "old-time fiscal religion" of classical political economy. Government spending became a goal unto itself in this political-economic mindset as politicians became unconstrained from the heritage of the historical fiscal constitution of budgetary balance. The public-debt problems that confront Europe and the United States today did not emerge in the past 10 years. The problem is deeply rooted in the interaction between Keynesian policies and the systemic incentives of democratic politics. "From Roosevelt's new deal onward, elected politicians have lived with the demonstrated relationship between favorable election returns and expansion in public spending programs," write Nobel Prize–winning economist James Buchanan and Richard Wagner ([1977] 2000, 75). Vote-seeking politicians would be acting against their self-interest within this environment by advocating fiscal restraint and responsibility. "Sober assessment," Buchanan and Wagner conclude, "suggests that, politically, Keynesianism may represent a substantial disease, one that can, over the long run, prove fatal for a functioning democracy" (57).

The problem is not just that the incentives within the democratic process produce shortsightedness in policy and bloated bureaucracies. As responsible public finance was replaced with functional finance aimed at macroeconomic management of aggregate demand, the relationship between the government and the economy shifted drastically. Government was no longer seen as a referee but instead became an active player in the economic game, and in fact became the overlord of the economy. "Functional finance," Wagner observes, "is the fiscal component of the Progressivist political agenda of a government that is unlimited by any constitutional limit on its scope of activity" (2013, 7). What is expected of government in meeting the demands of citizenry shifted drastically in the wake of the Keynesian erosion of the fiscal constitution. Adam Smith's "juggling tricks" were no longer avoided, but were instead embraced.

The economist Albert Hahn identified the fundamental flaws of Keynesianism in his book *The Economics of Illusion* (1949). For Keynesian remedies to have the force required, argued Hahn, the participants in the economy must remain ignorant of the policy steps being taken and their impact on economic factors. As Hahn put it, Keynesian thinking ignored the potential "compensating reactions" that arise as a response to the manipulation of monetary and fiscal policy. An inflationary theory of employment cannot solve the problem of unemployment any more than government spending can be the source of long-run economic growth and development. The belief that such discretionary and expansionary monetary and fiscal policy can correct flaws in the economy is the "economics of illusion." Economists trained in this tradition, said Hahn, "seem to have lost the ability to think along classical lines" (8). They are preoccupied with demand management and thus ignore the long-run costs of these policies.

Hahn was critiquing not merely economic forecasting, but the general exercise of trying to manage demand. "As long as the world is not entirely totalitarian," he wrote, "neither the objective data of the future nor the subjective reactions of millions of individuals can be predicted" (8). The *economics of control* in a real economy, as opposed to an abstract model, is an impossibility and incompatible with any notion of economic freedom. You can fool some of the people some of the time, but you cannot fool all of the people all of the time.

The logic of democratic politics that emerges from the interaction between vote-seeking politicians, and rationally ignorant, rationally abstaining, and especially interested voters is to concentrate benefits on well-organized and well-informed groups (who will provide campaign contributions and votes) in the short run, and disperse the costs on the unorganized and ill-informed (who are either not paying attention or are mistaken in their understanding) in the long run. Deficits and accumulated public debt are perhaps the best illustration of this logic playing out. Who pays for what and when?

The shift in the implicit constraint on fiscal policy that was wrought by the Keynesian revolution (or Keynesian confusion, as Hahn called it) has changed the behavior of politicians and citizens over the past 60 years. As Wagner has stressed: "A recipe for prudent fiscal conduct for an individual within a regime of wholly private property might be revised when society governance proceeds with an admixture of private and collective property" (2013, 7).

The expansion of public services since 1950 has been very popular among the electorate, but the costs of those policies have been hidden by economic growth, intergenerational transfers, and budgetary tricks. As economists Laurence Kotlikoff and Scott Burns argue in their recent book *The Clash of Generations* (2012): "Thanks to six decades of incredibly profligate and irresponsible generational policy, we can declare, *The United States* is bankrupt" (3). And, as they add, it is not bankrupt years from now; it is bankrupt right now. By their estimates, the true indebtedness of the United States is $211 trillion—the fiscal gap between the present values of future obligations minus future tax receipts.

Kotlikoff and Burns reach that figure by including various unofficial spending obligations that the government has assumed but kept off the books. In their narrative of our budgetary woes, these are mainly obligations to senior citizens, as political promises have resulted in "turning retirement into a well-paid, long-term occupation" (2). And these seniors are an extremely powerful interest group and have successfully lobbied to make sure that they get what is "owed" them, including having their benefits fully adjusted for inflation.

The economics of illusion, in other words, has been checkmated in this instance. Adam Smith's "juggling trick" of deficits, debt, and debasement has been truncated because the ability to inflate away the debt obligations has been limited with inflation adjustments built into the benefits package owed. Putting aside the issue of the costs associated with inflation to erode debt obligations, there is now the need to confront the consequences of the "profligate and irresponsible" fiscal practice. Adam Smith argued that the least dishonorable and least harmful policy a government could pursue in such a situation would be repudiation. But given the cultural situation in Europe and the United States, the rupture of the relationship between the citizens and the state that would result is perhaps too severe for any politician to accept.

As economist Luigi Zingales described the problem:

> Keynesianism has conquered the hearts and minds of politicians and ordinary people alike because it provides a theoretical justification for irresponsible behavior. Medical science has established that one or two glasses of wine per day are good for your long-term health, but no doctor would recommend a recovering alcoholic to follow this prescription. Unfortunately, Keynesian economists do exactly this. They tell politicians, who are addicted to spending our money, that government expenditures are good. And they tell consumers, who are affected by severe spending problems, that consuming is good, while saving is bad. In medicine, such behavior would get you expelled from the medical profession; in economics, it gives you a job in Washington. (2009, para. 24)

Expectations in Western democracies are for government to protect citizens from the vagaries of nature *and* the market; citizens are expected to be educated when they are young, and protected when they are old. Public-sector employment during the past 60 years was transformed through lobbying efforts from a secure though low-paying job to a secure job that paid the going rate on the market and provided a lucrative retirement package.

Blaming public unions for asking for improved benefits for their members or blaming elected officials for responding to those demands in order to win votes is like criticizing a wasp for stinging you when you step on its nest. The problem isn't the people; it is the institutional regime that produces this pattern of behavior.

A Half Century of Fiscal Irresponsibility and Counting

The economics of control and effective demand management have proved not only to be elusive in the success of their intended practical application, but also to possess long-term costs that have not been adequately accounted for in the decision-making process. The economics of illusion in practice results in a perpetual trading off of short-term economic emergency responses for long-term economic health. The cauldron of politics in times of perceived economic crisis is the worst place to expect sound economic policy to emerge. As economist Henry Hazlitt put it, "Emotional economics has given birth to theories that calm examination cannot justify" (1946, 124).

The idea that extraordinary circumstances may require a commitment to ordinary economics simply hasn't resonated with politicians, the public, or the economics profession as it evolved in the second half of the 20th century and continues to evolve to this day. But a return to the basic teachings of economics from Adam Smith to F. A. Hayek is what is required. This "mainline" of economic science stressed the role of property, prices, and profit/loss accounting in structuring incentives, mobilizing dispersed knowledge, and providing the required feedback to spur innovation and discipline wishful conjectures. It is within the institutional context of a private property market economy that the striving of individuals to better their own condition is transformed into publicly desirable outcomes. The "invisible hand" is a structure-induced outcome, and it does not require for its realization either perfectly rational actors or perfectly competitive markets. For Smith, as well as Hayek, the invisible hand mechanism operates in a world of very imperfect human beings interacting in a very imperfect world.

This understanding of the "mainline" of economic thought was lost during the Great Depression. A new "mainstream" of economic thought and public policy emerged and announced the end of the classical liberal political economy of Smith, David Ricardo, John Stuart Mill, Eugene von Böhm-Bawerk, Ludwig von Mises, and Hayek. This "mainstream" held that laissez-faire was viable only in a world of perfectly rational individuals interacting in a perfectly competitive market. Laissez-faire policies were appropriate only for the simple environment of a perfect world. But the modern world had introduced a new complexity along with the great material progress achieved. The economy was now prone to the abuse of monopoly power, the injustice of income inequality, the inefficiencies of external economies caused by urban living, and the instability of macroeconomics that resulted in the wretched threat of mass unemployment.

As a theory, Keynesianism filled an important void because it offered an explanation that unified the greatest resentment of modern capitalist society—the idle rich—with the great fear of capitalist society—mass unemployment. And Keynes's Cambridge colleagues also provided the theories of microeconomic inefficiency due to monopoly power, including the theory of imperfect competition, and the theory of externalities and market failure. By the mid-1940s, all the pieces of the "New Economics" were in place, and "Orthodox" or "Classical Economics" was held to be in disrepute.

The older Orthodox position that maintained that the public debt should follow responsible budgeting principles was overturned in favor of the new theory of functional finance. This "new Orthodoxy" argued that deficits and debt should not be balanced per se, but should be whatever was required to meet the policy objectives established by the government. Government spending became an end unto itself as a tool for maintaining full employment and macroeconomic stability. By 1950, this understanding of the role of government within the economy was deeply embedded in the mindset of politicians, the public, and the economics profession. The new mainstream of economic thought deviated significantly from what had been the mainline of economic teachings for the previous 150 years or so. The culture of government spending unconstrained by any notion of responsible budgeting resulted in a significant expansion of government throughout Europe and the United States.

Toward a Fiscal Constitution for a Free and Prosperous Republic

Thinking through how we might transition from our current situation of fiscal irresponsibility to one of responsible budgeting requires that we first recognize that the problem is not a purely technical one, but ultimately a philosophical, cultural, and institutional one. Philosophically, there needs to be a new consensus on a much more limited scope for government. To invoke the earlier analogy Keynes used, you cannot make a fat man skinny by tightening his belt. The challenge is not to starve the state of resources, but to starve it of responsibility. Government must simply be called on to do less, individuals and their communities called on to do more.

Culturally, there has to be a renewed appreciation for the self-governing capacity of human beings, and the citizens within the democratic order must embrace, as Alexis de Tocqueville said so aptly, "the cares of thinking and the troubles of living." A citizenry capable of self-governance helps democracy work, not by aiding the political process, but by circumventing politics and living a truly democratic life in relation with one to another.

Finally, even in the wake of a philosophical revival of limited government, and a cultural reawakening of democratic self-governance, the institutional structures of the state must be designed to constrain the natural proclivities of politicians. The philosopher David Hume argued long ago that in designing institutions of governance, the analyst must presume that all men are knaves ([1742] 1985). We must never forget the fundamental problem that government introduces into the question of social order and our ability to live better together—namely, that in our effort to curb private predation, we turn to the creation of the state, but in so doing we create the very real threat of public predation. The fundamental paradox of government as recognized by the Founders was that a constitution must first empower government, and then constrain it.

This institutional puzzle is solved by thinking seriously about countervailing forces. As Alexander Hamilton put it, use ambition to check ambition. The organization of government that James Madison crafted has built-in checks and balances, and sought to limit the ability of political factions to ease those checks on the accumulation of power and favor.

James Buchanan put the puzzle of the paradox of governance in a more modern context: can we establish a protective and productive state without unleashing the redistributive state to play havoc with our political order? Just as Hayek reluctantly had to conclude that the noble and inspiring project of the US Founders to limit the rule of factions had failed, we must conclude that Buchanan's puzzle has not yet found a successful solution in either theory or practice.

The fiscal difficulties faced by the countries in Europe and the United States did not emerge overnight, but are the consequences of decades of public policy. Keynesian economics as a tool for public policy and as an intellectual justification for the existing proclivities of politicians effectively relaxed if not eliminated any of the preexisting constraints on fiscal policy; the decades of profligate and irresponsible spending have adversely affected not only public-sector but also private-sector behavior.

It's the culture, stupid! The culture of the Western democracies that emerged in the wake of the Keynesian revolution and the pursuit of the economics of illusion threaten to destroy free-market capitalism and with that the long-term prosperity of the Western democracies of Europe and the United States. James Buchanan described himself as an optimist when he looked backward and a pessimist when he looked forward—an optimist because things hadn't gotten as bad as he had predicted, but a pessimist because the situation was indeed bleak.

In the second half of the 20th century, technological innovations combined with the opening of new trading opportunities (namely, China, but also India) produced economic growth that effectively masked—and thus sustained—the dysfunctions of our fiscal practice. But the dysfunctions are real and the bill is due. We cannot kick the grenade down the road any farther. The 60-year exercise in "fiscal child abuse," as Kotlikoff calls our fiscal practice, must finally come to an end. The demographics don't line up; the numbers don't add up.

References

Buchanan, James M., and Richard E. Wagner. [1977] 2000. *Democracy in Deficit: The Political Legacy of Lord Keynes*. Vol. 8 of *The Collected Works of James M. Buchanan*. Indianapolis: Liberty Fund.

Hahn, L. Albert. 1949. *The Economics of Illusion: A Critical Analysis of Contemporary Economic Theory and Policy*. New York: Squier Publishing Co.

Hazlitt, Henry. 1946. *Economics in One Lesson: The Shortest and Surest Way to Understand Basic Economics*. New York: Three Rivers Press.

Hume, David. [1742] 1985. "Of the Origin of Government." In *Essays, Moral, Political, and Literary*. Edited by Eugene F. Miller. Indianapolis: Liberty Fund.

Kotlikoff, Laurence J., and Scott Burns. 2012. *The Clash of Generations: Saving Ourselves, Our Kids, and Our Economy*. Cambridge, MA: MIT Press.

Smith, Adam. [1776] 1976. *An Inquiry into the Nature and Causes of the Wealth of Nations.* Chicago: University of Chicago Press.

Wagner, Richard E. 2013. *Deficits, Debt, and Democracy: Wrestling with Tragedy on the Fiscal Commons.* Cheltenham, UK: Edward Elgar.

Zingales, Luigi. 2009. "Keynesian Principles: The Opposition's Opening Remarks." *The Economist,* March 10.

Chapter 7

The Role of the Economist in a Free Society

The statesman who should attempt to direct private people in what manner they ought to employ their capitals, would not only load himself with a most unnecessary attention, but assume an authority which could safely be trusted, not only to no single person, but to no council or senate whatever, and which would nowhere be so dangerous as in the hands of a man who had folly and presumption enough to fancy himself fit to exercise it.

—Adam Smith
An Inquiry into the Nature and Causes
of the Wealth of Nations ([1776] 1976)

E conomics in the hands of its masters is an expert critique of rule by expertise. And even among its masters, there are many differing visions of the role of economics.

Ludwig von Mises and Intellectual Engagement with Controversy

Ludwig von Mises was embroiled in controversial disputes in economics from almost the beginning of his career. His work on monetary theory also addressed questions of monetary policy (1912). He not only debated fine points of theory with his application to monetary economics of the advancements in microeconomics achieved by the earlier generation of Austrian School economists, but he also strove to counter the pet theories and policies

Adapted from a speech at the Mont Pelerin Society 2019 regional meeting in Dallas, Texas. Published in three parts by the Library of Economics and Liberty on July 1, 2019; August 5, 2019; and September 2, 2019.

of various monetary cranks. In the process, he demonstrated the intellectual flaws and bankruptcy of ideas, such as state theories of money, underconsumption theories of the business cycle, and overproduction theories of industrial fluctuations.

Investment decisions, employment decisions, and consumption decisions all, in Mises's hand, were a consequence of subjective evaluations by individuals and the choices they make on the margin based on those evaluations. Money does not disturb the individual decision calculus, though it does both complicate and resolve the situation. Money complicates matters because it introduces a link into all exchanges. Money is one-half of all exchanges, and thus, if the monetary system is distorted, all exchanges will be distorted. The classical dichotomy still holds—real variables only affect real variables, and nominal variables only affect nominal variables—but there is now a demand to explain the process by which the economic forces at work reveal themselves throughout the system due to the "loose jointedness" of money in analysis.

Mechanical interpretations of the quantity theory of money distort our understanding every bit as much as denials of the quantity theory distort such understanding. And finally, money must also be recognized for its role as an aid to the human mind in the complex coordination of economic activity through time. Monetary prices on the market enable decision makers both to economize on the details they must process in investment, production, and consumption decisions and to ease the assessment of alternative decision paths. The ability to engage in monetary economic calculation enables decision makers to assess alternative plans, and the system selects from the array of technologically feasible plans those that are economically viable.

Studying this market process of calculation and coordination would define Mises's career as an economist—both on the negative side (the inability of socialism to engage in rational economic calculation) and the positive side (the ability of capitalism to do so and how that engenders a process of entrepreneurial discovery and creativity).

The conundrum in these discussions is to determine from the start what science is and what one's personal moral assessment of a social arrangement is. Max Weber—who had to grapple with the ongoing debates from what were referred to in his time as "socialists of the chair"—thought he provided rules of intellectual engagement that would solve the problem. The critical analyst, Weber argued, must restrict analysis to the examination of the effectiveness of chosen means in achieving given ends. There would be no disputing over the ends sought. Thus, even if the analyst found the ends deplorable, if those ends were satisfied by the chosen means, then the analyst's critique would be neutered. But if the analyst could show that the means chosen would not produce the ends sought, and even more so that they would produce results that worsened the social ills that were to be eradicated by the policy choices under examination, the critique would stand (Weber 1922).

Mises was fully persuaded by Weber's rules of intellectual engagement. His critical analysis of monetary policy, his analysis of socialism, and of interventionism were grounded in this "value-freedom" method. Moreover, his argument was that the history of political economy traced back to Adam Smith. A quick example in support of Mises's point is Adam Smith and David Hume's debate over the state sponsorship of religion, where their analysis of the logic of choice, organizational logic, and situational logic was shared, but their normative assessment of the consequences of the policy choices differed. Political economy, in this sense, is a value-relevant discipline only to the extent that the economic analysis undergirding it was as value neutral as humanly possible.

Controversy and Mises were not limited to the "big question" of the viability of the socialist system. He was clear: Socialism, by definition, sought to eliminate private ownership of the means of production, and in so doing, socialism condemned its own project from achieving its stated ends of rationalizing the process of production. Rather than rationalizing economic processes, socialism would produce economic chaos due to the inability to engage in rational economic calculation (Mises 1922).

Nothing in Mises's analysis of socialism was predicated on differences in the aspirations of socialism—whether we consider those aspirations economically, politically, or morally. Socialism could promise fraternity, equality, and solidarity because the rationalization of production was supposed to lead to such a burst of productivity that, following the revolution, mankind would be delivered from the Kingdom of Necessity to the Kingdom of Freedom. Alas, such high-minded aspirations, once subjected to the sober analysis of economics, would collapse under the weight of the impossibility of the chosen means to realize the given ends of socialism.

But what was true for Mises's analysis of socialism is also true for his analysis of the market process and the problem of monopoly. His focus was the role of prices and profit and the arguments for interventionism; and the monetary system and the consequences of the manipulation of money and credit on the economic system. Mises is engaged in means/ends analysis, not moral posturing; such sober analysis isn't always appreciated by those who would prefer it never be offered as a challenge to their policy preferences.

In *Human Action* Mises writes:

> It is impossible to understand the history of economic thought if one does not pay attention to the fact that economics as such is a challenge to the conceit of those in power. An economist can never be a favorite of autocrats and demagogues. With them he is always the mischief-maker, and the more they are inwardly convinced that his objections are well founded, the more they hate him. (1949, 67)

Thus, as he would state in *Economic Freedom and Interventionism*:

> The social function of economic science consists precisely in developing sound economic theories and in exploding the fallacies of vicious reasoning. In the pursuit of this task the economist incurs the deadly enmity of all mountebanks and charlatans whose shortcuts to an earthly paradise he debunks. (1990, 51–52)

Frank Knight and Confronting Intellectual Attacks

Frank Knight was just as blunt in his assessment of the situation. In his 1950 American Economic Association (AEA) presidential address titled "The Role of Principles in Economics and Politics," he states:

> My interest has of late tended to shift from the problems of economic theory, or what seem to be its proper concerns, to the question of why people so generally, and the learned elite in particular, as they express themselves in various ways, choose nonsense instead of sense and shake the dust from their feet at us. And also, why the theorist is so commonly "in the dog-house" among economists, as classified by academic faculty lists and books and articles in learned journals carrying the word "economic" in their titles. (1951, 2)

Intellectual shifts of thinking during the first half of the 20th century, Knight argued, had produced a literature in the discipline:

> Consisting largely of attacks on traditional views of the nature and function of economics, in which the term "orthodoxy" commonly appears as a "cuss-word," an epithet of reproach. The critics, aggressors, have more or

less explicitly advocated the abolition of an economics of economic principles and its replacement by almost anything or everything else, other principles if they can be found—psychological, historical, statistical, political,
or ethical—or no principles at all but factual description of some sector of
social human phenomena called "economic" for reasons not clear to me.
I cannot comment in detail on these fashions in thinking. The latest "new
economics," and in my opinion rather the worst for fallacious doctrine and
pernicious consequences, is that launched by the late John Maynard (Lord)
Keynes, who for a decade succeeded in carrying economic thinking well
back to the dark age, but of late this wave of the future has happily been
passing. (1951, 2)

One of the major issues with this move is that the economist is transformed
from a scientist, student of society, and social critic into a would-be adviser
to those in positions of power and privilege. But those in power have no use
for serious economic science and social criticism. Economics so conceived
is a nuisance, and little more. As Knight continued telling his colleagues at
the AEA meetings: "The serious fact is that the bulk of the really important
things that economics has to teach are things that people would see for themselves if they were willing to see. And it is hard to believe in the utility of trying to teach what men refuse to learn or even seriously listen to" (1951, 2–4).

And this fate is all the more true because of the changes in expectations
among the elite and the population concerning the role of government in
society. As Knight pointed out, challenges to the teachings of economics
have significant effect on the body politic because the denial of economic
principles changes politics:

> This same period of history has also seen a growing disregard for free eco-
> nomic institutions in public policy—increasing resort to legislative and
> bureaucratic interference and control, the growth of pressure groups employ-
> ing both political and "direct" action to get what they want, and with all this
> the debasement of the state itself, completely in much of the European world,
> from free forms to ruthless despotism. It is surely legitimate to ask whether
> there is some connection between the movement of economic thinking and
> that of political change. (Emmett 1999, 363)

Those in the resistance—which is of course what the Mont Pelerin Society was built to cultivate and sustain—must be willing to engage in the futile
crusade for economic literacy in the general population, to continually refine

our understanding of basic economics, and to persuade our peers in the discipline that there isn't anything boring about working with the persistent and consistent application of economic principles to understanding the way the world works in all its given diversity. Simple economics is *not* simpleminded, and clarity of exposition of the principles of economics is to be valued over quickness of mind and cleverness in presentation.

This commitment to sound economics—and to the role of the economist in society as a student of society, and as a social critic, but never as an adviser and social engineer—is what united Mises and Knight. They were both true radical liberals, but not Progressive Era intellectuals. It was, after all, the Progressive Era shift in intellectual temperament that was transforming the discipline of economics before their eyes.

Knight and Mises provide foundational arguments on the question of the role of the economist in a free society. The next masters to take on this challenge include Nobel laureates George Stigler, James M. Buchanan, and Ronald Coase. But this is an exploration for another day.

Friedman and Stigler

In 1946, two promising young economists, Milton Friedman and George Stigler, published a pamphlet for the Foundation for Economic Education critically examining housing policy titled *Roofs or Ceilings?* They concluded their essay with the following:

> A final note to the reader—we should like to emphasize as strongly as we can that our objectives are the same as yours: *the most equitable possible distribution of the available supply of housing and the speediest possible resumption of new construction.* The rise in rents that would follow the removal of rent control is not a virtue in itself. We have no desire to pay higher rents, to see others forced to pay them, or to see landlords reap windfall profits. Yet we urge the removal of rent ceilings because, in our view, any other solution of the housing problem involves still worse evils. (22)

In framing their analysis in this way, Friedman and Stigler were following the same approach that Mises laid out. Treat ends as given, and critically analyze the effectiveness of chosen means to achieve those ends. But the reaction to Friedman and Stigler's essay was telling. Intellectuals on the left either ignored or disregarded it, and intellectuals on the right condemned it as granting too much moral high ground to the egalitarian ethos. Both reactions illustrated the economist's plight as discussed by Frank Knight in his AEA address—why is nonsense so attractive to intellectuals, rather than sense, in matters of public policy? This is especially damning when, as Mises noted in *Human Action*, that "economic history is a long record of government policies that failed because they were designed with a bold disregard for the laws of economics." In other words, the stakes are high, and in the case of the housing policy being discussed by Friedman and Stigler, the consequences are dire and relatively visible.

The reactions to this episode in the two scholars' careers are instructive. Friedman would devote more of his efforts to engaging the public, becoming one of the leading public intellectuals of the 20th century, as well as a superstar in the world of elite scientific economists. Stigler—the student of Knight—would interpret the lesson differently and seek to follow the scientific strictures that follow from the criticism of economics as unscientific. He also would become a superstar in the world of the scientific elite. But he was never the public intellectual that Milton Friedman became. As he writes in a letter to Friedman in December 1948, "If a pure scientist—one believing only demonstrated things—is asked his opinion on policy, he must decline to answer—and listen to his intellectual inferiors give advice on policy. Hence the role of the pure scientist is terribly painful to assume in economics." This becomes Stigler's dictum; either economists can become preachers or they can become economists, and he believes they will have a nearly impossible task of being both. Thus, the correct choice to make is clear for the scholar/scientist. The economist as scientist must remain silent even when nonsense is being peddled.

Stigler may have taken this position one step too far, and in doing so lost the very means/ends analysis that is the stock-in-trade of economists as social critics. Insisting that one can productively infer intentions from outcomes changes the analyst's stance as the law of unintended consequences is pushed aside, and inefficiency in the choice of means with respect to ends is denied. Whatever is, it is postulated, must be efficient because if it wasn't, then things would already be different. So this means arguing over policy choices is arguing over values even when we pretend it isn't. And in doing so, this means we are preaching, not analyzing.

Which then is to be preferred—a dialogue among preachers, or a deep discussion among students of civilization over the liberal principles of justice and the good society? To hark back to Knight, the intellectual agenda in the second half of the 20th century could be summarized as the effort to elaborate a new liberalism for the postwar era. Civilization had just stared down its impending demise in the 1930–1950 period with the Great Depression and World War II, and three things seemed necessary to breathe life into a new and renewed liberalism worthy of that name.

First, it was vital to cultivate an appreciation for economic principles and the operation of a free-market economy, as well as their limitations as guides to understanding. The economic way of thinking had to be practiced and taught effectively, and that begins with teaching price *theory*, and exposing popular fallacies. Second, a democratic people needed to come to recognize not just the benefits, but also the limitations of political solutions to social problems. Intelligence in democratic action can result only through open and critical dialogue—democracy is essentially government by discussion—and thus the potential for fraudulent speech and political salesmanship must be recognized as a threat to the free society, and to the acceptance of the exploratory nature of all social action. What Knight, and later James Buchanan, would stress as the "relatively absolute absolute" is an essential component to any discourse about freedom and reform within a democratic society. Truth seeking in science is foundational to the enterprise, but the assertion of truth claims in politics is the path toward tyranny, and must be guarded against constantly. And third, according to Knight, a free society requires free and responsible individuals willing to shoulder the burden of living and thinking, so a renewed liberalism must be accompanied by an independent conception of the ethics of freedom. Knight's conundrum, as he put it, was that it was unclear that our human nature would be adaptable and resilient enough to live up to the challenge that liberation from the oppression of authoritarian rule demands.

Buchanan and Coase

That is some challenge. But it is a challenge that was picked up by others in this same tradition, such as Buchanan and Ronald Coase, and it set them apart from others who sought to pursue public policy in a more direct manner. Neither Buchanan nor Coase sought to engineer the policy environment to promote market-friendly policies. They were market economists because, as Buchanan would put it famously in his "What Should Economists Do?" essay (1964), they studied markets. Nothing more and nothing less. The

Buchanan-Coase project was one that studied exchange relations, and the institutions within which exchange takes place.

Buchanan, beginning in 1949, represented a radical departure from the emerging consensus in the economic analysis of the public sector. Though his analysis would sharpen over the coming decades, all the basic elements of his later approach are evident already in that earlier essay on "The Pure Theory of Government Finance." In particular, here Buchanan is already working with his criticism of the "fisc," which is a mythical unified government planner that chooses the optimal level of taxation and expenditure to reflect the known preferences of the democratic polity and is guided by the expertise of the economists. There is simply no stable social welfare function that the planner can maximize—there is no procedure for aggregating preference, there is no omniscient and benevolent planner, and there is no teleology of the economy as a whole. The economist, Buchanan would come to stress, has no privileged position in the political discourse of a democratic society.

Modern welfare economics, Buchanan insisted, reflected a utilitarian, engineering, and elitist mentality that must be rejected if we are to make progress in the field of political economy. It evolved as it did using the omniscience assumption as a resolution to difficult questions in political economy, but that "seems wholly unacceptable" (1960, 108). The neoclassical social welfare economics exercise can assert that it provides the economic foundation for the good society, but it can only do so by introducing various assumptions that lead to normative theorizing parading as positive analytics. With the tools of modern welfare economics in place, the observing economist is supposedly empowered to identify those welfare-enhancing positions *independent* of the individual behavior of the agents within the model because the all-knowing benevolent social planner can perfectly predict what individuals would in fact choose if faced with the circumstances postulated. Optimality and efficiency are, in this exercise, defined within the confines of this specific modeling exercise.

Rather than accept the presumption of omniscience, Buchanan sought to substitute the presumption of ignorance. The idea of *presumptive efficiency* does some of the work for Buchanan in this task of challenging the conventional wisdom. The economist who uses the notion of *presumptive efficiency* retains various features of the Paretian analysis. The observing economist makes judgments about "efficiency" and attempts to translate individual preferences to alternative social arrangements. These must be understood to be provisional statements, not precise ones. And, *they are offered only as hypotheses to be tested in the arena of collective action, and not as definitive policy choices.*

The economist cannot recommend policy A over policy B per se because without recourse to an objective social welfare function, and without the accompanying assumptions of omniscience and benevolence, there is *no scientific basis* for such a judgment. All policy discussions necessarily move us from the realm of the positive to that of the normative, and we only fool ourselves when we don't recognize this explicitly in our work in the field of welfare economics. "But," Buchanan insists, "there does exist a positive role for the economist in the formation of policy. His task is that of diagnosing social situations and presenting to the choosing individuals a set of possible changes." Buchanan continues, "He does not recommend policy A over policy B. He presents policy A as a hypothesis subject to testing. The hypothesis is that policy A will, in fact, prove to be Pareto-optimal. The conceptual test is *consensus* among the members of the choosing group, not objective improvements in some measurable social aggregate" (1960, 110).

Two points of emphasis in designing the "test" follow from this Buchanan perspective. First, the proposed changes must be accompanied by a true compensation scheme. Second, the proposed changes must be restricted to changes in the structural rules under which individuals make choices and interact with one another. Compensation is vital to this exercise because there will always be vested interests in the status quo, and as a result there will be motivated reasoning in the collective decision-making process. Buchanan does not attribute any normative weight to the status quo, as we will see; it is merely the starting state from which any discussion of change must begin. In ensuring intelligence in democratic action, the discourse among reasonable parties must transform motivated reasoning into indifference, and thus allow purely rational discourse concerning the consensus to be built. The political economist's job, in Buchanan's rendering, "is completed when he has shown the parties concerned that there exist mutual gains 'from trade.' He has no function in suggesting specific contract terms within the bargaining range itself" (1960, 112).

Ronald Coase also challenged the conventional wisdom of welfare economics as it was formulated in the 20th century. As he argues in an essay on "Saving Economics from the Economists":

> Government is increasingly seen as the ultimate solution to tough economic
> problems, from innovation to employment. Economics thus becomes a con-
> venient instrument the state uses to manage the economy, rather than a tool
> the public turns to for enlightenment about how the economy operates. . . .
> [I]t is hardly up to the task. (2012)

This is equivalent to Buchanan's thinking about the importance of the structural rules of the game, or as we will eventually see, F. A. Hayek's good gar-
dener cultivating a vibrant garden, rather than an engineer orchestrating
an economic miracle.

Robert Skidelsky (2005) wrote a magisterial three-volume biography
of John Maynard Keynes. It is important to note that he titled the second
volume *The Economist as Savior* to depict Keynes's intellectual and political
activities between 1920 and 1937. But not everyone agreed with Keynes
that economists were, or could be, saviors. It is hard to imagine more polar
opposites in their visions of the role of the economist in society than that
of Keynes and Hayek.

F. A. Hayek and the Pretense of Knowledge

When Hayek was awarded the Nobel Prize in Economic Science, he did not
fail to highlight this point to the chagrin of his host and his peers. In his Nobel
banquet toast, he said simply that if he had been consulted, he never would
have advocated awarding Nobel Prizes to economists for the simple reason
that no economic thinker should ever be provided with such public recognition, as it falsely provides a sense of authority that can be safely trusted to no
economist. But Hayek wasn't done there. In his Nobel Lecture titled "The
Pretense of Knowledge" he made the following claims: First, we economists
have indeed made a mess of things with our efforts at macroeconomic management of the Western economies. Second, economists are led to make a
mess of things because they have falsely adopted a methodology appropriate
for the natural sciences but inappropriate for the sciences of man. He dubbed
this intellectual mistake *scientism*. Third, a scientific discipline expected to be
able to deliver useful, practical knowledge—which in fact it is incapable of
producing—is a quick path toward charlatanism. Furthermore, this charlatanism is protected by vested interests within the economics profession and its
relationship with agents of the state. There is an alliance, in essence, between

scientism and statism, and there are self-reinforcing incentives that make this alliance difficult to break once it is forged. Fourth, unless this intellectual situation is resisted, not only will economic science be rendered worthless in terms of social understanding, but economists will become potential tyrants and destroyers of civilization ([1974] 1989).

Hayek's essay received a revise and resubmit from the very journal he helped edit during his time at the London School of Economics—*Economica*. That is a very strange fate for a Nobel lecture, but Hayek's message was very much outside the general tenor of the times. The idea of the economist as social engineer and economics as the science that guides the engineering was then, and is now, the dominant mindset across the political spectrum. This perspective shapes the advanced study of economics methodologically and analytically. But this wasn't always the case.

Colander and Freedman's *Where Economics Went Wrong*

The transformation of classical political economy into economic science, and from economic science to economic engineering, is the subject of David Colander and Craig Freedman's recent stimulating and important book *Where Economics Went Wrong* (2019).

The science of economics is different from the art of political economy, and the art of political economy must always begin with the recognition that we are natural equals, that economists have no privileged status in the democratic process of collective decision-making, and that the plurality of values must be weighed and incorporated into our public policy deliberations. The art of political economy must be practiced in a manner consistent with the demands of a self-governing democratic society. Just as Adam Smith argued that the only difference between the philosopher and the street porter was in the mind of the philosopher, in our time the only difference between the elite academic economist and the ordinary school teacher is in the mind of the economist. We are one another's equal in the democratic polity, and before the law.

Democracy by discussion is aimed at arriving at a consensus—an agreement—not at discovering deep truth. Truth is what science strives for; to claim truth in politics is the road to tyranny. That is a difficult pill to swallow, when so much economic nonsense abounds within political discourse, but one we must swallow if we are to avoid becoming Hayek's tyrants over fellow citizens and destroyers of the very civilization that unleashed the creative powers of a free people.

As Elinor Ostrom summed up the problem in *Governing the Commons*:

> The intellectual trap in relying entirely on models to provide the foundation for policy analysis is that scholars then presume that they are omniscient observers able to comprehend the essentials of how complex, dynamic systems work by creating stylized descriptions of some aspects of those systems. With the false confidence of presumed omniscience, scholars feel perfectly comfortable addressing proposals to governments that are conceived in their models as omnicompetent powers able to rectify the imperfections that exist in all field settings. (1990, 215)

And modern economics has evolved to fit comfortably into this mindset. Seeing like a state is categorically different from seeing like a citizen.

The Art of Political Economy

How then are we to practice economics and political economy if we take this idea of the art of political economy appropriate for a self-governing democratic society seriously? How should we deal with "experts" who govern over our fellow citizens instead of seeking to govern with them? The post–World War II consensus rejected the earlier classical liberalism of Adam Smith and John Stuart Mill. As Colander and Freedman write: "In the profession as a whole, Paul Samuelson unarguably became one of the early and most influential voices impatient to dump Classical Liberalism and replace it with a scientifically based policy" (2019, 46). Many will recognize Samuelson's neoclassical synthesis as the opposite of the teachings of Hayek and Milton Friedman. But consider the claim on the next page in Colander and Freedman's book: "Chicago may have lagged a step or two behind the pioneers of the new modernism, but they displayed few qualms in dispensing with the Classical Liberal approach. Instead, they formulated and embraced their own version of economic science, which opposed and countered the version of economic science being promulgated" (2019, 47).

Hayek's position of the economist as properly understood as a "student of civilization" was just as alien to Chicago as it was to the Massachusetts Institute of Technology; the modernist position must be seen as a decisive break with the grand tradition of political economy as initiated by the

Scottish moral philosophers of the 18th century and the British classical political economists of the 19th century. Colander and Freedman correctly identify Frank Knight and Jacob Viner as the key intellectual leaders of the older Chicago School during the interwar years of the 1920s and 1930s. "Graduate students and other young economists" throughout the profession, they argue, "embraced the cause of science-based theory and policy as providing the only reliable basis for either one." But they also point out that at least in the 1930s, "only Chicago and the London School of Economics (where Hayek and Lionel Robbins still ruled) provided any semblance of a sustained resistance to that abandonment [of classical liberalism] in that postwar era" (2019, 43).

Classical Liberalism

The abandonment of classical liberalism would only spread through the 1950s and 1960s. The Chicago School of Economics with Milton Friedman at the helm was a different beast from when Frank Knight was the driving intellectual. That Knightian perspective would instead be pursued within the Virginia School of Political Economy. But this approach, championed by James Buchanan and Ronald Coase, ran into obstacles that according to Colander and Freedman could not be overcome. Both public choice and law-and-economics would be transformed in the hands of others in a direction away from the classical liberal methodology, instead following the post–World War II Chicago School approach. As a result, the counterresistance to the abandonment was ignored by the mainstream of economic science. Both the science of economics and the art of political economy suffered as a result.

It might be useful to dig a bit deeper into the Virginia School of Political Economy. (I should add that George Mason University remains the final stronghold of this school within the profession.) Buchanan's position could be summarized with two statements he often made. First, economists must cease in their habit of offering economic advice as if to a benevolent despot. Second, in discussing public policy issues, economists must move the analysis to the level of rules and not limit the discussion to particular policies within the rules. This is Buchanan's "constitutional perspective," and it is reflected in his insistence that economists can never pick particular distributions of resources, but must always choose from among various rules of the game that will engender a pattern of exchange and production, and thus distribution.

Buchanan's position is directly attributable to the work of Frank Knight and Knut Wicksell. But he also would often stress the work of his University of Virginia colleague and also former Knight student Rutledge Vining. After Buchanan left UVA, he wrote in a letter to Vining on March 8, 1974:

> My own worry, which you do not express so directly as I do, stems from the step taken by such an idealized professional assistant when he takes it on himself to propose changes in structure, as if he has a direct line to God. This is the arrogance I talk about, and about which I think Frank Knight was also worried.

But Buchanan—in what might surprise the modern-day reader of this letter—singles out as a prime example of an economist violating this Knightian stricture none other than Milton Friedman. Friedman, Buchanan writes, "thinks and talks as if he is telling people what they should want, in terms of basic values, which is not at all his role, or so it seems to me. This is arrogant behavior, which Knight would never have engaged in." Buchanan admits that it is extremely difficult to avoid falling into this trap, but concludes that nevertheless "we should avoid this where possible."

So what should classical liberal political economists do? When Buchanan assumed the directorship of the Thomas Jefferson Center for Studies in Political Economy at UVA, he argued that the goal was:

> to carry on the honorable tradition of "political economy"—the study of what makes for a "good society." Political economists stress the technical economic principles that one must understand in order to assess alternative arrangements for promoting peaceful cooperation and productive specialization among free men. Yet political economists go further and frankly try to bring out into the open the philosophical issues that necessarily underlie all discussions of the appropriate functions of government and all proposed economic policy measures. They examine philosophical values for consistency among themselves and with the ideal of human freedom. (1958, 5)

This mission statement, I would argue, is completely consistent with the sort of classical liberal methodology that Colander and Freedman discuss in their book, and should be juxtaposed with a rule-by-experts approach whether on the right, left, or center. The mission statement is an indictment of the effort to see economics as providing the technical expertise that enables the efficient and judicious use of public policy to eradicate social ills. It is not an effort to ignore social ills, or to downplay their significance, but rather to discipline the way we discuss solutions to social ills and the role that economists play in a free and democratic society.

Conclusion

It is my hope that I have provided something to wrestle with about the role of economists in a free and democratic society. Economics in the hands of its masters, such as Hayek, is a masterful expert critique of rule by expertise, as Hayek (1952) described his own "Abuse of Reason" project where he followed the Humean dictum of using reason to whittle down the claims of reason. In his essay "Individualism: True and False," Hayek (1948) argued that the thrust of Adam Smith's system was to strive to find a social system where the institutions were so robust that bad men could do the least harm, rather than to find a system where the good and the wise could rule. To devise a system of governance in such a fashion, Hume's advice that we must presume that all men are knaves seems to be methodologically wise for the analytical task at hand. It is equally important for us to remember that knavery comes in multiple forms—namely, opportunism and arrogance. It might be that the "Fatal Conceit" is a more general problem than just in the attitudes of our socialist and interventionist colleagues in economics. It may be endemic to the modern mindset. And the antidote might require that economists be knocked off their pedestal as saviors of society and high priests of the modern order, and restricted once more to our status as students of civilization, and the lowly philosophers of social order.

References

Buchanan, James M. 1949. "The Pure Theory of Government Finance: A Suggested Approach." *Journal of Political Economy* 57 (6): 496–505.

———. 1958. "The Thomas Jefferson Center for Studies in Political Economy." *The University of Virginia News Letter* 32 (2): 5–9.

———. 1960. *Fiscal Theory and Political Economy: Selected Essays*. Chapel Hill: University of North Carolina Press.

———. 1964. "What Should Economists Do?" *Southern Economic Journal* 30 (3): 213–22.

Coase, Ronald. 2012. "Saving Economics from the Economists." *Harvard Business Review*, December.

Colander, David C., and Craig Freedman. 2019. *Where Economics Went Wrong: Chicago's Abandonment of Classical Liberalism*. Princeton, NJ: Princeton University Press.

Emmett, Ross B., ed. 1999. *Selected Essays by Frank H. Knight.* Volume 2: *Laissez-Faire: Pro and Con.* Chicago: University of Chicago Press.

Friedman, Milton, and George J. Stigler. 1946. *Roofs or Ceilings? The Current Housing Problem.* Irvington-on-Hudson, NY: Foundation for Economic Education.

Hayek, F. A. 1948. *Individualism: True and False.* Chicago: University of Chicago Press.

———. 1952. *The Counter-Revolution of Science: Studies on the Abuse of Reason.* Glencoe, IL: Free Press.

———. [1974] 1989. "The Pretence of Knowledge." *American Economic Review* 79 (6): 3–7.

Knight, Frank. 1951. "The Role of Principles in Economics and Politics." *American Economic Review* 41 (1): 1–29.

Mises, Ludwig von. 1912. *The Theory of Money and Credit.* Munich: Verlag von Duncker & Humblot.

———. 1922. *Socialism: An Economic and Sociological Analysis.* Jena, Germany: Gustav Fischer Verlag.

———. 1949. *Human Action: A Treatise on Economics.* New Haven, CT: Yale University Press.

———. 1990. *Economic Freedom and Interventionism.* Indianapolis: Liberty Fund.

Ostrom, Elinor. 1990. *Governing the Commons: The Evolution of Institutions for Collective Action.* New York: Cambridge University Press.

Skidelsky, Robert. 2005. *John Maynard Keynes: 1883–1946: Economist, Philosopher, Statesman.* New York: Penguin Books.

Smith, Adam. [1776] 1976. *An Inquiry into the Nature and Causes of the Wealth of Nations.* Chicago: University of Chicago Press.

Weber, Max. 1922. *Economy and Society.* Berkeley: University of California Press.

Chapter 8

Don't Be a "Jibbering Idiot": Economic Principles and the Properly Trained Economist

I am not here today to insult my fellow economists, but to hopefully inspire the young, aspiring economics teachers among you to learn your craft and to do your job. Teaching is a most worthy vocation, and the teaching of economics is especially needed today given the plethora of popular fallacies that occupy the public imagination and the public policy community.

But the problem is even deeper because our profession has fallen short in its job of teaching the basic principles of our discipline. Graduate students are too often trained in the technical tools of optimization and in deriving the theorems that constitute the equilibrium models with which they are taught to work. However, they no longer learn price theory, which analyzes the critical role that relative prices play in guiding human decision-making and the necessary adjustments on multiple margins that are required for adapting to changing circumstances.

Institutions, while no longer ignored, are merely mentioned, not analyzed, as Barry Weingast (2016) has emphasized in an essay, "Exposing the Neoclassical Fallacy." Again, graduate students are trained in sophisticated procedures of statistical testing, but largely remain ignorant of history and thus economic performance through time as a result of institutions and institutional change.

The consequence of this educational trajectory is that when graduate students find themselves in front of a classroom of undergraduate students after successfully completing their studies, they must either bifurcate their teaching lives from their research lives or attempt to dumb down their research results

Remarks delivered at the 42nd annual meeting of the Association for Private Enterprise Education, April 10, 2017, Lahaina, Hawaii. Published in *Journal of Private Enterprise* 32, no. 3 (2017): 9–15.

to communicate effectively with undergraduates. There is nothing inherently wrong with this, but economics without price theory is not *economic theory*, and measurement without theory isn't *empirically meaningful*. Students don't learn the beauty of economic theory, and they don't learn the empirical importance of economic history. In short, they don't learn how the world works; they don't learn the governing dynamics of human action and the mechanisms that produce the social cooperation under the division of labor that modern civilization depends on.

My speech title derives from a brilliant lecture by my teacher James Buchanan. In his essay "Economics and Its Scientific Neighbors," Buchanan ([1966] 2001) argued for the renewed commitment by the economist to the basic principles of the science. These principles have been refined through the evolution of economics, but the essential insight comes down from Adam Smith through F. A. Hayek—what I have called "mainline economics." In mainline economics, the "invisible hand" explanation of market order follows from the self-interest postulate via institutional analysis. The economic forces *at work* bring about systemic order and the pattern of exchange and production that realizes that the gains from social cooperation come about due to the incentives created by private property rights, the guiding influence of relative prices, the lure of entrepreneurial profits, and the discipline of losses. Shifts in the rules of the game will set in motion changes in incentives and information, and with that the learning from the feedback that actors receive.

Not only do different institutional arrangements possess different incentive effects, they also provide different informational signals that economic actors rely on in making their decisions and different feedback about how to learn, what to learn, and who is to take responsibility for learning. Economic theory enables us to see through this complex set of issues and to understand not just the *what happened* of economic history, but the *why* of what happened in economic history. As Buchanan says, it is these principles of economics that enable the ordinary scientist to rise to the height of genius in the ability to make sense out of the seemingly senseless ([1966] 2001, 7). It is a thing of beauty, and our students must be intellectually seduced by the aesthetic beauty of the logic of economic analysis in the hands of a master teacher.

As I alluded to already, James Buchanan was such a master of conveying the beauty of economic analysis, so I will rely on his insights throughout this talk to guide me through the points I want to make. First, let's consider the passage from which I derive my title. "As a 'social' scientist," Buchanan argued, "the primary function of the economist is to explain the workings of these institutions and to predict the effects of changes in their structures. As the interaction process that he examines becomes more complex, it is but natural that the task of the economic scientist becomes more intricate. But his central principle remains the same, and he can, through its use, unravel the most tangled sets of structural relationships among human beings" ([1966] 2001, 7).

Economics, properly understood, makes sense out of the complex web of human relations that constitutes reality. Buchanan writes:

> The economist is able to do this because he possesses this central principle— an underlying theory of human behavior. And because he does so, he quali- fies as a scientist and his discipline as a science. What a science does, or should do, is simply to allow the average man, through professional specialization, to command the heights of genius. The basic tools are the simple principles, and these are chained forever to the properly disciplined professional. With- out them, he is as a jibbering idiot, who makes only noise under an illusion of speech. ([1966] 2001, 7)

Rather than move increasingly away from the basic principles of our dis- cipline, Buchanan suggests, our job is to reaffirm and refine those principles and to deploy them to address ever more complex problem situations—to keep them, as he puts it, forever chained to our side as a properly disciplined professional economist. Forgive me for a slight detour here, but there is an important lesson to be learned from the great basketball coach and teacher John Wooden. The best book I have ever read on pedagogy is one about Wooden, titled *You Haven't Taught until They Have Learned* (Nater and Gallimore 2006), which I think many college teachers of economics would benefit from reading even if they had no interest whatsoever in basketball.

Anyway, Wooden at UCLA was loaded with All-American players during his run of 10 NCAA [National Collegiate Athletic Association] champion- ships. And despite the fact that his gym was full of the best players in the game at the time, and in the instance of a few, arguably the best players of all time, he began the first practice of every year with a lesson on how to put on your socks and tie your shoelaces. His reason was simple—you cannot play good basketball if your feet are not in good shape. An untied shoelace or a bunched-up sock could result in an inability to perform a basic task, and a blister might eliminate the ability to play altogether. First principles matter.

Attention to detail matters. One should never get bored with first principles or with exploring the intricate details if one wants to excel.

Now, back to economics. Fancy techniques are fine, and sophisticated tools are important, but not if they are acquired at the expense of basic principles. In that case, they are likely little more than activity without accomplishment, something that any serious and self-respecting economic scientist should avoid. But Buchanan fears we have lost this seriousness and self-respect for the discipline of economics. He challenges us all when he writes:

> Unfortunately, most modern economists have no idea of what they are doing or even of what they are ideally supposed to be doing. I challenge any of you to take any issue of any economics journal and convince yourself, and me, that a randomly chosen paper will have a social productivity greater than zero. Most modern economists are simply doing what other economists are doing while living off a form of dole that will simply not stand critical scrutiny. Beware the day for educators generally when the taxpaying public finds out that the king really has no clothes. ([1979] 2000, 28–29)

The problem, as Buchanan sees it, is that economics as a discipline has a public purpose, but modern economists have shirked that purpose and yet are still being rewarded as if they were earnestly working to meet their educational obligation. As he put it:

> I have often argued that there is only one 'principle' in economics that is worth stressing, and that the economist's didactic function is one of conveying some understanding of this principle to the public at large. Apart from this principle, there would be no general basis for general public support for economics as a legitimate academic discipline, no place for 'economics' as an appropriate part of a 'liberal' educational curriculum. I refer, of course, to the principle of the spontaneous order of the market, which was the great intellectual discovery of the eighteenth century. ([1977] 2000, 96)

Economics properly done is an invitation to inquiry, and the principles constitute a golden key that unlocks the deepest mysteries of the human experience. We live in a world of scarcity, and as a result, individuals must choose. In choosing, individuals face tradeoffs, and in negotiating those tradeoffs, they need aids to the human mind to guide them. Prices serve this guiding role, profits lure them, losses discipline them, and all of that is made possible by an institutional environment of property, contract, and consent. These are the basic principles from which we work in economics.

Economic analysis relies neither on any notion of hyperrational actors myopically concerned with maximizing monetary rewards, nor on postulating perfectly competitive markets. It relies simply on the notion that fallible yet capable human beings are striving to better their situations, and in so doing, they enter into exchange relations with others. Atomistic individualism and mechanistic notions of the market are, as Buchanan has stressed, nonsensical social science. Instead, economics as a social science is about exchange relations and the institutions within which those relationships are formed and carried out.

As Buchanan stressed in his essay "What Should Economists Do?," it is "man's behavior in the market relationship, reflecting the propensity to truck and to barter, and the manifold variations in structure that this relationship can take" that are "the proper subjects for the economist's study" (1964, 214). We study "markets" because markets are the institutional embodiment of the network of these exchange relationships. "A market is not competitive by assumption or by construction," Buchanan argued:

> A market *becomes* competitive, and competitive rules *come to be* established as institutions emerge to place limits on individual behavior patterns. It is this *becoming* process, brought about by the continuous pressure of human behavior in exchange, that is the central part of our discipline, if we have one, not the dry-rot of postulated perfection. A solution to a general-equilibrium set of equations is not predetermined by exogenously-determined rules. A general solution, if there is one, *emerges* as a result of a whole network of evolving exchanges, bargains, trades, side payments, agreements, and contracts which, finally at some point, ceases to renew itself. At each stage in this evolution towards solution, there are *gains* to be made, there are exchanges possible, and this being true, the direction of movement is modified. (1964, 218)

It is our job as teachers of economics to alert and emphasize to our students the manifold ways in which (a) individuals in the market are constantly adapting and adjusting, (b) coordinative processes of adjustment align the production plans of some with the consumption demands of others, and (c) the unintended yet reliable orderliness of this coordinative process emerges spontaneously because of the role that property, prices, and profit and loss play in guiding, cajoling, and disciplining individuals. This is how the price system impresses upon decision makers the essential items of knowledge required for plan coordination. This is how monetary calculation works to guide us amid a sea of economic possibilities and ensures that among the technologically feasible, only the economically viable projects are selected. This is how wealth is created and humanity is lifted from the miserable condition of extreme poverty to one where human flourishing is possible.

From a Buchanan perspective, basic economics can be conveyed in eight points:

1. Economics is a "science," but not like the physical sciences. Economics is a "philosophical" science, and the strictures against scientism offered by Frank Knight and F. A. Hayek should be heeded.
2. Economics is about choice and processes of adjustment, not states of rest. Equilibrium models are only useful when we recognize their limits.
3. Economics is about exchange, not about maximization. Exchange activity and arbitrage should be the central focus of economic analysis.
4. Economics is about individual actors, not collective entities. Only individuals choose.
5. Economics is about a game played within rules.
6. Economics cannot be studied properly outside of politics. The choices among different rules of the game cannot be ignored.
7. The most important function of economics as a discipline is its didactic role in explaining the principle of spontaneous order.
8. Economics is elementary.

When you are teaching, think about these eight points constantly. By pursuing them consistently and persistently, you will be able to demonstrate that you are a properly trained professional, and you will communicate to your students the intellectual beauty as well as the scientific power of economic theory. You also will avoid being a "jibbering idiot" in economics who confuses noise for speech in the analysis of human action in all walks of life. And in avoiding that fate, you will be able to communicate to your students how economics is both the most wildly entertaining social science and the most deadly serious. It is, in short, the scientific vehicle by which they can be transformed from ordinary observers to the height of genius, capable of making sense of the seemingly senseless and exploring the mysteries of man in his ordinary business of life.

References

Buchanan, James M. 1964. "What Should Economists Do?" *Southern Economic Journal* 30 (3): 213–22.

———. [1966] 2001. "Economics and Its Scientific Neighbors." In *The Collected Works of James M. Buchanan*. Volume 17: *Moral Science and Moral Order*. Indianapolis: Liberty Fund.

———. [1977] 2000. "Law and the Invisible Hand." In *The Collected Works of James M. Buchanan*. Volume 17: *Moral Science and Moral Order*. Indianapolis: Liberty Fund.

———. [1979] 2000. "General Implications of Subjectivism in Economics." In *The Collected Works of James M. Buchanan*. Volume 12: *Economic Inquiry and Its Logic*. Indianapolis: Liberty Fund.

Nater, Swen, and Ronald Gallimore. 2006. *You Haven't Taught until They Have Learned: John Wooden's Teaching Principles and Practices*. Morgantown, WV: Fitness Information Technology.

Weingast, Barry R. 2016. "Exposing the Neoclassical Fallacy: McCloskey on Ideas and the Great Enrichment." *Scandinavian Economic History Review* 64 (3): 189–201.

Chapter 9

Information and Knowledge: Austrian Economics in Search of Its Uniqueness

I am wiser than this man; it is likely that neither of us knows anything worthwhile, but he thinks he knows something when he does not, whereas when I do not know, neither do I think I know; so I am likely to be wiser than he to this small extent, that I do not think I know what I do not know.

—Socrates[1]

Since the mid-1930s, Austrian economics has found itself in a strange position with regard to the mainline of economic thinking. Many of the theoretical innovations introduced by scholars working within the Austrian tradition were understood by economists to be fully incorporated into standard neoclassical economics by the early 1930s. Developments in economic thinking during the 1930s in retrospect call that claim into question. No doubt, many economists in the 1930s understood that tastes were subjective, that microeconomic analysis must be grounded in methodological individualism, that production plans must be coordinated with consumption demands through time, and that the incentives that the market economy engenders possess strong self-regulating tendencies. Lionel Robbins's (1932) statement of the methodology and methods of analysis neatly summarized the main Austrian tenets for an English-speaking audience and was widely accepted by economists.

But in the wake of the Great Depression, this orthodox consensus broke down. The new economics of Keynes decidedly moved away from

Society for the Development of Austrian Economics presidential address, Southern Economic Association meeting, November 2001, Tampa, Florida. Published in *Review of Austrian Economics* 15, no. 4 (2002): 263–74.

the methodological individualist position and questioned the self-regulatory robustness of the market economy. Instead of relying on market forces to self-correct for errors in investment, the government was given the policy role of correcting for market instability.

In addition to the Keynesian revolution in macroeconomics, economists started to develop arguments about the microeconomic inefficiency of the market economy. The theories of imperfect competition and monopolistic competition were developed by Edward Chamberlin and Joan Robinson during the 1930s. Moreover, the argument of Adolf Berle and Gardiner Means about the separation of ownership and control within the modern corporation was presented to suggest another way in which the modern era deviated significantly from the earlier model of capitalist efficiency. Finally, these macroeconomic and microeconomic arguments served as the background for the emerging argument for market socialism as developed by Oskar Lange and Abba Lerner.[2] The underlying logic of Lange's model was that through the use of standard price theory, he could demonstrate the theoretical possibility of market socialism, and given this demonstration the practical desirability of market socialism over the instability and inefficiency of real-world capitalism.

In the wake of both the rise of Keynesianism and market socialism, Ludwig von Mises and F. A. Hayek started to emphasize the nuances with the Austrian understanding of the market economy that had tended to be glossed over in the pre-1930s intellectual climate in economic science. The work by Mises stressed the dynamic and competitive entrepreneurial process, whereas Hayek stressed the informational processing capability of the market economy. Both stressed the necessary institutional conditions for these arguments to hold—namely, private property, freedom of contract, and limited government. Moreover, both made favorable reference to each other's arguments as essential components to forming a correct understanding of the nature of the market economy.[3] It was not just that the Keynesian, monopolistically competitive, and market socialist arguments were politically wrong, they were wrong because they were built on a foundation of economics that fundamentally misconstrued economic life.

Ironically, during the 1930s and 1940s, both Mises and Hayek maintained that their understanding of economic life represented the *mainstream of economic thinking*. It was really only with the generation of Austrian economists trained in the 1950s (namely, Murray Rothbard and Israel Kirzner) that the idea of a modern and unique Austrian School of economics began to take hold of the imagination of scholars.[4] But what exactly were the defining characteristics of this unique school of thought?

Murray Rothbard (1962) emphasized the rejection of mathematical modeling and statistical inference as the basic tools of economics analysis. Rothbard, instead, focused on the consistent application of methodological individualism and methodological subjectivism. The defining characteristic, in other words, to Rothbard was the praxeological method—including a firm commitment to apriorism. Israel Kirzner (1973), while not disputing the claims of Rothbard, emphasized the uncertainty inherent in all economic decisions and the entrepreneurial nature of the market process. Ludwig Lachmann (1977), who was also a significant contributor to the literature on a unique Austrian School, emphasized the radical subjectivist stance. In Lachmann's mind the Austrian School matured with each step along the consistent adoption of subjectivism—the move from subjectivism of value to subjectivism of expectations.[5]

While not disputing the arguments put forth by Rothbard, Kirzner, and Lachmann, I want to suggest that perhaps Austrians ought to ground their argument for uniqueness not along methodological grounds, but instead in their analytical contributions to our understanding of the epistemic-cognitive properties of alternative institutional arrangements. It is this recognition of the contextual nature of the relevant economic knowledge that actors must work with within an economic system that represents the unique contribution of the modern Austrian School to our understanding of the price system and the market economy.

Distinguishing Knowledge and Information

Two major developments in economic theorizing occurred when time and information were incorporated into the analysis of the market economy. Rather than a static and full information world, economists were set to analyze action in time and the acquisition of information. But in order to accommodate these factors in the standard model, the strategy followed was to treat time and information as either constraints or objective commodities.[6] Information, for example, was divided into bits and pieces dispersed throughout the economic system that maximizing agents must acquire in making a decision.

Standard models of search presume that agents follow Bayes's law for updating their priors as they learn through the search process. This guarantees that the actors are not merely passive reactors to given information, but instead are willing to adjust their priors as they acquire more information. The general rule is that they will continue to collect information until the expected marginal benefit of continued search equals the marginal cost of continuing the search.[7] While adjustment through learning is evident in the basic model, the actors in the model are nevertheless rather mechanical learners. "Nothing will ever occur," Stephen Littlechild has pointed out, "for which they are not prepared, nor can they ever initiate anything which is not preordained" (1977, 7). Interpretation and skillful judgment in the face of the unforeseen, not to mention creativity, are not captured in the Bayesian learning process.

Standard search theory—while clearly an improvement over the full information models that preceded it—tends to rely on its own form of complete information. The model presupposes that the underlying probability distribution is known to agents and that the question is one of them searching for information under conditions of risk, not uncertainty (in Knight's sense). In short, complete information is available, but agents are imperfectly informed and have to engage in a deliberate process of gathering the information that is relevant to their decision-making.

As information economics developed, Austrian writers repeatedly raised the distinction between risk and uncertainty to distinguish their position—in many instances calling upon Mises's distinction between case and class probability in human decision-making to make their point. It is not my point to rehash this position, with which I am in essential agreement, but to insist that the semantic point about the meaning of risk and uncertainty is *not* what is driving the Austrian criticism. Instead, the point is raised by writers in this intellectual tradition because something fundamental about the price system and the market economy is lost when information and learning is treated in a mechanical manner.

Identifying precisely what is lost in the explanation will lead us to what is unique about the Austrian research program on the market economy. I am going to argue that the definitions of *knowledge* and *information* are really what underpin the dispute. Semantic disputes have often bogged down progress in economics.[8] A prominent example would be the capital theory debates in the 1930s and 1940s, where Knight thought of capital in monetary terms, whereas Hayek thought of capital in goods terms. Of course, in monetary terms capital is homogenous, but in goods terms capital is heterogeneous. But Knight and Hayek talked past each other (see Boettke and Vaughn 2002).

Economics, as all specialized fields, has its own jargon. Economists often redefine terms to fit with their meaning. *Elasticity*, a term we use to describe how sensitive human behavior is to changes in price, is a favorite example— why not just use the word *sensitive*? Textbooks often use the term *sensitivity* in the definition of *elasticity*. *Competition* is another favorite example in the Austrian literature. Textbook economics uses the term *competition* to define a state of affairs where in fact the activity of competition ceases. Well, I want to suggest that the terms *information* and *knowledge* have also been translated into economic language in a manner that distorts their standard meaning. To incorporate information and knowledge into the standard economic model, the concepts were conflated and treated as a commodity that was *deliberately* bought and sold in the market.

Merriam-Webster's Collegiate Dictionary defines *information* as "the communication or reception of knowledge or intelligence; knowledge obtained from investigation; facts or data." *Knowledge*, on the other hand, is defined as "the fact or condition of knowing something with familiarity gained through experience or association; acquaintance with or understanding of a science, art, or technique; the range of one's information or understanding." In short, information is a flow concept, whereas knowledge is a stock notion. However, economists have tended to view information as both a stock and flow and eliminate the discussion of knowledge as discovery of the previously unknown.

The Austrians objected to this conflation of information and knowledge. But since Hayek had already used the term *knowledge* in his 1937 and 1945 essays to connote the use of existing as well as the discovery of new knowledge, and the term *information* was already being employed in a particular way by other economists to describe objective bits, they tended to employ the term *knowledge* to discuss the subjective component, the discovery factor, and the tacit domain.

Knowledge is ever changing and is multifaceted, whereas information is something fixed. In other words, information is the stock of the existing known, while knowledge is the flow of new and ever-expanding areas of the known. As G. L. S. Shackle put it, "So far as men are concerned, *being* consists in continual and endless fresh knowing" (1972, 156). While the Austrian, or subjectivist, definition of *knowledge* as a flow flies in the face of the dictionary definition, it does distance itself from the conflation of information and knowledge that exists in the standard textbooks.

To illustrate the difference, perhaps the following example might work. Consider a basic learning-by-doing model and the example of solving a technical issue in engineering. Given a certain problem, a student at the Massachusetts Institute of Technology realizes that the answer lies in a textbook somewhere on the library shelves, but does not know in which book the correct formula is to be found. A standard search model can be deployed. Our MIT student will search the textbooks to find the needed formula up to that point where the expected marginal benefit of continued search equals the marginal cost of continued search. As our student progresses from freshman year to senior year, she gets more proficient in doing these searches. But what is absent from this exercise is that as our engineering student works with the existing texts, she may well be in the process of creating the new texts that will occupy the library shelves as she uses the existing information to solve different problems or to launch new avenues of inquiry that were previously not thought. The Austrians want to emphasize not just the proficient use of existing information, but the discovery and use of new knowledge that comes into being only because of the context in which actors find themselves acting.[9]

In addition to a discussion of the discovery and use of knowledge, the Austrians have often emphasized another dimension absent from standard treatments of information—the interpretation and skillful judgment embodied in the use of knowledge. It is often remarked about the internet nowadays that information is vast, but knowledge is scarce. This phrase gets at the basic Austrian concern. In making economic decisions, we do not just passively react to information, but must actively interpret the information we receive, and pass judgment on its reliability and its relevance for our decision-making.

If you are looking for the unique Austrian research program, I contend, it is to be found in this emphasis on these knowledge aspects of the economic process. Of course, there are other differences between Austrian economists and their neoclassical brethren. Some of these differences are vital. But the claim to the uniqueness of the Austrian contribution lies, I believe, in the treatment of information and knowledge.

Information and Knowledge within the Austrian Literature

To illustrate my point, I plan to examine the discussion of information and knowledge in the work of four major Austrian economists—Hayek, Fritz Machlup, Kirzner, and Don Lavoie. A more ambitious task would be to also discuss Mises's (1922, 1949) contributions to this literature because his treatment of economic calculation, the intellectual division of labor, and the entrepreneurial market process is the genesis of these later contributions. But Mises did not explicitly distinguish between information and knowledge in his work since the conflation of the terms was not yet fully evident in the economics literature.

Hayek's research program took the "knowledge" turn with his 1937 essay "Economics and Knowledge." I interpret the main point of that essay to be that the knowledge that defines the equilibrium state of affairs emerges within the process leading to that equilibrium state rather than existing anterior to that process. Without the market process to generate it, the relevant knowledge would not exist. Economists, Hayek warned, cannot continue to assume given knowledge.

A secondary point of that essay was to suggest that while the logic of choice is a necessary component of an explanation of the market process, it is not sufficient. The logic of choice must be complemented with empirical examination of how learning takes place within alternative institutional settings. Within a private property order, the competitive market process will direct economic actors—all pursuing their own individual logics of choice—to engage in activities that will dovetail with the actions of others to coordinate plans through time. Outside the context of the private property order, Hayek contended, the individual pursuit of their goals is not powerful enough to ensure plan coordination. In fact, it is in this 1937 essay that we first get a statement of a theme that Hayek will emphasize throughout his career—namely, that what we call economic rationality emerges because of a certain institutional setting and is not a behavioral postulate of economic analysis.

Hayek's most famous essay "The Use of Knowledge in Society" (1945) pursues a slightly different approach to these issues. Aspects of his essay emphasize the informational efficiency of the price system. His famous tin example, for example, highlights how the price system economizes the amount of information that economic actors must process in order to act successfully within the market. It is this insight that many economists within the information economics research program have picked up from Hayek and examined. But Hayek also emphasized in that 1945 essay that the knowledge of the market process is not of the type that can be treated as a statistic and instead is knowledge of particular time and place that agents deploy in making their decisions on the spot. Agents outside of a particular institutional context do not have the relevant knowledge for decision-making within that context. Knowledge, in other words, is concrete and contextual and not abstract.

Starting in the 1950s, Fritz Machlup began a series of studies on innovation and the knowledge industry. In these works, Machlup defines *knowledge* as a commodity and attempts to measure the magnitude of the production and distribution of this commodity within a modern economy. In short, Machlup was the first modern economist to address the question of the "information economy" that is so often talked about today. Machlup divided the knowledge industries into five categories: (a) practical knowledge, (b) intellectual knowledge, (c) pastime knowledge, (d) spiritual or religious knowledge, and (e) unwanted knowledge. In *The Production and Distribution of Knowledge in the United States*, published in 1962, Machlup estimated that knowledge production in 1958 was almost 29 percent of the gross national product (GNP). Later work following up on Machlup estimates that the growth of the knowledge industry was actually quite modest compared with other components of GNP. The knowledge industry went from 29 percent in 1958 to 34.3 percent of GNP in 1980.

However, Machlup's division of the knowledge industry into various categories does not address the question of knowledge of time and place, the importance of interpretation and skillful judgment. Thus, while Machlup certainly contributed to our understanding of knowledge as a commodity, he did not address the questions upon which Hayek sought to reorient economic research.

Throughout the 1960s and 1970s, Israel Kirzner, building on the work of Mises and Hayek, developed his theory of the entrepreneurial market process. Entrepreneurs in Kirzner's understanding of the market economy represent the driving force that ensures the relative efficiency of competition processes within a system of clearly defined and strictly enforced private property rights. The entrepreneur perceives previously unrecognized opportunities for mutual gain and by acting on them directs the economic system to a more coordinated state of affairs than had previously existed. In short, entrepreneurial arbitrage is the equilibrating force within the market economy.[10]

In the process of articulating his theory of entrepreneurial behavior, Kirzner had to revisit the issues of knowledge that Hayek raised in his 1937 and 1945 essays. Kirzner tended to emphasize two aspects of knowledge which do not permit it to be treated as a fixed commodity. First, Kirzner's entrepreneurial theory emphasizes the subjective perception of opportunity. A profit opportunity that is known to all will be realized by nobody; so while all actors possess some aspect of entrepreneurial alertness, they cannot all be alert to the same opportunities with the same level of proficiency in alertness. This differential recognition of entrepreneurial opportunities for profit raises the issue of contextual knowledge within the competitive market process. This context-dependent nature of our knowledge is the second aspect of knowledge that Kirzner's theory of the entrepreneurial market process raises. Unfortunately, Kirzner does not address this aspect head-on.

Don Lavoie picked up on Kirzner's work on the nature of the entrepreneurial market process and revisited the socialist calculation debate and the problems of centralized economic planning (1985b). In his follow-up book on piecemeal economic planning, Lavoie (1985a) reinforced the ideas of Mises, Hayek, and Kirzner with the theories of knowledge in science and society advanced by Michael Polanyi to show that the knowledge-problem critique of socialist central planning applied with equal force to supposedly more modest attempts at national economic planning, such as industrial policy.[11] The tacit domain of our knowledge addresses the issue of context, but does so in a manner that focuses on learned and skillful judgment in the use of knowledge. "Learning," Lavoie writes, "is an enhancement of our interpretive powers and our tacit understanding of an unfolding reality rather than the simple accumulation of data" (1985a, 58).

In Lavoie's writings, we get an explicit treatment of the market as a cognitive process. Not only does the price system economize on the information economic decision makers must process, but the entire market system generates a level of social intelligence that no one mind or group of minds could approximate.[12] These insights of Lavoie, however, are blurred in treatments that conflate information and knowledge and treat the universe as essentially known rather than in a constant flux of unending discovery.

Hayek's emphasis on the market as a device for social learning—in particular, the role of entrepreneurial competition in stimulating that learning—is developed by Lavoie and harnessed to address the arguments for comprehensive central planning (e.g., Marxian central planning), aggregative notions of planning (e.g., Leontief input–output analysis), and piecemeal planning (e.g., industrial policy, etc.). The data that are relevant for the most essential decisions within a market economy, Lavoie contends, are fundamentally uncollectible and are embedded instead in the decisions of time and place and acted on by decision makers through their active interpretation and the exercise of skillful judgment.

Information Economics and the Market Process

The awarding of the Nobel Prize to Joseph Stiglitz, George Akerlof, and Michael Spence in 2001 was richly deserved. Information economics has transformed the way economists think about the economic system. I will not comment on Spence's essential writings on signaling in labor markets, but restrict my comments to Stiglitz and Akerlof because they raise the issue of the connection between information asymmetries and market failure.[13] If the market is viewed as an epistemic-cognitive process, as I contend the Austrian writers tend to do, then asymmetries are what drive the entrepreneurial process. The successful entrepreneur perceives the imperfection in the current arrangement of affairs more accurately than others, and he acts on that information to earn a profit and in so acting brings new knowledge into existence. In others words, today's inefficiency is tomorrow's profit opportunity for those who recognize it and act on it to better satisfy the demands of consumers.

In Stiglitz's work on the informational efficiency of the market system (mostly written with Sanford Grossman), he argues that private information once revealed will become public information and thus the private information that agents have that could be used to their benefit will cease to be valuable once publicly revealed through the market. This leads him to conclude that markets will underproduce the requisite information for the efficient allocation of resources. It is my contention that this argument overestimates the efficiency of equilibrium prices and completely disregards the informational content of disequilibrium prices. To Stiglitz, the dynamic adjustment processes that disequilibrium prices set in motion are simply ignored in his treatment of the market economy. In Stiglitz's theory, the efficiency postulates attributed to the competitive model are highly fragile to deviations from the ideal conditions.[14] The Austrians, on the other hand, argue that the competitive market process is highly robust with regard to its efficiency properties even in situations far from the ideal. Today's inefficiency is tomorrow's profit opportunity for those who act to improve the situation and bring the underlying variables of tastes and technology more in line with the induced variables of prices and profit and loss that exist on the market. Stiglitz argues for fragility because the price system is informationally inefficient, whereas the Austrians contend that disequilibrium prices spur economic actors to adjust their behavior in a less erroneous direction than before.

Akerlof's discussion of "lemons" suffers from the same sort of problem I suggest plagues Stiglitz's system.[15] Admittedly, Akerlof does raise the market responses to the lemons problem in passing in his famous paper, but he does not really emphasize those institutional responses to the potential problem of asymmetry. What Akerlof perceives as problems in market systems have actually given rise to entrepreneurial solutions, as private actors situated in particular time and place have adjusted their behavior to realize the mutual gains from exchange. As Hayek argued:

> The confusion between the objective facts of the situation [e.g., Akerlof asymmetries] and the character of human responses to it tends to conceal from us the important fact that competition is the more important the more complex or "imperfect" are the objective conditions in which it has to operate. Indeed, far from competition being beneficial only when it is "perfect," I am inclined to argue that the need for competition is nowhere greater than in fields in which the nature of the commodities or services makes it impossible that it ever should create a perfect market in the theoretical sense. (1948, 103–4)

It is competition that prods actors to behave in a manner more conducive to "rationality" and the coordination of economic plans. Without the competitive market process, the knowledge necessary for actors to plot their course in the economic sea of possibilities would not exist. It is not that it would be difficult to find; it is literally that the knowledge would remain unknown. The ability of the market process to reveal hitherto unknown possibilities and spur economic actors to act on this new and fresh knowledge to better themselves by satisfying the demands of others is what lies at the heart of the comparative institutional case for the market economy as a superior institution for coordinating our economic affairs.

It is the contention of the Austrians, from Hayek to Lavoie, that, as Kirzner writes:

> [T]he market performs a crucial function in discovering knowledge nobody knows exists; that an understanding of the true character of the market process depends, indeed, on recognizing this crucial function; and, finally, that contemporary economists' unawareness of these insights appears to be the result of otherwise wholly laudable attempts to treat knowledge objectively—that is, as consisting entirely of units of available information that are to be acquired only through calculated expenditure of resources. (1979, 139)

Conclusion

The Austrian economists have indeed found themselves in a strange position since the 1930s. Prior to the 1930s, the contributions of the economists from Vienna were widely recognized as significant advancements in the emerging neoclassical hegemony. However, during the 1930s, the Austrians were blindsided by two forces. First, the new economics of Keynes seemed to be a step backward from the neoclassical economics the Austrians were part of, yet younger economists and policymakers flocked to the Keynesian system. Mises and Hayek thought this popularity would be short-lived given that the theory was grounded in an economics of abundance and was really only a policy doctrine for the time, rather than a refinement of neoclassical economics. Little did they know the sway that Keynesian doctrine would hold in the scientific and public policy communities for over 40 years.

Second, Mises and Hayek were taken aback again by the use of neoclassical arguments, namely, Walrasian equilibrium theory, to argue in favor of market socialism. In the market failure literature, the models of imperfect and monopolistic competition and the Berle-Means hypothesis about the separation of ownership and control were deployed to question the efficiency of the market economy. The Walrasian conditions for market efficiency were then adopted for the model of market socialism, and the argument was made that socialism could achieve in theory exactly the same results as capitalism could, and in practice it could outperform capitalism.

To Mises and Hayek, these arguments must have seemed not just wrong, but intellectually bizarre. Somehow neoclassical economics had taken a drastic turn for the worse. In trying to figure out how this turn took place, Mises and Hayek embarked on a very innovative stage of their careers as they separately articulated the nature of the entrepreneurial market process and the cognitive function that process served. Most economists failed to appreciate the innovative nature of the work of Mises and Hayek in the 1940s. Many fail to do so to this day.

It has been my contention that the innovative aspect of their work is to be found in their discussions of knowledge and the distinction between knowledge and information that follows from their work. By focusing our analytical attention on our cognitive imperfections, Hayek sought to articulate how we can cope with, and in fact exploit, this situation to realize the unforeseen and unpredictable from which we will benefit as the course of events unfolds through time. "If there were omniscient men," Hayek wrote in *The Constitution of Liberty*, "if we could know not only all that affects the attainment of our present wishes but also our future wants and desires, there would be little case for liberty. And, in turn, liberty of the individual would, of course, make complete foresight impossible. Liberty is essential in order to leave room for the unforeseeable and unpredictable; we want it because we have learned to expect from it the opportunity of realizing many of our aims. It is because every individual knows so little and, in particular, because we rarely know which of us knows best that we trust the independent and competitive efforts of many to induce the emergence of what we shall want when we set it" (1960, 29).

Notes

1. From Plato, Apology 21d (Cooper 1997, 21). I am using this quote in the hope of capturing for the reader three possible cognitive states we human beings find ourselves in. There are times when we act when we know that we don't know (rational ignorance); when what we think we know ain't so (stupidity); and when we don't know that we don't know (utter ignorance). Standard search theory reduces our cognitive condition to one of rational ignorance. The work of my colleague Bryan Caplan (2001a, 2001b) tends to focus on how even stupidity can be rational within certain institutional contexts, while the writings of the Austrians tend to focus on utter ignorance of human beings and how the institutions of the market arise to cope with this ignorance, even though the actors themselves could not know these institutions serve this function. In fact, I think one way to put F. A. Hayek's main contribution to our understanding of the price system is that we benefit from its functioning without having to be aware of its functioning. It is my contention that while all three cognitive states exist, recognizing our ignorance is an essential step

in developing a theory of the creative market process that has been the main theoretical task the Austrian economists have taken upon themselves in the post–World War II period.

2. For a documentary history of the socialist calculation debate, see Boettke (2000).

3. On the close intellectual relationship between Mises and Hayek with regard to the argument against socialism, see Boettke (1998). A contrasting point of view is presented by Joseph Salerno (1990, 1993).

4. See Boettke and Leeson (2003) for a discussion of the evolution of modern Austrian economics since 1950 and the resistance Mises and Hayek demonstrated to the idea of a unique Austrian School. As late as the 1960s, Mises and Hayek still both argued in print that the main contributions of the Austrian School had been fully absorbed into the mainstream of economic thinking.

5. Perhaps the most illuminating way to see the common ground, as well as the differences, among Rothbard, Kirzner, and Lachmann is to examine their different contributions to *The Foundations of Modern Austrian Economics* (Dolan 1976). In the decade following this volume, the differences were highlighted, but a large degree of common ground has also tended to be forgotten in the subsequent literature. That common ground consisted of a commitment to methodological individualism, methodological subjectivism, and the notion of the market process as opposed to the equilibrium economics. The implications of these commitments included the rejection of the mathematical method as the primary tool for theory development and the rejection of standard techniques of statistical inference for the testing of theory. Logic and evidence were championed by Rothbard, Kirzner, and Lachmann in their scientific work in economics, but natural language and traditional historical scholarship were employed rather than mathematical modeling and statistical analysis.

6. For a criticism from an Austrian perspective of standard economic treatments of time and information, see O'Driscoll and Rizzo (1985).

7. Kirzner makes an important point with regard to standard search theory: the theory cannot "avoid making the assumption that, before undertaking the search, one already knows enough about the territory to be able to calculate rewards and costs. So that, if we are to view the acquisition of knowledge as deliberately undertaken, one must postulate some prior knowledge not acquired through deliberate search or learning activity" (1979, 142). The paradox of knowledge—what Kirzner calls the Boulding-Shackle paradox—is that in discussing the acquisition of knowledge in a deliberative manner, we must know what it is that we want to know before looking for it. But this notion of knowledge misses completely the idea that there is knowledge that we ought to know, that we do not know. Kirzner, as we will see, argues that it is precisely the entrepreneur's function within a market economy to discover that which was previously unknown.

8. Paul Samuelson used to argue that the two major sources of confusion in economics are (a) calling the same thing different names and (b) calling different things the same name. He, of course, used this argument to advocate the use of mathematics

to eliminate ambiguity. But as Kenneth Boulding pointed out in reviewing Samuelson's *Foundations of Economic Analysis*, "Conventions of generality and mathematical elegance may be just as much barriers to the attainment and diffusion of knowledge as may contentment with particularity and literary vagueness. . . . It may well be that the slovenly and literary borderland between economics and sociology will be the most fruitful building ground during the years to come and that mathematical economics will remain too flawless in its perfection to be very fruitful" (1948, 247). Boulding's prediction has proved prophetic. Nevertheless, I do think Samuelson's point about the two sources of confusion are valid and relevant to the current discussion, even if I think it is precisely the mathematical modeling research strategy that was followed by Leonid Hurwicz, Roy Radner, Joseph Stiglitz, and others that produced many of the problems I am going to highlight with regard to information economics.

9. Hayek sums up the position nicely when he writes: "Even the statement of the problem as one of utilizing knowledge dispersed among hundreds of thousands of individuals still over-simplifies its character. It is not merely a task of utilizing information about particular concrete facts which the individuals already possess, but one of using their abilities of discovering such facts as will be relevant to their purposes in particular situations. This is the reason why all the information accessible to (rather than already possessed by) the individuals can never be put at the disposal of some other agency but can be used only if those who know where the relevant information is to be found are called upon to make the decisions. Every person will discover what he knows or can find out only when faced with a problem where this will help, but can never pass on all the knowledge he commands and still less all the knowledge he knows how to acquire if needed by somebody else" (1973–1979, vol. 3, 190, fn. 7).

10. This claim, of course, was the source of the great debate in Austrian economics between Kirzner and Lachmann that dominated the intellectual agenda between the mid-1970s and mid-1980s (see Vaughn 1994, 112–61).

11. Lavoie also emphasizes the problem of power inherent in planning efforts. As he stated, "Planning does not accidentally deteriorate into the militarization of the economy; it is the militarization of the economy" (1985a, 230).

12. Lavoie (1985a, 65–76) uses an argument by analogy to discuss the generation of social intelligence in an ant colony, the market system, and the scientific community. In each case, the emergent orders described are not merely complex orders, but orders that achieve a level of complexity that extends beyond that attainable to constituent parts. In short, the whole is greater than the sum of its parts; "social intelligence that is greater than the intelligence of any of its individuals" (1985a, 66).

13. Representative publications of Stiglitz and Akerlof include *Whither Socialism?* (1994) and *An Economic Theorist's Book of Tales* (1984), respectively.

14. My colleague Bryan Caplan is fond of pointing out the fallacy implied in Stiglitz's argument. Caplan points out that the assumptions normally thought of as necessary for general competitive equilibrium are really just sufficient conditions. If you

have those ideal conditions, you will have a general competitive equilibrium, but the absence of those conditions does not necessarily imply that general competitive equilibrium will not be achieved (even if that result is more unlikely).

15. For an examination of Akerlof's lemons arguments and a proposed Austrian market process theory response, see Steckbeck and Boettke (2001).

References

Akerlof, George A. 1984. *An Economic Theorist's Book of Tales*. New York: Cambridge University Press.

Boettke, Peter J. 1998. "Economic Calculation: The Austrian Contribution to Political Economy." *Advances in Austrian Economics* 6: 131–58.

———, ed. 2000. *Socialism and the Market: The Socialist Calculation Debate Revisited*. 9 volumes. New York: Routledge.

Boettke, Peter J., and Peter T. Leeson. 2003. "The Austrian School of Economics (1950–2000)." In *Blackwell Companion to the History of Economic Thought*, edited by Warren J. Samuels, Jeff E. Biddle, and John B. Davis, 445–53. Oxford: Blackwell.

Boettke, Peter J., and Karen Vaughn. 2002. "Knight and the Austrians on Capital and the Problems of Socialism." *History of Political Economy* 34 (1): 153–75.

Boulding, Kenneth E. 1948. "Samuelson's Foundations: The Role of Mathematics in Economics." *Journal of Political Economy* 56 (3): 187–99.

Caplan, Bryan. 2001a. "Rational Ignorance vs. Rational Irrationality." *Kyklos* 54 (1): 3–26.

———. 2001b. "Rational Irrationality and the Microfoundations of Political Failure." *Public Choice* 107 (3/4): 311–31.

Cooper, John M., ed. 1997. *Plato: Complete Works*. Indianapolis: Hackett.

Dolan, Edwin G., ed. 1976. *The Foundations of Modern Austrian Economics*. Kansas City: Sheed and Ward.

Hayek, F. A. 1937. "Economics and Knowledge." Reprinted in F. A. Hayek. 1948. *Individualism and Economic Order*. Chicago: University of Chicago Press.

———. 1941. "The Meaning of Competition." Reprinted in F. A. Hayek. 1948. *Individualism and Economic Order*. Chicago: University of Chicago Press.

———. 1945. "The Use of Knowledge in Society. Reprinted in F. A. Hayek. 1948. *Individualism and Economic Order*. Chicago: University of Chicago Press.

———. 1948. *Individualism and Economic Order*. Chicago: University of Chicago Press.

———. 1960. *The Constitution of Liberty*. Chicago: University of Chicago Press.

———. 1973–1979. *Law, Legislation and Liberty*. 3 volumes. Chicago: University of Chicago Press.

Kirzner, Israel M. 1973. *Competition and Entrepreneurship*. Chicago: University of Chicago Press.

———. 1979. *Perception, Opportunity, and Profit*. Chicago: University of Chicago Press.

Lachmann, Ludwig M. 1977. *Capital, Expectations, and the Market Process*. Kansas City: Sheed, Andrews and McMeel.

Lavoie, Don. 1985a. *National Economic Planning: What Is Left?* Washington, DC: Cato Institute.

———. 1985b. *Rivalry and Central Planning: The Socialist Calculation Debate Reconsidered*. New York: Cambridge University Press.

Littlechild, Stephen. 1977. "Change Rules, OK?" Inaugural lecture delivered at the University of Birmingham, May 28, 1977.

Machlup, Fritz. 1962. *The Production and Distribution of Knowledge in the United States*. Princeton, NJ: Princeton University Press.

Mises, Ludwig von. [1922] 1981. *Socialism: An Economic and Sociological Analysis*. Indianapolis: Liberty Fund.

———. [1949] 1966. *Human Action: A Treatise on Economics*. 3rd ed. Chicago: Henry Regnery.

O'Driscoll, Gerald P., and Mario J. Rizzo. 1985. *The Economics of Time and Ignorance*. Oxford: Blackwell.

Robbins, Lionel. 1932. *The Nature and Significance of Economic Science*. London: Macmillan.

Rothbard, Murray N. 1962. *Man, Economy and State*. 2 volumes. Princeton, NJ: Van Nostrand.

Salerno, Joseph T. 1990. "Ludwig von Mises as a Social Rationalist." *Review of Austrian Economics* 4: 26–54.

———. 1993. "Mises and Hayek Dehomogenized." *Review of Austrian Economics* 6 (2): 113–46.

Shackle, G. L. S. 1972. *Epistemics and Economics*. New York: Cambridge University Press.

Steckbeck, Mark, and Peter J. Boettke. 2001. "Akerlof Problems, Hayekian Solutions." Unpublished manuscript.

Stiglitz, Joseph E. 1994. *Whither Socialism?* Cambridge, MA: MIT Press.

Vaughn, Karen I. 1994. *Austrian Economics in America*. New York: Cambridge University Press.

Chapter 10
What Should Classical Liberal Political Economists Do?

Prelude

It is a great honor for me to be part of this celebration of the ideas of James M. Buchanan. I had the great fortune to study with Buchanan in 1984, precisely at a time when he had been strongly rumored to be the favorite to win the Nobel Prize. Though he did not have that honor bestowed upon him then, he eventually did win the prize in 1986. In many ways, I was in the last group of students that studied with him prior to the increasing demands of his post-Nobel commitments.

I was fortunate for another significant reason. Buchanan's mantra at the time was "Dare to be different." The Center for Study of Public Choice had just moved from Virginia Tech to George Mason University, and he insisted that we should not strive for conventionality in our approach to economics and political economy. "Who wants to be," he would say, "a pale version of MIT on the Potomac?" Buchanan conveyed to us the importance of doing "economics with attitude." Yet he insisted that we never isolate ourselves, but be professionally engaged; and that, while not being conventional, never adopt intellectual strategies that would result justly in professional isolation. In short, he instilled in students the desire to be bold and creative, but also to be taken seriously as a scholar within the disciplines of philosophy, politics, law, and economics.

Buchanan was the type of scholar and teacher who asked questions and challenged conventional wisdom. He also insisted that in order to ask bold questions and challenge standard results, one needed to master the elementary principles

Paper presented at the George Mason University conference "James M. Buchanan: A Celebration of Scholarship," September 28–29, 2013. Published in *Constitutional Political Economy* 25, no. 1 (2014): 110–24.

of the discipline of economics, most notably the persistent and consistent application of opportunity-cost reasoning, and the principle of spontaneous order of the market economy. Students were expected to think and rethink the elementary principles of economics. Borrowing from Herbert Spencer, Buchanan stressed to his students that "it takes varied iterations to force alien concepts upon reluctant minds." His message was, learn the elementary principles of economics and the technical implications for applied areas of analysis in public economics and comparative institutional analysis, and then strike out in a bold and creative fashion in theoretical exploration and applied political economy.

As a scholar and a teacher, it was obvious that Buchanan had a deep commitment to a particular perspective in political economy—methodologically, analytically, and even one might say ideologically. Yet his approach was not that of a "normative political economist," but rather that of positive political economy. This can be seen in his treatment of the status quo and his deployment of the compensation principle. The status quo is not accorded any normative standing in his analysis beyond the simple point that it defines the start state of all analysis of social change. And the compensation principle—in other words, voluntary agreement—is the only criterion for social change. The positive political economist's proposals for reform are "restricted to those social changes that may be legitimately classified as 'changes in law,' that is, changes in the structural rules under which individuals make choices" (Buchanan 1959, 200).

Buchanan was the champion of the methodological individualist perspective across the social sciences and even the humanities, given his individualistic and contractarian perspective in political philosophy. Throughout his career, Buchanan was a dogged scholar, but he was never dogmatic as that would be the ultimate sign of intellectual laziness. Question everything and everyone; nothing is sacred, Buchanan would insist. But he also encouraged us to explore the questions associated with a society of free and responsible individuals and to ponder what rules will enable us to live better together while simultaneously respecting individual autonomy and generating economic prosperity.

Finally, as a scholar and a teacher Buchanan's greatest gift to his students was his ability to convince them that his academic success was purely a function of work ethic.

Kenneth Boulding and Gordon Tullock were two other superstar professors that I studied with at this time, and in both instances replicating their path seemed impossible. Their work, it seemed, was all inspiration, whereas

Buchanan's was perspiration. Of course, both impressions were wrong—Boulding and Tullock worked tirelessly at their scholarly craft, and Buchanan was a genius of rare analytical abilities. But his emphasis on work ethic and professionalism was an extremely important gift he gave to those who studied with him. For those slightly out of sync (or in actual fact radically out of sync) with the prevailing wisdom in the economics profession, Buchanan insisted that a successful career and lasting impact was within your grasp if only you were willing to think long and hard enough, and to work on your craft as a writer of scholarly papers. Buchanan often asked us, as a way to stress his point about having a lasting impact, would you rather be an intellectual celebrity in your lifetime (think John Kenneth Galbraith) or write works that could potentially be read 100 or 200 years from now (think Adam Smith)? In the way Buchanan communicated this tradeoff, and the values he instilled in his students, the preferred choice was obvious: the goal was to strive to produce works that could potentially be read 100 or 200 years from now, even if that meant you would not receive the benefits of academic celebrity in your own lifetime.

James Buchanan was a genius as an economist and political economist, but he was also an inspiring teacher. He was my professor, and I consider myself very fortunate to have been touched by greatness. It is indeed a great honor to celebrate his life and scholarship on this occasion.

Introduction

James M. Buchanan (1919–2012) pursued an approach to economics and political economy that stressed the following:

- Economics is about exchange and the institutions within which exchanges take place.
- The political economist should not act as if he or she were providing advice to a benevolent despot.
- The positive political economist can combine the reformist zeal that often attracts individuals to the discipline with the scientific demands of positive economic analysis by shifting intellectual attention to the "rules of the game."
- The most important function that economics plays as a public science is its didactic role in teaching the elementary principles of economics and cultivating an appreciation of the spontaneous

order of a market economy so that citizens can become informed participants in democratic decision-making.

- The contemporary classical liberal political economist, building on this position, must capture the imagination of scholars, intellectuals, and the public concerning (a) justice of the liberal order, (b) freedom and responsibility of the individual within the liberal order, and (c) the vision of a self-ordering market economy within the right institutional framework.

These focal points in Buchanan's work are interconnected, and are not disparate interests of his.

The point of this chapter will be to show the interconnections by way of examining arguments in three papers that spanned three decades, though I will not address them in chronological order. The three papers are "What Should Economists Do?" (1964); "Positive Economics, Welfare Economics, and Political Economy" (1959); and "Politics without Romance" (1979). I will try to highlight the unifying theme in these papers that produces a Buchanan-inspired political economy. From the perspective of this analytical framework, I will then discuss the challenges that Buchanan saw for contemporary classical liberals and the opportunities for meeting those challenges that the collapse of communism and the financial crisis of 2008 represent. I conclude by stressing the continuity as well as the evolution of Buchanan's work in political economy throughout the eight decades of research output that represent the body of his work.

The Task of the Political Economist

After World War II, economics was transformed from a tool of social criticism and philosophical understanding to a tool of social control and applied policy engineering. Buchanan was among a handful of economists who resisted this transformation. His revered teacher Frank Knight actually argued that the idea of the economist as a trained policy expert who could engage in social control was an affront to democratic values (see Knight 1960).

One of Buchanan's biggest concerns from the beginning of his career was that this transformation of the discipline would entail the cost of losing the common knowledge of the political economists from decades earlier. This included not only elementary propositions, such as opportunity-cost reasoning and the mutually beneficial aspects of trade, but more social philosophical issues with respect to the appropriate institutional framework for a society of free and responsible individuals. As reflected in the citation trail of Buchanan from his earliest professional writings, the common knowledge of the political economists included specific arguments about methodological individualism, and market theory and the price system. There is, as Milton Friedman once insisted, only good economics and bad economics. But what constituted Buchanan's notion of good economics was not only the self-interest postulate and the "invisible hand" theorem, but the institutional analysis through which the derivation of the invisible hand theorem emerges from the basic behavioral postulate of self-interest. Private property, free pricing, and profit and loss accounting all work to signal and direct economic actors to realize the mutual gains from trade. These insights, Buchanan recognized, were found in the 18th-century Scottish moral philosophers David Hume and Adam Smith; the British classical economists David Ricardo and John Stuart Mill; the Austrian School economists Ludwig von Mises, Joseph Schumpeter, F. A. Hayek, and Israel Kirzner; and the Chicago School tradition of Frank Knight and Henry Simons. The methodological, analytical, and social philosophic contributions of these different strands of economic thought were all part of the common knowledge of the economist and political economist in the 1940s, only to be under threat of oblivion by the late 1950s with the rise of an institutionally antiseptic and pure formal theory of market failure and a social engineering perspective on public economics.

Buchanan's resistance took on a new significance as a result. In "What Should Economists Do?" (1964), he argued that the analytical focus on the efficient allocation of resources had resulted in economists turning a blind eye to the very process by which that efficient allocation could reasonably be obtained and the specific institutional environment required for the process to emerge in that direction. It is too intellectually easy to slide from the analytical point about individuals realizing the mutually beneficial gains from trade, and the constant agitation in the market until all those gains from trade are exhausted, to the idea that one can engineer the optimal solution through correct policy designs. This is not only a problem confronted by models of socialist planning, it is also an endemic feature in public economic models concerning tax and subsidies to counter market failures, and the regulation of economic affairs. Allocative efficiency is a by-product of an economic process within a specific institutional setting, not a defining goal of the system.

If the economic problem is conceived exclusively as one of allocation, Buchanan warned, then economic study becomes little more than an exercise in "applied maximization of a relatively simple computational sort" (216). If this is all there is to economics, the discipline would best be left to applied mathematicians. The advances Buchanan witnessed in economics during the 1940s and 1950s were in fact primarily improvements in "computing techniques, in the mathematics of social engineering" (216). In writing "What Should Economists Do?" Buchanan was trying to insist that these contributions be put in the proper perspective. These developments can be recognized as improvements in the applied mathematics of managerial science, but they are not, and should not be seen as, contributions to economics properly understood.

"Economists 'should' concentrate their attention on a particular form of human activity," Buchanan argued, "and upon the various institutional arrangements that arise as a result of this form of activity" (213–14). Furthermore, "the elementary and basic approach" he advocated would place "the 'theory of markets' not the 'theory of resource allocation' at center stage" (214). The most serious problem with the post–World War II textbook economics that emerged was not that it was unrealistic, as Buchanan is quick to admit all models are abstractions from reality. The scientific question is matching the level of abstraction with the research purpose such that we get models of appropriate abstraction. The textbook consensus by 1960, however, had resulted in a flawed model of the world because of "its conversion of individual choice behavior from a social-institutional context to a physical-computational one" (218). As a result, Buchanan argued, "nonsensical social science" emerged and the older institutionalist critics of economics proved to be "broadly on target in some of their attacks" (218).

It was indeed time for a fundamental reconsideration of the economist's project. "A market is not competitive," Buchanan argued, "by assumption or by construction. A market *becomes* competitive, and competitive rules *come to be* established as institutions emerge to place limits on individual behavior patterns. It is this *becoming* process, brought about by the continuous pressure of human behavior in exchange, that is the central part of our discipline, if we have one, not the dry-rot of postulated perfection" (218, emphasis in original). Neither maximizing behavior nor general competitive equilibrium is to Buchanan the defining characteristic of market analysis, but instead the "continual evolution of the exchange process" that emerges from the Smithian propensity to truck, barter, and exchange.

Looking at the economic process through this window, Buchanan argued, results in the recognition that "the market" does not have an overarching end. The market is not a means to the accomplishment of anything in particular. In this sense, it has no teleology at all; it just is an ongoing process of exchange and production. The market is "the institutional embodiment of the voluntary exchange processes that are entered into by individuals in their several capacities. That is all there is to it. Individuals are observed to cooperate with one another, to reach agreements, to trade. The network of relationships that emerges or evolves out of this trading process, the institutional framework, is called 'the market'" (219).

Economists should be "market economists" without any normative implication. "Learning more about how markets work means learning more about how markets work" (222). But such a straightforward message is not always easy to understand. Economics is about exchange *and* the institutions within which exchange takes place.

Individuals attracted to economics, however, are often so because they not only want to understand the world but would like to change it for the better. The scientific demand for positive analysis is apparently at odds with the normative impulse that attracts individuals to advanced study in the discipline of economics and political economy. Again, the post–World War II consensus was misleading in that the social engineering embedded in economics as a tool of social control presented a formal theory of public economics such that normative theorizing masqueraded as positive analysis.

A close reading of Buchanan's "The Pure Theory of Government Finance" (1949) will reveal that he had already identified the critical problem from the very beginning of his career. The state is not a single coherent entity, and that entity is not omniscient, omnipotent, and benevolent. This is the origin of Buchanan's rendering of the Wicksellian wisdom that economists in the field of public economics cannot act as if they are offering advice to a benevolent despot. Buchanan's paradigmatic exercise is to ask how one does public economics when you do not have recourse to reference a benevolent and omniscient unified state entity, and furthermore, as he developed in the wake of his critique of Arrow's theorem, no coherent social welfare function can be maximized.

Economics as social engineering is illegitimate, yet economics attracts reformers. Untrained reformers are mere ideologues—whether right or left doesn't matter, ideologues exhibit the sin of intellectual laziness. On the one hand, Buchanan denies the economist-as-dentist metaphor, and instead argues that the belief in that model of the economist results in a dull profession of ideological eunuchs. On the other hand, Buchanan deplores the demagoguery of the ideological warrior. So how precisely can the political economist satisfy the reformist zeal that attracts interest, and avoid the pitfalls of social engineering on the one hand, and demagoguery on the other, while maintaining a commitment to positive science?

In "Positive Economics, Welfare Economics, and Political Economy" (1959), Buchanan presents his solution to this conundrum. In essence, positive political economy is comparative institutional analysis. The positive role that the economist can play in policy formation is one of "diagnosing social situations and presenting to the choosing individuals a set of possible changes" (127). The scope for those changes must be limited to "those social changes that may legitimately be classified as 'changes in law,' that is changes in the structural rules under which individuals make choices" (131).

In the starkest way possible, it is important to remember that while Adam Smith identified the human propensity to truck, barter, and exchange, Thomas Hobbes and others had also identified the human propensity to pillage and plunder unless constrained. Whether men are Smithian or Hobbesian in their behavioral propensities is a function of the rules of the game under which they operate. If the costs of raping, pillaging, and plundering are less than the benefits, then the "society" under examination will indeed resemble the Hobbesian jungle. If the costs of predation are raised, and the benefits of cooperation are greater, then Smithian wealth creation through realizing the mutual gains from trade will be the foundation of the social order.

The political economist contributes to science and reform by analyzing alternative institutional arrangements, and offering changes in the rules of the game as hypotheses to be tested in the arena of collective action. In devising such changes in the rules of the game, Buchanan stresses two critical building blocks. The first building block concerns the position of the status quo. The positive political economy of reform must begin with the "here and now," and never some imaginary start state where opposition to change is nonexistent. In doing this, Buchanan is not attributing any normative weight to the status quo. All he is doing is insisting that "it is what it is," and that must be the starting point of any assessment of relevant alternatives.

The second building block follows from the recognition that we begin with the "here and now," and that is the compensation principle. Any shift in the rules of the game will change the nature of the payoffs in the game. Those who currently gain from the status quo will lose, while others currently not in a position of privilege with respect to existing institutions will gain from the change. The winners must compensate the losers in the proposed change, not because the losers have any normative claim to their existing benefits but because unless compensated the beneficiaries of the status quo will fight to defeat any proposed changes in the structure of rules.

In "Politics without Romance" (1979), Buchanan argues, "It seems to be nothing more than simple and obvious wisdom to compare social institutions as they might exist rather than compare romantic models of how such institutions might be hoped to operate" (47). Rule changes must be filtered by an analysis of knavery, both the arrogant and opportunistic varieties. A robust theory of political economy thus challenges both the assumption of omniscience and benevolence.

"By any comparison with politics," Buchanan argued, "economic theory is *simple*" (50). Political exchange is far more complex than economic exchange within a system of well-defined and enforced property rights. There are two reasons for this. First, the set of political exchanges that produce agreement on the "rules of the game" must precede economic exchange. Orderly trade takes place within an established legal structure. Second, within the established legal structure, political exchanges produce external benefits and costs to a far greater extent than the simple rendering of two trading partners realizing the mutual gains from trade in the economy.

Two levels of political exchange must be studied. The formation of the rules of the game is the constitutional level of analysis, and the strategic play of the political game within the established rules of the game constitutes the ordinary analysis of politics. In Buchanan's rendering of constitutional political economy, the two levels of analysis must be engaged as you cannot answer the relevant questions unless the social philosophical analysis of "good" rules is informed by the "predictive analysis of how different political institutions will operate." The science of economics in this manner interacts with social philosophy to produce political economy.

A Stocktaking before Proceeding

In examining briefly these three pivotal papers, an idea of what a Buchanan-inspired political economy looks like emerges and with it, what such political economists should do in their work. Economics is about exchange, and the institutions within which those exchanges take place. Political economists must recognize the two levels of analysis. And with the aid of the positive science of economics, they can propose changes to the structural rules of the game. Neither the economist nor the political economist has a privileged position in the democratic process of collective decision-making, but the knowledge provided by the economist and the political economist is an essential input to understanding both, the political-legal-economic nexus and the efforts to reform that system through proposed changes in the rules.

A Buchanan-inspired political economy exhibits the following characteristics:

- Analytically egalitarian agents are present.
- The behavior of the actors in the different realms is symmetrical.
- Actors within political, legal, and market contexts are denied the assumptions of omniscience and omnipotence.
- The public purpose of the economist and political economist is to teach "students" about the principles of spontaneous order in the market economy, and the institutional arrangements that either are conducive to peaceful cooperation and productive specialization or thwart the efforts to realize social cooperation under the division of labor.

To reflect on this a bit more, consider that Alexander Hamilton asked his readers in Federalist No. 1 whether the constitution of the new nation would be the product of accident and force, or choice and reflection. Buchanan's answer 200 years later was that we should be unwilling to live by rules that are thrust upon us by accident and force. Instead, the political economist must opt for rules that come from choice and reflection, and that enable individuals to live better together. This is, in part, why Buchanan could declare—*Why I, Too, Am Not a Conservative* (2005).

Post-Socialist Political Economy

The formative years of Buchanan's political economy were the decades following World War II, and it was in opposition to a formalistic version of economics that desensitized a generation of economists to comparative institutional analysis. The last decades of his career, however, saw a general recognition of the role of institutions in determining economic performance, particularly the role of private property rights and freedom to contract and trade. Buchanan's post-Nobel era coincided with the challenges of the post-socialist political economy. Institutional problems do indeed demand institutional solutions. But how do you get the process of institutional transformation underway in a world where the problem was precisely the institutional framework in the first place?

The political economy reality of the 1990s and 2000s was a situation where for most of the pressing questions the world under examination was one defined by a dysfunctional institutional framework, and a population pool with great social divisions along ethnic and religious lines. In such an environment, how is it that the political economist can suggest a set of rules that diverse groups can live by and in cooperation with one another? How can they turn their differences into advantages that can be successfully exploited? How can they turn their potential conflicts into opportunities for social cooperation?

No doubt the growth of the social democratic welfare state in Western democracies in the post–World War II era represented a major intellectual challenge to classical liberal political economists. F. A. Hayek, Milton Friedman, and James Buchanan all rose to meet that challenge head-on in their respective ways in the 1940–1980s period. However, the problems of post-socialism were different, and the problems that post-socialism presented to the Western democracies themselves were also different. Consider the following passage from Buchanan and Tullock's *The Calculus of Consent*:

> The evolution of democratic constitutions from the discussion of rational individuals can take place only under certain relatively narrowly defined conditions. The individual participants must approach the constitution-making process as "equals" in a special sense of this term. The requisite "equality" can be insured only if the existing differences in external characteristics among individuals are accepted without rancor and if there are no clearly predictable bases among these differences for the formation of permanent coalitions. On the basis of purely economic motivation, individual members of a dominant and superior group (who consider themselves to be such and who were in the possession of power) would never rationally choose to adopt constitutional rules giving less fortunately situated individuals a position of equal partnership in governmental processes. On noneconomic grounds the dominant classes might choose to do this, but, as experience has so often demonstrated in recent years, the less fortunately situated classes will rarely interpret such action as being advanced

in their favor. Therefore, our analysis of the constitution-making process had little relevance for a society that is characterized by a sharp cleavage of the population into distinguishable social classes or separate racial, religious, or ethnic groupings sufficient to encourage the formation of predictable political coalitions and in which one of these coalitions has a clearly advantageous position at the constitutional stage. ([1962] 1999, 80)

Such cleavages are what emerge in the dysfunctional political economy of failed and weak states (see Rajan 2004). The inability to find rules that enable diverse groups to live in harmony with one another plagues not only the failed and weak states of Africa, Latin America, and the Middle East, but also transitioning economies in Eastern and Central Europe and the former Soviet Union. With the new wave of globalization in the last decade of the 20th century, the tensions among groups in one country often spill over to tensions in other countries through the migration of conflict and disharmony.

Buchanan and Tullock were quick to say that one should not be so quick to dismiss their analysis of constitution making in the face of diversity and conflict. "So long as some mobility among groups is guaranteed, coalitions will tend to be impermanent" (80). They insist that their analysis of the calculus of consent will only break down in a situation where a constitutional democratic order is, strictly speaking, impossible.

I tend to agree with them that we should not overstate the intractability of rule establishment in even extremely unlikely circumstances. The sort of constitution making from the ground up that one finds in the work of Elinor Ostrom is, of course, such an example. Faced with the social dilemma of common pool resources, Ostrom (1990) examined the great diversity of institutional forms that a variety of groups have stumbled upon in their effort to govern the commons. She identified across cultures and across time various long and enduring practices that were, at the local level, successful at avoiding the predicted outcome of the tragedy of the commons. How? Well, it is important to remember the distinction between form and function in rules—or to use her language, rules in form versus rules in use in the institutional analysis of development.

To boil down the argument, faced with a commons problem, economists typically suggest that assignment of private property rights will solve the dilemma. But how? Property rights internalize the costs and benefits of decisions on resource use, and they do so by assigning responsibility, limiting the access of others to the use of your property, and establishing penalties when others violate your property rights. The fascinating aspect of Ostrom's work is the diverse institutional arrangements adopted by groups of individuals in their effort to govern the commons that are functionally equivalent to private property rights in limiting access, assigning responsibility, and introducing penalties, but do not take the particular form of private property rights.

The reason I bring up Ostrom's work in relation to Buchanan and post-socialist political economy is that her work forces us to consider the move away from an exogenous rule formation process as Buchanan argued in classic papers such as "Ethical Rules, Expected Values, and Large Numbers" (1965). If the rules of the game are to be analyzed as parametric, then the sort of intractability in the face of cleavage is a serious problem for the relevance of *The Calculus of Consent* to the problems political economists have been grappling with since 1989, and especially since 2001. This is not the intellectual fate of Buchanan's political economy if, instead, we can agree that what we have learned is simply the primacy of the framework in political economy analysis and, that we should take Buchanan's own plea seriously: "The economist should not be content with postulating models and then working within such models. His task includes the derivation of the institutional order itself from the set of elementary behavioral hypotheses with which he commences" ([1968] 1999, 5).

Institutional problems demand institutional solutions, and those institutional solutions are found in a blend of constructivism and spontaneous order; they do not condemn us to either pure accident and force or choice and reflection. Although Buchanan certainly had reservations about an evolutionary approach of rule formation, his contractarianism cannot be written off as entirely inconsistent with it. Consider this quote by Hayek in volume 1 of *Law, Legislation and Liberty*:

> At the moment our concern must be made clear that while the rules on which a spontaneous order rests, may also be of spontaneous origin, this need not always be the case. Although undoubtedly an order originally formed itself spontaneously because the individuals followed rules which had not been deliberately made but had arisen spontaneously, people gradually learned to improve those rules; and it is at least conceivable that the formation of a spontaneous order relies entirely on rules that were deliberately made. (1973, 45)

The point that Hayek makes about individuals learning to improve rules is where he intersects with Buchanan. If positive economics as a nonnormative science teaches us to put constraints on our utopias, then it also puts constraints on our choices of the rules during the "constitutional moment." In this sense, Buchanan's and Hayek's insights are not mutually exclusive, but inform us how rules are adopted by individuals. Although the Constitutional Convention was based on the "choice and reflection" of the Founders, the constraints on the utopia they wished to establish had evolved in England centuries before based on a common-law tradition. Their "choice and reflection" was not an act of pure rational constructivism, but a conscious, yet *learned adoption* of previously evolved rules upon which they wished to improve. Indeed, the conscious adoption of rules by "choice and reflection" is not the creation of rules ex nihilo, but the recognition and awareness of which rules have served us best overtime, including those rules that may have originally been thrust upon us by "accident and force." As Buchanan stated, "political economy has a non-normative role in discovering 'what is the structure of individual values'" (1959, 207).

It is through the individuals' rational experimentation within groups struggling to cope with social dilemmas, and the testing of rules that may turn situations of dire conflict into opportunities for peaceful social cooperation and productive specialization among free individuals that we find the evolving constitutional order. This sort of examination of the endogenous formation of the framework of rules—even in the "hard cases" (see Leeson 2010)—has, in my opinion, the potential to capture the imagination of a new generation of political economists. It has historical roots in the evolved "constitutional" structure of England, and thus blends with elements of a constitutional construction among the Founders in the United States. The positive political economy of endogenous rule formation is directly applicable to the study of reform efforts in failed and weak states. As Rajan (2004) argued, the orthodox model that assumes a working institutional framework that protects property rights and ensures freedom of contract is simply not helpful for the study of much of the political economy of the world.

A conventional reading of Buchanan might suggest that the sort of analysis that he provides of the constitutional contract in say *The Limits of Liberty* ([1975] 2000) conflicts with the sort of endogenous rule formation that we have been talking about. But that tension, I want to suggest, is only apparent. First, the reader should keep in mind Buchanan's promise that a genuine institutional economics would follow from the economist studying the derivation of the institutional framework itself from the ordinary behavioral postulates they work with. Second, there are at least two social dilemmas that Buchanan's project in constitutional political economy identifies. The first is the problem of private predation that he attempts to capture in his depiction of the Hobbesian jungle. But once the monopoly apparatus of coercion is established, that is, the state, then the analysis must turn to curbing the possibility of public predation. This leads to the enduring puzzle of political economy that Buchanan identified so clearly: how can we empower the protective and productive state without unleashing the redistributive state?

The classical liberal political economist should be prepared, as Buchanan was, to grapple with the tough issues of distributive justice that justify the demands for the expansion of the redistributive state. Here again, technical economics on factor pricing and wage determination must align with the more dynamic and process-oriented theory of the market economy, and become the background information of the social philosophical discussion of the justice of the liberal order. The Buchanan vision of political economy is one where the structure of the rules permit neither discrimination nor dominion in the body politic. While not a romantic conception of political economy, it is an inspiring normative aspiration, and one that follows naturally from the consistent and persistent application of the "rule of law" to issues of political arrangements and public policy.

Slapped by the Invisible Hand? The Financial Crisis of 2008

In a somewhat shocking manner, the financial crisis of 2008 had a profound effect on Buchanan. He believed that the crisis demonstrated the intellectual excess of undisciplined libertarianism, and the intellectual bankruptcy of the "New" Chicago School of economics as opposed to the "Old" Chicago School of economics in which he was educated. His reasoning was straightforward: how markets function is a consequence of the rules of the game under which they operate. It is always important to stress that a "free market" is not a market free of rules. If the rules are rigged so that you can privatize profit but socialize risk, then don't be surprised when individuals engage in riskier behavior. Absent the institutional environment, markets are not capable of operating in the same manner as in the presence of private property rights institutions.

The "New" Chicago School, Buchanan argues, had proceeded in their analysis of financial markets and the macroeconomy as a whole as if institutions didn't matter and the invisible hand of the market economy could be relied on to guide markets on the right path independent of the framework of rules governing the economic game. Of course, the idea that economists assume that self-interest alone could result in social order is not new to the modern Chicago School economists. But this actually isn't the position that Adam Smith held. Smith's professors in Glasgow and in Oxford both pursued their self-interest, but the systemic incentives produced under the different payment schemes of the respective schools affected the behavior of the professors. The same is true of the behavior of religious leaders in a state-sponsored church versus religious leaders in a church that must compete each Sunday to put in the seats individual souls in need of saving, and put dollars in the collection plate to pay for the spending.

Basic economic reasoning from the time of Adam Smith through James Buchanan stressed that the self-interest hypothesis must be squared with the invisible hand postulate not through a set of additional behavioral postulates, but through a thoroughgoing institutional analysis. It is true that the butcher, the baker, and the brewer provide our dinner not due to feelings of solidarity and benevolence, but as result of their pursuit of self-interest. The point, however, is that their self-interest guides them to coordinate the division of labor so we can enjoy our dinner precisely because they operate within a system of property, prices, and profit and loss. Absent the three Ps of property, prices, and profit and loss, individuals will be devoid of the incentives and information required to continually innovate and coordinate their plans to realize the gains from trade and the gains from innovation.

The collapse of communism in the late 1980s, and the collapse of the house of cards that constituted modern finance in the 2000s, have both demonstrated the necessity of the institutional framework in any political economy analysis of our world. Markets operate in a "socially efficient" manner if and only to the extent they are embedded in a set of rules that guides them in that direction. Absent a framework of rules concerning property, contract, and consent, the market system is likely to be dysfunctional. The financial crisis of 2008 demonstrates not that the invisible hand can slap, but that even the most robust and capable hand cannot function if the skeletal structure is broken or absent.

Conclusion

In describing the formation of the Thomas Jefferson Center for Studies in Political Economy, James Buchanan stated that the scholars associated with the center

> strive to carry on the honorable tradition of "political economy"—the study of what makes for a "good society." Political economists stress the technical economic principles that one must understand in order to assess alternative arrangements for promoting peaceful cooperation and productive specialization among free men. Yet political economists go further and frankly try to bring out into the open the philosophical issues that necessarily underlie all discussions of the appropriate functions of government and all proposed economic policy measures. (Buchanan 1958)

That basic message as to what the classical liberal political economist should do remains the same. It falls on each generation of political economists to embrace the challenges of their day, while at the same time stressing the enduring principles of the discipline that can be traced back to Adam Smith and the great scientific conversation that he initiated. Political economists study exchange and the institutions within which exchange takes place, and examine how alternative institutional arrangements either promote or hinder the realization of social cooperation under the division of labor.

Buchanan often described himself as a pessimist when he looked to the future, but an optimist when he looked back in time because the situation hadn't turned out to be as bad as he thought it would. It is my sincere hope that in embracing a Buchanan-inspired political economy, and facing the challenges of our time, as we go forward with our research and teaching, the vision of a classical liberal order of a society of free and responsible individuals will inspire the intellectually curious and imbue in them greater social understanding, and ultimately be a cause for optimistic social change.

References

Buchanan, James M. 1949. "The Pure Theory of Government Finance: A Suggested Approach." *Journal of Political Economy* 57 (6): 496–505.

———. 1958. "The Thomas Jefferson Center for Studies in Political Economy." *The University of Virginia News Letter* 32 (2): 5–9.

————. 1959. "Positive Economics, Welfare Economics, and Political Economy." *Journal of Law and Economics* 2 (October): 124–38.

————. 1964. "What Should Economists Do?" *Southern Economic Journal* 30 (3): 213–22.

————. 1965. "Ethical Rules, Expected Values, and Large Numbers." *Ethics* 76 (1): 1–13.

————. [1968] 1999. *The Collected Works of James M. Buchanan.* Volume 5: *The Demand and Supply of Public Goods.* Indianapolis: Liberty Fund.

————. [1975] 2000. *The Collected Works of James M. Buchanan.* Volume 7: *The Limits of Liberty: Between Anarchy and Leviathan.* Indianapolis: Liberty Fund.

————. 1979. "Politics without Romance: A Sketch of Positive Public Choice Theory and Its Normative Implications." *IHS: Journal, Zeitschrift des Instituts für Höhere Studien* (Vienna) 3: B1–B11.

————. 2005. *Why I, Too, Am Not a Conservative: The Normative Vision of Classical Liberalism.* Cheltenham, UK: Edward Elgar.

Buchanan, James M., and Gordon Tullock. [1962] 1999. *The Collected Works of James M. Buchanan.* Volume 3: *The Calculus of Consent: Logical Foundations of Constitutional Democracy.* Indianapolis: Liberty Fund.

Hayek, F. A. 1973. *Law, Legislation and Liberty.* Volume 1: *Rules and Order.* Chicago: University of Chicago Press.

Knight, Frank H. 1960. *Intelligence and Democratic Action.* Cambridge, MA: Harvard University Press.

Leeson, Peter T. 2010. "Anarchy Unbound: How Much Order Can Spontaneous Order Create?" In *The Handbook of Contemporary Austrian Economics,* edited by Peter J. Boettke, 136–53. Cheltenham, UK: Edward Elgar.

Ostrom, Elinor. 1990. *Governing the Commons: The Evolution of Institutions for Collective Action.* New York: Cambridge University Press.

Rajan, Raghuram. 2004. "Assume Anarchy?" *Finance and Development* 41 (3): 56–57.

Chapter 11

Context, Continuity, and Truth: Theory, History, and Political Economy

I
t is a great honor for me to give the Liggio Lecture at Atlas Network's Liberty Forum. Leonard Liggio truly was the Ambassador of Liberty throughout his amazing career. He was also a great friend and mentor to many of us. My first interactions with Leonard were through the Institute for Humane Studies in the early 1980s, and as a teacher, and as a mentor. My last interactions with Leonard were through our work together with the Fund for the Study of Spontaneous Orders in the 2000s and 2010s. In between, Leonard became a constant source of encouragement in my career, of ideas of interest to pursue, of connections to develop within the network of scholars as a graduate student, and then as a faculty member. At my first job, Leonard arranged for the Liberty Fund catalogue of books to be donated to my university library.

Leonard pushed me to submit my work to be considered for awards, such as the Hayek Prize from the Mont Pelerin Society, and he also championed my membership with MPS early in my career—and now I am president of that organization. Leonard arranged to get me invited to Liberty Fund conferences, and even to be hired by Liberty Fund to consult on a project to reinvigorate the economic wing of its conference and publishing program. Leonard also encouraged me to attend the History of Economics Society meetings, as well as those of the American Economic Association, the Association of Private Enterprise Education, the Public Choice Society, and the Southern Economic Association. Leonard argued that professional engagement for scholarship and network building was important to one's career. He celebrated my faculty appointments at New York University and

Fifth annual Liggio Lecture presented at the Atlas Network's Liberty Forum and Freedom Dinner, New York, 2017.

then at George Mason University, and he convinced me to apply to be part of the Templeton Freedom Project.

As you can tell, Leonard's support, encouragement, and intellectual example were indispensable in my own development as an academic economist. Leonard always exhibited deep, not surface level, learning across disciplines, but especially history and intellectual history—so *scholarship*. Leonard always exhibited respect for others, not strategic manipulation, and mutual respect in the community of learners—so *left* and *right*. And finally, Leonard, while always curious and always respectful, was also firmly planted in the sciences of human action—so *Mises* and *praxeology*. And by praxeology, Leonard meant not a restrictive methodological/epistemological stance, but instead the application of the methods associated with the economic way of thinking beyond the study of the market process to all walks of human actions and interaction.

Leonard tells us in his biographical notes that when he first came to study with Mises after reading *Human Action* upon its publication in 1949, the Mises seminar was devoted at that time to his presentation of the materials that would become *Theory and History* (1957). This is important because Leonard was studying history and engaged in the literature in European political, legal, and economic history, as well as intellectual history of classical liberalism, in particular the French liberal tradition of Jean-Baptiste Say and Frédéric Bastiat. In short, it is always important to remember that as a scholar, Leonard was both a historian and a historian of ideas, and he weaved between these seamlessly to address liberty and power from the Middle Ages to the 20th century.[1]

So on this occasion, I believe it is appropriate to take a moment to acknowledge Leonard Liggio's life of scholarship, teaching, mentorship, and institutional entrepreneurship. Leonard identified, encouraged, connected, and created opportunities for many of us in this room, and without his presence in our lives we may very well not be here right now. We all owe him so much.

And for my talk, I hope to suggest one way we can repay that intellectual debt. The most obvious is to be a good steward to the intellectual tradition of classical liberalism. The great Frédéric Bastiat once wrote that we should never fear an artful critique of our position, but always fear an inept defense. It is our responsibility to be the best scholars and teachers of classical liberal political economy that we can be—to think clearly, speak clearly, and write clearly, and to tackle tough questions and take on, in the most rigorous and sophisticated way possible, the popular fallacies of our age that tend to cut against the argument for a society of free and responsible individuals.

With this task in mind, what I want to talk about today is the dilemma of our day in carrying out that task. There is, I contend, an intellectual crisis in both the fields of intellectual history and in the discipline of history more generally. It is a crisis regarding the status of truth seeking in the disciplines. A new generation of critical theorists are seeking to poke holes in the history of economic theory and liberal political economy, and to demonstrate the inherent inefficiency, instability, and immorality of the capitalist system. And just to hopefully ignite some stimulating conversation, I am going to suggest that economic approaches that are not rooted in the Misesian and Hayekian economic way of thinking that Leonard championed are decidedly ill-equipped to face these new challenges. Instead, they lead to the abandoning of the disciplines of history and intellectual history. And if we economists abandon history—in both senses—we leave our past to the kindness of our enemies.[2] This is an extremely vulnerable position to find oneself in. Yet this is where we are. Leonard would want us to correct that, so let's do that.

What is truth in the social sciences and humanities? During the 1970s and 1980s, as the positivist philosophical program came under increasing scrutiny, among the postpositivist positions articulated was postmodernism, and among postmodernists were critical theorists and deconstructivists. It is one thing to claim that social scientists cannot hermetically seal themselves off from ethical values and various biases and pursue purely objective analysis, but it is quite another thing to claim that this means that the entire enterprise of "objective" analysis is a sham. To say knowledge of the social world—and knowledge of our efforts to understand the social world—is embedded in an intricate matrix of values, social meanings, and contextualization does not imply that there are no basic facts of the situation, or that there are no ways to adjudicate between competing explanations or theoretical frameworks. Of course, facts do not speak for themselves, and thus all knowledge of the social world demands *contextualization* and recognition of its *social construction*. But also, not all interpretations of events are equally as grounded, and not all arguments are equally valid. Progress in the social sciences and humanities can be made.

Most economists are trained to avoid such murky epistemological waters. But even in their practice they don't. Rather, they just avoid recognizing that they are drowning in them. To say that "if something is important, we must measure it" bleeds too quickly into the claim that whatever we can measure, we should claim as being important. It is not! Now is not the time to discuss in any detail the various shortcomings of the empirical project in the social sciences, except to note that the substitution of sophisticated statistical analysis for more narrative history does not solve the problems that have plagued social science and history since their very beginning. The only way to "solve" them is to recognize them, and embrace multiple forms of evidence and multiple methods of analysis.

But many economic historians argue that this is precisely not the way to solve the problem. Instead, they insist we must just count, count correctly and thoroughly. But let me be clear, nobody should be against counting. In fact, counting can fix a lot of confusion in social sciences and history. When F. A. Hayek edited *Capitalism and the Historians* (1954), basic counting was used to challenge the prevailing opinions about the immiseration of the working class during the Industrial Revolution. And more recently, Deirdre McCloskey stresses in her history of the Great Enrichment that you cannot answer empirical questions philosophically, so we have to count when doing responsible history. But she is still doing history.

In a recent paper, Robert Margo (2017) explored the progress economic historians have made over the past generation within the economics profession. How he measured progress, however, was whether economic historians looked in their work more and more like economists and less like historians. In other words, if you pick up an article in the *Journal of Economic History* (JEH) and compare it with the *Journal of Political Economy* (JPE), what do you see with regard to words, formulas, tables, and charts? By Margo's measure, what has happened over the past 20 years is that the form and substance of articles in the *JEH* and the *JPE* have become increasingly indistinguishable from each other.

Economists count, and economic historians count, they don't read so much as they once did, they don't contextualize as was once expected, and they certainly don't look for meanings associated with the human condition historically contemplated. Economic historians in essence have ceded history to the historians; they do economics but by counting and calculating with data from the deeper past, rather than the more recent past or the present. But let's not get confused. These economic historians are economists and thus they approach their research and produce results that look the same as their fellow economists. Margo tells us not to fear, though, since economists have better employment opportunities and higher compensation. He is, of course, right on this last point. But what happens if economic historians abandon *history*?

We already know the answer—we get new histories of capitalism, which focus on exploitation of man, monopoly power, alienation, and periodic crises. Capitalism is plagued by inefficiency, suffers instability, and is characterized by injustice (see, e.g., Beckert 2015). Effectively addressing these arguments requires more than counting. It might be important here to remember that there is a world of difference between being heard and being listened to. So in the exchange between historians of capitalism and economic historians of capitalism, insisting on counting by the economists while ignoring all the other issues—including the problems with power, politics, culture, and the long shadow of past imperfections—means one might be heard, but not listened to, and moving the intellectual climate of opinion requires earning such a hearing. Counting, in other words, is a necessary component for the explanation of capitalism, but not sufficient.

History is more than counting. It requires contextualization and comparative analysis, and to do that sound economic theory is critical. Enter once again Mises's *Theory and History*—economists need to be *economists*, not mathematicians and statisticians, in order to do economic *history*. The problem with the contemporary histories of capitalism is weak theory more so than innumeracy, though innumeracy doesn't help. Too many historians of capitalism are arguing that the legacy of slavery and colonization benefited the West and not trade, technological innovation, and entrepreneurial creativity. They see the world in negative-sum terms, they misunderstand the institutional preconditions for realizing productive specialization and peaceful social cooperation among diverse and often distant people. In short, they have a bad theory of economic development and the role that a private property market economy plays in that process of material progress. Deirdre McCloskey refers to economic development as "trade-tested betterment," and much of the modern history of capitalism is allergic to this way of thinking about it. History is too important to be left to the "historians." I am arguing that this bad intellectual state of history is a consequence of economists abandoning economic history and the intellectual history of classical and modern political economy and economics to their intellectual enemies.

But the problem that must be addressed isn't limited to bad history. The intellectual history of economics is also experiencing its own crisis. Reading the history of economic theory can be divided into at least three broad approaches: (a) internal logic of arguments in texts, (b) ideas in context, and (c) hermeneutics of suspicion. Other fine distinctions can be introduced, such as Whig, contra-Whig, antiquarian, and instrumental (see Boettke 2000). The classic task for economists from prior to Adam Smith until the post–World War II era was for economists to engage in close textual readings of arguments and to assess the strengths and weaknesses of different arguments on their own internal consistencies, the comparative analysis with other arguments, and the correspondence with the issues in the world that the theories were being developed to address.

Economics evolved during its first 150 years as a philosophical subject. During the past 70 years, economics has shifted from being a philosophical science to becoming a mathematical and statistical science. The transformation of economics can actually be traced to the turn of the 20th century, but it was not completely accomplished until after World War II—as before that the more philosophical thinkers existed side-by-side with the more scientific thinkers in the elite corners of the profession. Amartya Sen argued in *On Ethics and Economics* (1987) that economics as a discipline exists on an intellectual production possibility frontier between economics as a moral science and economics as social engineering. Since he was interested in reintroducing ethical discourse into economics, Sen argued that the economics profession was operating in the corner solution of social engineering and it was time for the profession to trade off and move back toward moral sciences. Of course, he doesn't advocate a corner solution in that direction either, but just significant movement back toward political economy and social philosophy.

Studying the shifting intellectual landscape of economics is the task of historians of economics. The exercise of intellectual history in political economy and economics improved when close textual reading was complemented by contextualization in the same way that political theory was contextualized with the Cambridge School of intellectual history, and our understanding of the evolution of ideas improved. Scholars and scientists do not work in a vacuum, but instead always within an intellectual, organizational, social, and cultural context. Ideas are not necessarily context dependent, but the way ideas are communicated, which ideas coalesce into a consensus, and which ones get cast aside are context dependent. This is why the evolution of ideas is never smooth, but always full of fascinating twists and turns defined by missteps, wrong turns, and the continual reevaluation of arguments. Thus, the potency of the contra-Whig position in intellectual history. The Whig tradition of intellectual history basically argues that all that is good in the ancients is embodied already in the moderns, so there really is not much value besides antiquarian tastes in reading Adam Smith or David Ricardo or John Stuart Mill.[3] But what if due to the misallocation of intellectual resources that results from following intellectual fads and fashions, critically important ideas from the past have not exhausted their evolutionary potential? If this is the case, then ideas from an older thinker can remain part of our extended present, and could in fact be a vital input into contemporary theory construction.

As economists, this disruptive and disjointed evolution of ideas becomes even more fascinating when we place ourselves in the model of intellectual development itself. The economics of economics, or more broadly the sociology of science matters. In one sense, it is a natural outgrowth of putting ideas in context. But in another way, it opens up another avenue of research and exploration. We can study the incentive structures of science and scholarship, including how professional activities in any discipline are organized. Funding, positions, and prestige must be addressed alongside the assessment of ideas and their application to the world of affairs. Again, our understanding of the process of scientific advancement is improved when we explore the "organization of inquiry."

But here is a critical point to remember about an economics of economics: to be effective, it has to be grounded in sound economic theory. Sound economics doesn't focus our attention on matters of personal psychology and strict adherence to preference and motivation-based explanations. Instead, the focus of attention is on the systemic incentives that alternative institutional arrangements produce in commercial and noncommercial life, including science and scholarship. In an analysis so pursued, the advancement of science and the tracking of truth do not depend on the individual motives of those involved, but on the institutional incentives and the ability of the organization of inquiry to produce a constructive conversation in which views are subject to continual contestation.

The honorable tradition of liberal political economy sought first and foremost to explore the technical principles necessary to understanding how alternative institutional arrangements affect our ability to realize productive specialization and peaceful social cooperation. In developing this line of thinking, political economists adopted a sort of analytical egalitarianism—a basic behavioral symmetry. People are people, my mom used to say, but so did my teachers James Buchanan and Gordon Tullock. Same players, *different rules*, result in different outcomes.[4] The critical point to take away from economics is that its explanatory thrust is to be found in institutional variation, not in behavioral differences among people. Methodologically and analytically, the question then becomes how best to study institutional variation.

But isn't it easier to focus on behavioral differences? Bad people do bad things. Stupid people do stupid things. So we want to avoid bad and stupid people, and trust in good and smart people. Such a perspective is problematic on many levels. But for our purposes here, let's just state that once we move away from institutional variation, and instead look for our explanations in differences among people, we invite the caricature that we sort individuals into: (a) those who are stupid, (b) those who are evil, and (c) those good and smart people who agree with me. Such a division doesn't result in learning, and when taken to its limits, it destroys the trust among scholars in the quest for human understanding.

The real problem with preference-based/motivation-inferring explanations of intellectual history—as opposed to close textual exegesis and the attempt to place ideas in their historical, philosophical, cultural context—is that personal psychology of ideas comes to be stressed rather than an assessment of arguments and adjudication of evidence for positions. Not only is personal psychology stressed, judgment is passed on the motives inferred (often never proved as this is often impossible to do so). So the hermeneutics of suspicion questions not arguments and evidence. And in much of the literature on neoliberalism, such as the work on Milton Friedman, F. A. Hayek, James Buchanan, and the legacy of the Mont Pelerin Society, the logic of their arguments is ignored, the empirical evidence related to their arguments is unexamined, but the supposed financial motivations and "will to power" take center stage and intellectual positions are tied to remote political realities such as Chile, or the global financial crisis.

This is our current intellectual climate. The history of capitalism by historians has resurrected arguments that were effectively challenged from Hayek's *Capitalism and the Historians* (1954) to Nathan Rosenberg and L. E. Birdzell's *How the West Grew Rich* (1987), and of course the monumental trilogy by Deirdre McCloskey on the bourgeois era (2006, 2010, 2016). And the history of neoliberal thought and economics in general suggests that these theories and approaches didn't emerge in *The Clash of Economic Ideas* (2012) as my colleague Larry White so brilliantly demonstrates, but instead through manipulation of the scientific process through unjustified positions of power in intellectual affairs obtained through the unwarranted intrusion of funding sources that have corrupted science. *The Merchants of Doubt* (Oreskes and Conway 2011) style of argument isn't limited to nuclear power, tobacco, and climate change, but now spreads to the new learning in Chicago price theory and industrial organization, monetarism and macroeconomic policy, public choice and constitutional political economy, and Austrian economics and libertarianism. The *House of Cards* conspiratorial style of "storytelling" about intellectual history identifies "evil geniuses" who devise "master plans" and find the funding from "dark money." Along the way, they have not only absconded with prestigious academic positions that are well funded and led to Nobel Prizes, but they have also ruined national economies and destroyed the hopes and dreams of the average individual, not to mention the oppression of their opponents.

These works—whether we are talking about Philip Mirowski and Dieter Plehwe (2009), Avner Offer and Gabriel Soderberg (2016), or Nancy MacLean (2017)—are easy reading. The story flows easily from their pens. They are entertaining narratives about the intellectual world in the same way as watching Frank Underwood in the Netflix series *House of Cards* manipulate the politics of D.C. to rise to the presidency. But just as *House of Cards* doesn't portray political reality accurately—it is not a public-choice analysis of democratic processes—these critiques of the "neoliberal thought collective" fall short of accuracy. As my good friend Michael Munger (2008, 2015, 2018) said of one of these works, it exalts "truthiness" over truth.

Among a certain group of progressive intellectuals who have been challenged by the developments in economic theory associated with the Austrian, Chicago, UCLA, and Virginia schools that effectively poked holes in the Keynesian consensus in the decades following World War II with a rejuvenated microeconomics to challenge the hegemony of macroeconomics, and the innovative development of property rights economics, public-choice economics, law and economics, and market process economics, the ability to dismiss rather than having to provide counterarguments was (is) just too attractive. If they can discredit and delegitimize arguments, why would they need to address them? Again, Frank Underwood has no legitimate claim to the office, right?

But rather than end on a note of scolding those I disagree with most about the intellectual descent into an unproductive hermeneutics of suspicion, I

want to warn us—classical liberal scholars and intellectuals—about following a similar path. There is an allure, after all, to those ideological blinders,
but it is a tragedy whenever we are seduced to pursue narratives that exhibit
only truthiness at the expense of truth tracking. We must always remember Bastiat's dictum: never fear an artful criticism, but always fear an inept
defense. Nothing worse, Bastiat warns, could happen to a good cause. True
liberalism is a good cause.

A key to Leonard Liggio's approach to history and intellectual history
was no doubt the story of liberty versus power, but Leonard didn't take the
easy way out. He didn't argue that the economics profession, for example,
was plagued by corruption and confusion due to major funding by those
in political power. Austrian economics faced barriers, but Leonard Liggio's
argument was to aspiring professors: face those barriers head-on and just do
better work—work that others in the profession will have to pay attention
to, and work that tracks truth. Never settle for comfortable "truthiness"
that fits with your ideological priors. So yes, we should acknowledge that
when we put economists in the model of economics itself, it does matter
with regard to the structure of incentives within the organization of inquiry.
But that doesn't exhaust the narrative we tell; it is just one component. Our
primary focus begins with the most charitable interpretation of arguments,
a close and critical examination of the arguments, and a careful weighing
of the evidence. As I said, Leonard taught us all to be better and to stress
scholarship, to find common ground with other scholars *left* and *right*, and to
practice *praxeology* to the high standard set by Mises, Hayek, Kirzner, and
others in our quest to understand the human condition. To do that we must
recognize the tragedy that results when ideological blinders block scholarship and our continual learning. Let's live up to the standard Leonard set
as a lifelong learner, and follow his lead in how he encouraged us to pursue
and produce scholarship of impact, be teachers that excite, and be mentors
that connect to a growing intellectual network.

Notes

1. See the three-part biographical sketch on Leonard at the Liggio Project.
2. I owe the recognition of this basic dilemma that economists face to my colleague
   David Levy. Levy gives a classic example of this in his book *How the Dismal Science
   Got Its Name* (2002). Most commentaries uninformed about the economic content

of the disputes of the time believe the name derives from some Malthusian observation or the disciplinary insistence on scarcity and constraints, but Thomas Car-
lyle and his literary cohort were attacking classical economists for their analytical
egalitarianism and their refusal to accept a natural hierarchy of mankind. It was
the classical economists, Levy documents, that opposed the institution of slavery,
as well as argued that the Irish were not inherently inferior to the English. Thus, if
economists abandon our history, we let others, who are either unaware or unwilling
to understand, tackle the arguments that were actually made by economists in the
time being discussed. Instead, they read back into the past the discourse that they
are most familiar with and that fits most comfortably into their ideological priors.

3. The classic statement of Whig history of economic thought is George Stigler's (1969)
   in "Does Economics Have a Useful Past?" In 1976, McCloskey asked "Does the
   Past Have Useful Economics?" Part of my purpose here is to recommend that our
   contemporary situation demands that we reexamine these questions and reengage
   the interrelationship between theory and history in our study of the past and the
   present.

4. See the first chapter in the public-choice primer *Government Failure* written by Tullock,
   Seldon, and Brady and republished in 2005. Chapter 1 is titled "People Are People:
   Elements of Public Choice Theory." Also see Buchanan's "Same Players, Different
   Games: How Better Rules Make Better Politics" (2008).

References

Beckert, Sven. 2015. *Empire of Cotton*. New York: Vintage.

Boettke, Peter J. 2000. "Why Read the Classics in Economics?" Library of Economics
and Liberty, Liberty Fund, Indianapolis.

Buchanan, James M. 2008. "Same Players, Different Games: How Better Rules Make
Better Politics." *Constitutional Political Economy* 19 (3): 171–79.

Hayek, F. A., ed. 1954. *Capitalism and the Historians*. Chicago: University of Chicago Press.

Levy, David M. 2002. *How the Dismal Science Got Its Name*. Ann Arbor: University of
Michigan Press.

MacLean, Nancy. 2017. *Democracy in Chains*. New York: Vintage.

Margo, Robert A. 2017. "The Integration of Economic History into Economics." NBER
Working Paper No, 23538, National Bureau of Economic Research, Cambridge,
MA.

McCloskey, Deirdre N. 1976. "Does the Past Have Useful Economics?" *Journal of Economic Literature* 14 (2): 434–61.

———. 2006. *The Bourgeois Virtues: Ethics for an Age of Commerce*. Chicago: University of
Chicago Press.

———. 2010. *Bourgeois Dignity: Why Economics Can't Explain the Modern World*. Chicago:
University of Chicago Press.

———. 2016. *Bourgeois Equality: How Ideas, Not Capital or Institutions, Enriched the World*. Chicago: University of Chicago Press.

Mises, Ludwig von. 1957. *Theory and History*. New Haven, CT: Yale University Press

Mirowski, Philip, and Dieter Plehwe, eds. 2009. *The Road from Mont Pelerin*. Cambridge, MA: Harvard University Press.

Munger, Michael C. 2008. "Blogging and Political Information." *Public Choice* 134 (1/2): 125–38.

———. 2015. "L'Affaire LaCour: What It Can Teach Us about Academic Integrity and 'Truthiness.'" *Chronicle of Higher Education*, July 10.

———. 2018. "On the Origins and Goals of Public Choice: Constitutional Conspiracy?" *The Independent Review* 22 (3): 359–82.

Offer, Avner, and Gabriel Soderberg. 2016. *The Nobel Factor*. Princeton, NJ: Princeton University Press.

Oreskes, Naomi, and Erik M. Conway. 2011. *Merchants of Doubt*. New York: Bloomsbury Press.

Rosenberg, Nathan, and L. E. Birdzell Jr. 1987. *How the West Grew Rich: The Economic Transformation of the Industrial World*. New York: Basic Books.

Sen, Amartya. 1987. *On Ethics and Economics*. New York: Wiley.

Stigler, George J. 1969. "Does Economics Have a Useful Past?" *History of Political Economy* 1 (2): 217–30.

Tullock, Gordon, Arthur Seldon, and Gordon L. Brady. 2005. *Government Failure: A Primer on Public Choice*. Washington, DC: Cato Institute.

White, Lawrence H. 2012. *The Clash of Economic Ideas*. New York: Cambridge University Press.

Chapter 12

Fearing Freedom: The Intellectual and Spiritual Challenge to Liberalism

The vision of the eighteenth-century philosophers which enabled them to describe a social order that did not require the centralized direction of man over man may yet stir excitement. Free relations among free men—this precept of ordered anarchy can emerge as principle when successfully renegotiated social contract puts "mine and thine" in a newly defined structural arrangement and when the Leviathan that threatens is placed within new limits.

—James Buchanan
The Limits of Liberty

In "The Soul of Classical Liberalism" (2000), James Buchanan argued that modern advocates of the liberal order must move beyond the mid-20th-century project of "saving the books" and "saving the ideas" and instead embrace the challenge of "saving the soul" of liberalism. His argument is fairly straightforward: the vast majority of modern defenders of classical liberalism are scientific economists, and they base their defense on the logic and evidence that they work with. But these insights understandably do not translate easily into the popular imagination.

The prospects for establishing a genuine liberal order, however, turn on capturing the intellectual imagination of a significant segment of the population. I am in complete agreement with Buchanan, and I myself had a "mindquake" similar to the one he experienced when as a student he was introduced to the vision of the spontaneous ordering of the free-enterprise market economy. Once that vision was in my head, it is in retrospect hard to imagine any other path that I could have pursued professionally. However, like Buchanan, I do

Published in *The Independent Review* 18, no. 3 (2013/14): 343–58.

also wonder why so few of my classmates who listened to the same lectures and read the same books had the same reaction to the material.

The expectation, Buchanan told his readers, that the teacher of economics could effectively communicate the principles of economics to the broad class of the intelligentsia as well as to the masses was grounded in hubris and folly. Instead of limiting our articulations to the teachings of a science and stressing policies that should be supported due to our enlightened self-interest, he argued, we need to provide a coherent "vision" of a social system that is simultaneously romantically, aesthetically, and morally pleasing. The liberal promise of individual autonomy, generalized economic prosperity, and domestic and international peace, of course, can provide (and has provided) such a coherent vision. As Deirdre McCloskey (2006, 2010) has recently stressed, where bourgeois virtues are respected and bourgeois activities are attributed dignity in the popular imagination, modern economic growth is made possible. Where the popular imagination rejects such virtues and despises such activities, poverty, ignorance, and squalor follow for the masses. Yet we must still be struck by the reality that very few folk songs are written as odes to commerce and capitalism, and many are written to celebrate class struggle and socialism.

Liberalism, at least economic liberalism, has an image problem. And Buchanan wanted those who value liberalism to address this problem head-on rather than continuing to deny its existence. In order to embrace the challenge, we must first fully understand it. To do that, I examine here the themes Buchanan raised in three essays that focus our attention on the critical issues. They are, in chronological order, "The Potential and Limits of Socially Organized Humankind" ([1988] 1991), "The Soul of Classical Liberalism" (2000), and "Afraid to Be Free" (2005). The underlying economic analysis in all three essays is Buchanan's fundamental point that the same players acting under different rules will produce different games. The explanatory focus is on the rules of the game and their enforcement rather than on behavioral assumptions of the actors under examination per se. But it should be remembered at all times in the discussion that a Buchanan-inspired political economy treats the actors as analytically egalitarian, insists on behavioral symmetry across the different realms, and denies to the human actors under investigation in the context of market, legal, political, and social processes any notion of omniscience, benevolence, and omnipotence. These points are "given" in Buchanan's approach to political economy and social philosophy.

In these three essays, however, Buchanan pushed the analysis in novel directions. In "The Potential and Limits of Socially Organized Humankind," he raised the issue of justice; in "The Soul of Classical Liberalism," the issue of vision; and in "Afraid to Be Free," the issues of liberty and responsibility. I discuss each of these critical issues and then offer a suggested reconstruction of Buchanan's political economy and social philosophy that can embrace the challenges and provide a coherent vision of a society of free and responsible individuals.

In such a society, people have the opportunity to participate in the ongoing conversation of democratic deliberation that constitutes collective action in their society, to prosper in a market economy based on profit and loss, and to live in and be actively engaged with caring communities. A free society, I argue, is a good society, and a self-governing citizenry must be willing to embrace the "cares of thinking" and "troubles of living," as Alexis de Tocqueville ([1835–1840] 2003) stressed so many years ago. But an appropriately structured political economy of a free society—one that exhibits neither dominion nor discrimination in human relationships—will not be one that individuals should fear, but one that will constitute an inspiring vision that can capture the population's imagination.

Was Justice a Missing Component in Classical Liberalism?

"The great scientific discovery of the eighteenth century," Buchanan argued, "out of which political economy (economics) emerged as an independent academic discipline, embodies the recognition that the complementary values of liberty, prosperity, and peace can be attained" ([1988] 1991, 244). As long as the state provides the appropriate laws and institutions—the rules of the game and their enforcement—individuals can be left alone to pursue their own projects while realizing the values of liberty, prosperity, and peace through mutually beneficial exchange with one another.

The classical liberal ideal was never fully realized because—although the intellectual vision captured the essential role of the state in providing the required infrastructure—there was a lack of attention to the distinction between the political structure and political intervention into the socioeconomic game. As a result, the structural constraints required to limit the negative consequences of politicized interventions were not established. Within a few generations, the classical liberal ideal failed to inspire.

Buchanan postulated that critical to the failure to continually inspire was that the classical liberal list of liberty, prosperity, and peace was incomplete because it omitted justice. The injustice of capitalist distribution inspired instead the socialist vision. The idea of justice—in both its Aristotelian senses of commutative justice and distributive justice—captures the intellectual imagination. The classical liberal vision is one consistent with commutative justice (equity in the process), but its relationship to distributive justice (equity in outcomes) has always been dubious at best. Note how the failure to distinguish between the structure of rules and the politicized interventions into the game results in the blurring of the distinction between commutative and distributive justice in practice. If the political infrastructure permits differential treatment in the political process, such as special-interest-group politics and rent-seeking behavior, then the fairness of the structure itself is vulnerable to challenge, and a demand for a more equitable distribution of resources gained in that flawed process seems natural.

The incompleteness of the classical liberal infrastructure permitted an alignment between those with a justice-driven moral purpose and the interest-motivated constituencies, and it resulted in discriminatory politics that erodes the rule of law. In *The Limits of Liberty* ([1975] 2000), Buchanan argued that the public capital embodied in the protective and productive functions of government can be eroded through the redistributive politics of the "churning state" (see also de Jasay [1985] 1998). The constitutional puzzle from this perspective is one of empowering the protective and productive state without unleashing the redistributive state. But this puzzle cannot be solved as long as the question of justice is not met head-on, and, instead, those having an interest-driven motivation can align with those having a moral-driven motivation to challenge the legitimacy of the economic and social order.

Effectively countering the distributive-justice critique of the market order requires both a reinvigorated defense of the constitutional order of limited government and an appropriate understanding of the operation of the market economy itself. Distributive justice within the context of the ongoing market process cannot be viewed as a question of "just division" but instead must be understood as emergent from the pattern of exchange, production, and resource use. There is no "fixed pie" to be divided up among the participants; the process of producing the pie—the exchange relations among participants and the resource use based on buying decisions within the process—determines how big the pie grows. The size of the economic pie, in other words, is not invariant to the way "we" choose to divide up the pie. Policymakers could, if they so desired, decide that they will confiscate the existing stock of oil reserves, and it would not affect the current supply of oil. But it would have a drastic effect on the future exploration and discovery of oil reserves.

Economic theory per se remains silent on the question of whether profits are deserved or not, but it speaks quite clearly and loudly about the consequences of popular answers to that question. The political economist must take those consequences into account when offering structural reform suggestions. Political machinations that undermine the generality of the rules and instead yield benefits to some at the expense of others must be constantly identified and resisted in a renewed defense of the justice of the classical liberal order. Only by so doing will the 21st-century political economist complete his 18th-century counterparts' program and demonstrate the logical affinity between liberty, prosperity, peace, and justice.

Can the Invisible Hand Inspire a New Generation?

The challenges that Buchanan identified for the future of classical liberalism include not only those related to the infrastructure and the question of justice, but also the piercing of the "romantic vision" of politics with a scientific understanding of the reality of ordinary politics and an appreciation of the workings of Adam Smith's "invisible hand" in the market order. Only in this manner can the political economist convince fellow citizens of the relative inefficiency of ordinary politics and demonstrate the relative efficiency of the market order.

Ludwig von Mises presented the dilemma that 20th-century economists and political economists faced due to the romantic assumptions of the state's omniscience and benevolence ([1949] 1966, 692). That the state should be in control of the use and distribution of resources logically followed. Mises pointed out:

> This inference became logically inescapable as soon as people began to ascribe to the *state* not only moral but also intellectual perfection. The liberal philosophers had described their imaginary state as an unselfish entity, exclusively committed to the best possible improvement of its subjects' welfare. They had discovered that in the frame of a market society the citizens' selfishness must bring about the same results that the unselfish state would seek to realize; it

was precisely this fact that justified the preservation of the market economy in their eyes. But things became different as soon as people began to ascribe to the *state* not only the best of intentions but also omniscience. Then one could not help concluding that the infallible state was in a position to succeed in the conduct of production activities better than the erring individuals. It would avoid all those errors that often frustrate the actions of entrepreneurs and capitalists. There would no longer be malinvestment or squandering of scarce factors of production; wealth would multiply. The "anarchy" of production appears wasteful when contrasted with the planning of the *omniscient* state. The socialist mode of production then appears to be the only reasonable system, and the market economy seems the incarnation of unreason. ([1949] 1966, 688)

In the post-socialist political economy of the 21st century, the socialist god may in fact be dead, but an appreciation of Smith's "simple system of natural liberty" is far from possessing a general consensus among the intelligentsia. Our dilemma today is as follows: Modern classical liberal economists have been somewhat successful at challenging the efficacy of centralized state control of production, reflecting a mild success in pecking away at the romantic assumptions of the state's benevolence and omniscience. That said, they have significantly underestimated how the "churning state" is able to harness the morally driven philosophical critique of capitalism in order to serve special-interest-group motivations. Milton Friedman's "iron triangle" means that there will always be a significant resistance to classical liberal reforms that must be taken into account in any discussion of the transformation of politics (Friedman and Friedman 1984, 41–51). There is, Friedman argued, an asymmetry between the resistance to increase the size of government and to decrease it. The constituencies of beneficiaries of programs, politicians, and bureaucracies align to ensure that efforts to dismantle programs face much stronger resistance than efforts to create new programs or expand existing programs.

The rhetoric and reality of the financial crisis of 2008 only reinforced the lack of faith in laissez-faire. Rhetorically, blame has been inappropriately placed on the unhampered marketplace, when the reality is that government policies that disproportionately favored some constituencies and sheltered them from the self-regulation of the marketplace were the cause. If policies that privatize profits but socialize risk are in place, nobody should be surprised that market participants will respond by assuming unsustainable levels of risk while earning large returns in the gamble even after the losses are accounted for. Gambling with other people's money is always in the gambler's interest. Instead of focusing our analytical attention on the weaknesses in the institutional structure that permitted this predictable behavior to emerge, our collective attention has been on the behavior itself—as if it were solely a consequence of moral shortcomings associated with those in finance and commerce more generally. The intellectual challenge for the 21st-century classical liberal is great. But with great challenges, comes great opportunity.

The public-debt crises in Europe as well as those facing many US states, such as California, highlight the reality that the current approach to spending without paying cannot continue indefinitely. The public conversation must turn away from political wrangling over "austerity" measures and grapple seriously with questions not just of governmental scale, but more importantly of governmental scope. For classical liberals, this means switching the conversation from "starving the beast of resources" to "starving the beast of responsibility." As the conversation turns to the appropriate role of government in a society of free and responsible individuals, the only way that the argument can turn in favor of the system of natural liberty is if there is "a generalized willingness to leave things alone, to let the economy work in its own way, and outside of politicized interference" (Buchanan [1988] 1991, 248). The populace must regain a faith in the laissez-faire principle of classical liberal political economy in its finest moments.

Our modern experience with the internet, global commerce, the international division of labor, and technological developments in general provides ample material to build a reinvigorated and intellectually attractive image of the spontaneous order of economic life and the simultaneous achievement of liberty, prosperity, peace, and justice. The efficiency of the market order and the ongoing march of technological progress are not due to postulated perfection of man or the market or both, as textbook economics is often portrayed as providing, but is instead due to the very imperfections of man in his seeking of improvements and to the continual becoming of the emergent market order (see Buchanan 1964, [1982] 1999). Today's inefficiency is tomorrow's profit opportunity for the entrepreneur who can act on it to eliminate the identified inefficiency.

The old and stale debate of the 20th century that moved through the years from perfect market versus perfect state to imperfect market versus perfect state and then to imperfect market versus imperfect state must be recast. First, the role of the government in economic affairs should be at best focused on the institutional infrastructure—the rules of the game and their enforcement. Politics is to be limited conceptually to questions about the appropriate structure of government. Policy—by which I mean politicized choice within the rules—must be significantly restricted to avoid the churning state machinations discussed earlier. Voluntary agreement and freedom of association must be permitted to work themselves out through time. Second, a significant portion of the population must understand the power of the market to marshal individuals' ordinary motivations and lead them to realize the benefits of social cooperation under the division of labor.

One of the great scientific truths of the "invisible hand" is that the participants do not have to grasp (in fact cannot grasp) the overall operation of the system but are guided only by their own private interests in particular contexts. But it may very well be the case that while we don't have to understand the spontaneous order of the free-market economy in order to benefit from it, a significant portion of the general public might need to grasp the basic scientific principles and the aesthetic beauty of the "invisible hand" in order for it to be sustained in the face of ordinary political pressures for expediency. This is where the modern world should be the greatest aid to the economics teacher because the world of the internet that we experience every day in so many direct ways enables us to realize social cooperation through exchange relations with folks from distant lands who do not speak the same language, do not follow the same religion, and possess different conceptions of the good and the just. The anonymous cooperation that defines the marketplace has never been so evident and yet so directly experienced as it is in the smorgasbord that is the World Wide Web.

Should We Fear Freedom?

Cultivating a generalized willingness to leave things alone among the informed population is possible only with a citizenry capable of true self-governance in the Tocquevillian sense. Unless the citizenry is willing to embrace the "cares of thinking" and the "troubles of living," any hope for widespread acceptance of a visionary renewal of the laissez-faire principle will remain beyond our grasp.

James Buchanan once argued that "man wants liberty to become the man he wants to become" ([1979] 1999, 259). But what if man shies away from liberty rather than embracing the agony of choice because he would rather enjoy the leisure of security from choice? The problem that confronts the modern classical liberal, Buchanan (2005) postulated, is not the managerial socialism of the 20th century or even the "nanny state" of paternalistic socialism, but the people's desire to remain in the infantile state of demanding a parent to protect them from the vagaries of life and provide them with economic security. Vincent Ostrom (1997) focused on this problem as one of the factors that threatens the operation and continuation of well-functioning democratic societies. The key source of vulnerability for viable democratic living is how the "sickness in the state" resulting from the unconstrained machinations of interest-driven politics can breed a "sickness in the people" as their self-governing capabilities become atrophied.

The classical liberal vision is one of a society of free and responsible individuals. For our purposes, it is important to stress both the individual's freedom to choose a path of life according to his or her own volition and the acceptance of the burden of the responsibility of the choices made. Of course, it is hard for any of us in the Western professorial class to wax on about the benefits of taking on the responsibility of steering a course through the sea of economic possibilities, as we have been privileged with a position of tenure while being engaged in scientific and creative pursuits with almost complete autonomy. In short, our lives are unrealistic compared with our fellow citizens' everyday lives.

Can you imagine the lack of economic dynamism if everyone in the economy had the protected life of a tenured university faculty member? We don't have to even imagine such a world because in many ways the European labor market has sought to institutionalize something along these lines for the better part of the past 50 years, resulting in the PIGS countries (Portugal, Italy, Greece, and Spain) having consistent and persistent double-digit unemployment, creeping close to 30 percent in both Greece and Spain. As Casey Mulligan (2012) has argued, if policies raise the cost of hiring, don't be surprised when less hiring goes on. Policies designed to protect individuals from competition in the labor market and to secure against all the vagaries of economic change raise the costs of labor and provide a new layer of obstruction to economic progress.

The policy issues just raised highlight some perverse consequences regarding economic outcomes, but there are also issues of autonomy and dignity associated with individuals accepting the burden of responsibility. As Buchanan argued, "The thirst or desire for freedom, and responsibility, is perhaps not nearly so universal as so many post-Enlightenment philosophers have assumed. What share of persons in varying degrees of bondage, from slavery to ordinary wage salary contracts, really want to be free, with the accompanying responsibility for their own choices?" (2005, 24). If the number of people who are willing to shoulder the responsibility for their own choices is a distinct minority, then the majority will deem the institutional infrastructure of a classical liberal order inadequate. "The lacuna in classical liberalism," Buchanan pointed out, "lies in its failure to offer a satisfactory alternative to the socialist-collectivist thrust that reflects the pervasive desire for the parental role of the state. For persons who seek, even if unconsciously, dependence on the collectivity, the classical liberal argument for independence amounts to negation" (2005, 24).

But the classical liberal need not limit his or her vision to "leave me alone" and can extend to a strong sense of community and even, dare I say, collective purpose. The classical liberal ideal is not just a society of free and responsible individuals who have the opportunity to prosper through participation in a market economy based on profit and loss but also envisions those same individuals as living in and actively engaged with caring communities. It is these caring communities, as Richard Cornuelle ([1965] 1993) repeatedly argued, that allow a society of free individuals to give concrete meaning to the idea that the state can be starved of responsibility because private members of society individually and collectively can work to fill the gap. In other words, we don't need to fear freedom, but rather to embrace freedom, including the freedom of association to join communities of varying degrees of civic engagement.

The Importance of the Question of Anarchy

James Buchanan considered himself a "philosophical anarchist" because of his normative affinity with a philosophy of complete autonomy of the individual. Theoretically, he believed in the right of secession down to the level of the individual. But, practically, he demurred because our social existence requires collective action.

Buchanan lumped all anarchist theories with other "romantic" political theories. And, historically contemplated, Buchanan was clearly right in this judgment. Anarchistic political thought from William Godwin to Mikhail Bakunin was romantic in precisely the sense Buchanan intended—requiring a perfecting transformation of humanity for the social system to work. However attractive such theories are philosophically, they must be rejected because of the need for hard analytics to access alternative institutional arrangements in diverse human societies.

In *The Limits of Liberty* ([1975] 2000), Buchanan turned his attention to exploring the escape, by means of a constitutional contract, from the Hobbesian jungle that practical anarchy would condemn us to. He then turned to how we can avoid the collapse into Leviathan once we have achieved the escape. Through successful collective action at the constitutional level, a state is constituted, but now comes the task of institutional design such that the protective and productive state is operating effectively without unleashing the negative force of the redistributive state. If the redistributive state evolves unchecked, we devolve into the churning state—where interest groups are pitted against each other in a "war of all against all" in a zero-sum game. Buchanan would like to see a world of non-zero-sum games—only positive-sum games.

I have gone into this background because it is my assessment that Buchanan's normative caricature of anarchism results in a blind spot in traditional classical liberal political economy. After the financial crisis of 2008, Buchanan pinpointed the problem as one of an overly optimistic faith on the part of modern Chicago economists that market behavior can check itself without a proper framework of rules to discipline the behavior of market participants. There is much to be said for Buchanan's position, and we will provide a much better analysis of the financial crisis if we move the analysis to the level of rules and the institutional framework.

Economic analysis is ultimately about exchange and the institutions within which exchange takes place. As Buchanan wrote in *The Demand and Supply of Public Goods*:

> Appropriately thorough analysis should include an examination of the institutional structure itself in a predictive explanatory sense. The economist should not be content with postulating models and then working within such models. *His task includes the derivation of the institutional order itself from the set of elementary behavioral hypotheses with which he commences.* In this manner, genuine institutional economics becomes a significant and an important part of fundamental economic theory. ([1968] 1999, 5, emphasis added)

Thus, an appropriately thorough institutional economics would not just stress the necessity of the framework but explain both the origins of the framework and the mechanisms in operation to sustain the framework. Here, I think our constitutional analysis, by pigeonholing "anarchism" into the normative camp, misses the critical insights that can be learned from the empirical project of the positive political economy of anarchism (or "anarchy without romance").

First, we have a wealth of information about the institutional transformations that took place in medieval societies as they moved from personal exchange to impersonal exchange (see, e.g., Benson 1990; Greif 2006). Such work explores institutional prerequisites for the birth of modern economic growth, while emphasizing self-enforcement and self-regulation, evolutionary experimentation with a diversity of rules, and some mix of top-down and bottom-up rule design and establishment. The state is no doubt a major player, but the state is not a single unified entity either.

This point actually had a significant intellectual influence on Buchanan's work in public finance, as evidenced not only in his 1949 essay "The Pure Theory of Government Finance," but in subsequent works that reflect the influence of the Italian public-finance theorists on his work after his Fulbright year (1955/56). Public economics must proceed, according to Buchanan, without the delusion of state omniscience and benevolence. "Real rather than idealized politics, with real persons as actors—these were the building blocks in the Italian constructions, whether those of the cooperative-democratic state or the ruling class-monopoly state" ([1986] 1999, 17).

Second, the positive political economy of anarchism can excite the intellectual imagination of the next generation of 21st-century classical liberal political economists. Questions of anarchy can push the limits of what it means to be free and give us an appreciation of the self-governing capacities of individuals. In this way, research in the area creates a fruitful connection with the art and science of association and notions of bottom-up constitutional rules that uncover the inspiration and importance of power and voice for citizens. The project is not about "saving the books" or "saving the ideas," but of going onward and upward with the older ideas and making them new and relevant, and in the process taking the ideas developed by Adam Smith, F. A. Hayek, and James Buchanan and pushing them to logical implications that those brilliant individuals were unwilling to. We must recognize that the noble and inspiring projects of Smith in the realm of theory and James

Madison in the realm of action have failed to sustain subsequent generations' intellectual interests. The project needs to be recovered in order to
be reconstructed; but if left in the old formulation, it will confront the same
limitations it faced the previous time, when it proved to be so vulnerable to
intellectual critique and political manipulation.

A critical point of emphasis in Buchanan's work is that public finance
implies a political theory. Most public economists engage in their work with
only an implicit recognition of the underlying political theory. Buchanan
wanted his fellow public economists to make that recognition explicit. His
political theory was a version of contractarianism. The leap out of the
Hobbesian jungle was accomplished through a social contract. In his stylized treatment, Buchanan was forced to turn a blind eye to the myriad ways
in which individuals and groups can turn situations of conflict into opportunities for social cooperation.[1] Instead, he produced a stylized analytical
"history" of freedom in constitutional contract and the structural organization of government that in many ways overtheorizes the social contract and
"underhistories" the way in which rules are subjected to trial and error as
conflict-resolving mechanisms within and between groups.

Buchanan did this for an important reason—he distinguished between
the games we play within a given set of rules and the choices we make
over the rules of the game. He had a great analytical "faith" that, within
the appropriate set of rules, the order that will result within the process of
its emergence will in fact be a socially desirable one. The market process
exhibits a strong tendency toward (a) realizing the mutual gains from trade,
(b) inducing the innovations that will result in least-cost technologies being
used in production, and (c) responding to the diverse demands of the most
willing consumers by providing them with the goods and services they desire
when they desire them. In short, within the right institutional framework, the
economic forces at work tend to continuously agitate action until exchange
efficiency, production efficiency, and product-mix efficiency emerge. To deny
this is to deny the fundamental logic of the economic way of thinking.

Although not denying this strong tendency and in fact relying on it,
Buchanan put the emphasis on the activity of the market that brings about
that tendency—the dynamic competition and entrepreneurial adjustments,
the learning and adaptation to changing circumstances, the very becoming
of the competitive market process. He focused his attention on the reconciliation process among diverse market participants, the working out of their

differences through exchange. Consider closely the argument Buchanan provided in "What Should Economists Do?" (1964) or much later in "The Market as a Creative Process" (Buchanan and Vanberg [1991] 2000). The market has no grand teleology toward which it is heading, though its participants certainly do. The order of the market is indeed an emergent order. Yet the market is not chaotic; it possesses the strong tendency toward realizing the gains from trade and innovation and toward producing social cooperation under the division of labor.

The fundamental question that must be raised is one of application of the rules-selection process to the choice among frameworks of rules themselves. I argue that in his efforts to reinvigorate classical liberal political economy, Buchanan failed to incorporate the scientific knowledge that we have learned from the historical evolution of rule regimes from medieval times and the emergence of capitalism. Of course, for the operation to take place, we must recognize that there is some level at which metarules are in operation. For Europe, it has been hypothesized that the lack of a unified empire like the ones in Russia or China resulted in a healthy competition between the decentralized states, enabling the birth of modern capitalism (see, e.g., Rosenberg and Birdzell 1987). Russia and China no doubt had political competition going on, but the metarule situation of a unified empire meant that the competition took a different form from the trial-and-error policies of economic freedom experienced in divided Europe. In failing to incorporate this historical knowledge into his account, Buchanan missed the opportunity to fully learn from the empirical puzzle of failed and weak states and of transitioning economies. It is precisely situations where the rules of the game are up for grabs that the task of the political economist must include *"the derivation of the institutional order itself from the set of elementary behavioral hypothesis"* ([1968] 1999, 5, emphasis added).

By divorcing the constitutional project from the empirical puzzle, Buchanan was able to develop a rational-choice model of rulemaking with choosers who are devoid of their humanity—not through the typical modeling exercise of omniscience, but through an atypical move of depriving actors of concrete incentives through the veil of uncertainty. What if, instead, we must examine constitution making in a world of diverse populations (heterogeneous agents), in large-group settings, and perhaps in a situation defined by recent and deep conflicts? This is the world that political economists have been addressing in the post-socialist context, in the postwar context, in the

African, Latin American, and Middle Eastern context. Conceptually, constitution making is an exercise of choice over the rules by which we will play the social game. Theoretically, it makes sense to think of justness as fairness, and thus we strive for rules that permit neither dominion nor discrimination.

Anarchy can be read as synonymous with chaos, or absence of law, in which case its operation depends on either the transformation of humanity or the normative embrace of nasty, brutish, and short existence. This is how Buchanan read those who sought to discuss endogenous rule formation. But the "economics of anarchy" literature can proceed along a different line than either Buchanan or Winston Bush (1972) took—or than David Friedman (1971) or even more recently Jack Hirshleifer (1995) or Avinash Dixit (2004) took. Research on the positive political economy of anarchism simply means the theoretical and empirical discussion of the endogenous formation of rules of the game in the absence of a monopoly provider of the rules. To assume that we can have a monopoly provider that has the capacity to exogenously impose rules on the population that reflect the consensus of the governed is as heroic an assumption as any that traditional public-finance theory operates under.

So although Buchanan was not an anarchist, and in fact was highly critical of the libertarian anarchists with whom he intellectually engaged, the sort of intellectual reinvigoration of classical liberal political economy he envisioned might require taking the analytical anarchist turn more seriously. Buchanan didn't see it that way, as he extended his fundamental criticism of libertarianism to Hayekian evolutionism in general. There simply is, in his analysis, no processes of selection over the rules within the evolutionary process that would ensure the choice of good rules and the weeding out of bad ones. But he never really engaged the strongest arguments against his position in this regard because he was content to dismiss the moral theory of anarchism as possessing a certain philosophical desirability but practical shortcomings.

Although his own work—for example, *The Limits of Liberty* ([1975] 2000)—distanced him from the radical libertarianism of the Murray Rothbard, David Friedman, and even Robert Nozick varieties, it nevertheless set the analytical groundwork for later engagement with "analytical anarchism." It is the latter work—which provides the theoretical puzzle for collective action—that forms the basis for the "positive political economy of anarchism" as an empirical project in modern political economy. By remaining blind to this literature and the possibilities it has to offer, contemporary constitutional political economists are missing out on the greatest set of "natural experiments" of the ideas and concepts they work with. As we move onward and upward with the Buchanan project, it is my opinion that work on the endogenous formation of the rules of the game among large, diverse, and often divided populations must take center stage. Anarchy, in other words, cannot be dismissed out of hand as a relic of romantic political philosophy but instead must be embraced as the empirical reality that has formed the basis of some of the most pressing issues in comparative political economy over the past 30 years in non-Western societies.

Conclusion

Hayek remarked in his essay "The Intellectuals and Socialism":

> We must make the building of a free society once more an intellectual adventure, a deed of courage. What we lack is a liberal Utopia, a program which seems neither a mere defense of things as they are nor a diluted kind of socialism, but a truly liberal radicalism which does not spare the susceptibilities of the mighty (including the trade unions), which is not too severely practical, and which does not confine itself to what appears today as politically possible. We need intellectual leaders who are willing to work for an ideal, however small may be the prospects of its early realization. They must be men who are willing to stick to principles and to fight for their full realization, however remote. ([1949] 2005, 128–29)

In many ways, only Milton Friedman and James Buchanan took seriously Hayek's challenge to classical liberals in the closing decades of the 20th century. Milton Friedman emphasized the power of the market and the tyranny of controls in *Free to Choose* (Friedman and Friedman 1980), and Buchanan emphasized the freedom that is made possible through constitutional contract in *The Limits of Liberty* ([1975] 2000). Both sought to capture the embodied wisdom in the historical practice of Hayek's *The Constitution of Liberty* (1960), as best exemplified in the United Kingdom and the United States.

Milton Friedman's challenge to the classical liberals of the 21st century was a practical one. Rhetorically, he argued, the classical liberal political economists of the 20th century had won the battle of ideas, but in political practice they had lost the battle of implementation. Thus, the challenge was for them to find in the policy space not only incentive-compatible public policies, but incentive-compatible strategies for implementing those policies. Classical liberal economists cannot just wish away the problems that interest-motivated politics represents with wishful thinking about the power of ideas to change the world.

Buchanan's challenge is more "spiritual" than Friedman's and, ultimately, more in line with Hayek's demand that we make the building of a free society an act of intellectual excitement and courage. To Buchanan, the case isn't just about the ruthless efficiency of the market, but about the vision of a society that exhibits neither discrimination nor dominion. Such a society can be made possible only through the establishment of an institutional structure that constrains ordinary politics while also providing the appropriate rules that enable the "invisible hand" of the market to operate.

"The larger thesis is that classical liberalism," Buchanan argued, "as a coherent set of principles, has not secured, and cannot secure, sufficient public acceptability when its vocal advocates are limited to the second group. Science and self-interest, especially as combined, do indeed lend force to any argument. But a vision of an ideal, over and beyond science and self-interest, is necessary, and those who profess membership in the club of classical liberals have failed singularly in their neglect of this requirement" (2000, 112). Economics alone cannot do the job but must be joined by social philosophy. Through the interaction between economics and social philosophy, a conception of the "good society" can emerge to capture the public imagination.

As we move forward with our focus as 21st-century intellectuals, the reality of failed and weak states, the recent birth of emerging democracies postcommunism, and the emerging rules of a new international economic order all form the context of our time and place. Making the distinction between the two levels of analysis, pre- and postconstitutional levels, that is the hallmark of the Buchanan approach is a necessary but not sufficient intellectual move. In addition, 21st-century political economists must be unwilling to treat rules and their enforcement as given and instead must focus their intellectual attention on the emergence and establishment of the rules of the game themselves. We can see how institutions transform situations of conflict into opportunities for realizing the gains of social cooperation by witnessing how groups across a variety of countries and cultures engage in bottom-up constitution making to solve their societal problems. We can learn to live better together and establish a social order that simultaneously achieves liberty, prosperity, peace, and justice. Such a vision of the "good society" can and must inspire the citizenry not only with the scientific demonstration of the efficacy of freedom, but also with the aesthetic beauty and spiritual meaningfulness of the extensive social cooperation that are possible among free individuals.

Note

1. Consider, for example, the important passage in *The Calculus of Consent* where Buchanan and Tullock explicitly state: "Therefore, our analysis of the constitution-making process has little relevance for a society that is characterized by a sharp cleavage of the population into distinguishable social classes or separate racial, religious, or ethnic groupings sufficient to encourage the formation of predictable political coalitions and in which one of these coalitions has a clearly advantageous position at the constitutional stage" ([1962] 1999, 81). But as I argue, it is precisely this sort of environment that is most relevant for modern political economy to grapple with, not the stylized analytical exercise of producing a constitutional-level agreement from behind a veil of uncertainty—though I also argue that Buchanan and Tullock are underselling their contribution to the exercise of constitution making from the bottom up and in a conflict-prone world.

References

Benson, Bruce L. 1990. *The Enterprise of Law: Justice without the State*. San Francisco, CA: Pacific Research Institute.

Buchanan, James M. 1949. "The Pure Theory of Government Finance: A Suggested Approach." *Journal of Political Economy* 57 (6): 496–505.

———. 1964. "What Should Economists Do?" *Southern Economic Journal* 30 (3): 213–22.

———. [1968] 1999. *The Collected Works of James M. Buchanan*. Volume 5: *The Demand and Supply of Public Goods*. Indianapolis: Liberty Fund.

———. [1975] 2000. *The Collected Works of James M. Buchanan*. Volume 7: *The Limits of Liberty: Between Anarchy and Leviathan*. Indianapolis: Liberty Fund.

———. [1979] 1999. "Natural and Artifactual Man." In *The Collected Works of James M. Buchanan*. Volume 1: *The Logical Foundations of Constitutional Liberty*. Indianapolis: Liberty Fund, 246–59.

———. [1982] 1999. "Order Defined in the Process of Its Emergence." In *The Collected Works of James M. Buchanan*. Volume 1: *The Logical Foundations of Constitutional Liberty*. Indianapolis: Liberty Fund, 244–45.

———. [1986] 1999. "Better Than Plowing." In *The Collected Works of James M. Buchanan*. Volume 1: *The Logical Foundations of Constitutional Liberty*. Indianapolis: Liberty Fund, 11–27.

———. [1988] 1991. "The Potential and Limits of Socially Organized Humankind." In *The Economics and Ethics of Constitutional Order*. Ann Arbor: University of Michigan Press, 239–51.

———. 2000. "The Soul of Classical Liberalism." *The Independent Review* 5 (1): 111–19.

———. 2005. "Afraid to Be Free: Dependency as Desideratum." *Public Choice* 124 (1): 19–31.

Buchanan, James M., and Gordon Tullock. [1962] 1999. *The Collected Works of James M. Buchanan*. Volume 3: *The Calculus of Consent: Logical Foundations of Constitutional Democracy*. Indianapolis: Liberty Fund.

Buchanan, James M., and Viktor J. Vanberg. [1991] 2000. "The Market as a Creative Process." In *The Collected Works of James M. Buchanan*. Volume 18: *Federalism, Liberty, and the Law*. Indianapolis: Liberty Fund, 289–310.

Bush, Winston. 1972. "Individual Welfare in Anarchy." In *Explorations in the Theory of Anarchy*, edited by Gordon Tullock, 5–18. Blacksburg, VA: Center for Study of Public Choice.

Cornuelle, Richard C. [1965] 1993. *Reclaiming the American Dream*. New Brunswick, NJ: Transaction Publishers.

De Jasay, Anthony. [1985] 1998. *The State*. Indianapolis: Liberty Fund.

Dixit, Avinash K. 2004. *Lawlessness and Economics: Alternative Modes of Governance*. Princeton, NJ: Princeton University Press.

Friedman, David D. 1971. *The Machinery of Freedom: Guide to a Radical Capitalism*. New York: Harper and Row.

Friedman, Milton, and Rose Friedman. 1980. *Free to Choose: A Personal Statement*. New York: Harcourt Brace Jovanovich.

———. 1984. *Tyranny of the Status Quo*. New York: Harcourt Brace Jovanovich.

Greif, Avner. 2006. *Institutions and the Path of the Modern Economy: Lessons from Medieval Trade*. Cambridge: University of Cambridge Press.

Hayek, F. A. [1949] 2005. "The Intellectuals and Socialism." In *The Road to Serfdom: With "The Intellectuals and Socialism."* London: Institute of Economic Affairs, 105–29.

———. 1960. *The Constitution of Liberty*. Chicago: University of Chicago Press.

Hirshleifer, Jack. 1995. "Anarchy and Its Breakdown." *Journal of Political Economy* 103 (February): 26–52.

McCloskey, Deirdre N. 2006. *The Bourgeois Virtues: Ethics for an Age of Commerce*. Chicago: University of Chicago Press.

———. 2010. *Bourgeois Dignity: Why Economics Can't Explain the Modern World*. Chicago: University of Chicago Press.

Mises, Ludwig von. [1949] 1966. *Human Action: A Treatise on Economics*. 3rd ed. Chicago: Henry Regnery.

Mulligan, Casey B. 2012. *Redistribution Recession: How Labor Market Distortions Contracted the Economy*. New York: Oxford University Press.

Ostrom, Vincent. 1997. *The Meaning of Democracy and the Vulnerabilities of Democracies: A Response to Tocqueville's Challenge*. Ann Arbor: University of Michigan Press.

Rosenberg, Nathan, and L. E. Birdzell Jr. 1987. *How the West Grew Rich: The Economic Transformation of the Industrial World*. New York: Basic Books.

Tocqueville, Alexis de. [1835–1840] 2003. *Democracy in America*. London: Penguin Books.

Chapter 13

Rebuilding the Liberal Project

We must make the building of a free society once more an intellectual adventure, a deed of courage. What we lack is a liberal Utopia . . . truly liberal radicalism. . . . The main lesson which the true liberal must learn from the success of the socialists is that it was their courage to be Utopian which gained them the support of the intellectuals. . . . Unless we can make the philosophical foundations of a free society once more a living intellectual issue, and its implementation a task which challenges the ingenuity and imagination of our liveliest minds, the prospects of freedom are indeed dark. But if we can regain that belief in the power of ideas which was the mark of liberalism at its greatest, the battle is not lost.

—F. A. Hayek
"The Intellectuals and Socialism" (1949, 433)

L iberalism is in need of renewal. Too much time and effort has been put into repackaging and marketing a fixed doctrine of eternal truths rather than rethinking and evolving to meet new challenges. True liberalism today faces a serious problem from ideas emerging from a new generation of socialists on the left and from conservative movements on the right, some of which claim to follow liberalism's own time-honored teaching about the sanctity of private property rights and freedom of association.[1] Both sides are fueled by populist rhetoric and disillusionment born of discomfort from having to adapt to an ever-changing globalized world.

The challenges of a globalized world are not new, just as fear of the "other" is not a new challenge to true liberalism. As F. A. Hayek pointed out

Edited version of a paper presented at the special meeting of the Mont Pelerin Society in Stockholm, November 3–5, 2017. Originally published in Centre for Independent Studies' *Policy Magazine* 33, no. 4 (2017): 25–35.

repeatedly, the moral intuitions that are a product of our evolutionary past, which are largely in-group morals, often conflict with the moral requirements of the great globalized society (Hayek 1979).

We, as true liberal radicals—and in our capacity as scholarly students of civilization, as teachers of political economy and social philosophy, and as writers and public intellectuals—must aid in the cultivation of more mature moral intuitions if the great benefits of the globalized society are to be sustained (Buchanan 2000).[2] Left and right populism agitates against such an effort at cultivating the sensibilities of the cosmopolitan liberal, and instead promotes parochial and in-group political thought and action. And both left and right populism are based on poor economic reasoning.

The contemporary arguments deployed identify with traditional criticisms of the market economy based on inefficiency, instability, and injustice but, as in the past, cannot correctly identify the sources of those social ills in the existing reality of our times. Just as the great economic voices of the post–World War II era, such as Hayek, Milton Friedman, and James Buchanan, had to counter these arguments with careful research and effective prose, so too must the current generation of true liberals if there is to be scientific progress, scholarly wisdom, and practical sanity in addressing the social ills of our times.

The Populist Threat to a Free and Peaceful Society

In the United States and the United Kingdom, the populist threat can be seen on both the left and the right as evident in the rhetoric of Bernie Sanders and Jeremy Corbyn, respectively, and the populist electoral events of 2016 in the victory of Donald Trump in the US presidential race, as well as the Brexit vote in the United Kingdom.

Being anti-establishment should never be enough to bring intellectual joy to a true liberal.[3] The progressive elite establishment in Western democracies has indeed, as Hayek said in his Nobel Prize address, "made a mess of things" with economic policy, and with legislation that has undermined the rule of law ([1974] 1989, 3). True liberals must be vociferous critics of the intellectual errors committed by the progressive elite, and the empirical consequences that such errors have brought in their wake.

True liberal radicalism has always pulled on the nostril hairs of the pretentious and arrogant in positions of power who thought they could choose better for others than they could for themselves. Adam Smith, for example, warned:

> The statesman, who should attempt to direct private people in what man-
> ner they ought to employ their capitals, would not only load himself with
> a most unnecessary attention, but assume an authority which could safely
> be trusted, not only to no single person, but to no council or senate what-
> ever, and which would nowhere be so dangerous as in the hands of a man
> who had folly and presumption enough to fancy himself fit to exercise it.
> (1776, 478)

Ludwig von Mises was quick to remind his audience, "It is impossible to understand the history of economic thought if one does not pay attention to the fact that economics as such is a challenge to the conceit of those in power" ([1949] 1998, 67). And, of course, Hayek diagnosed the consequences of *The Fatal Conceit* (1988). True liberalism is a subtle and nuanced expert critique of the rule by experts. It uses reason, as Hayek put it, to whittle down the claims of Reason. If liberalism is not successful in this effort to expose the pretense of knowledge, then those experts risk becoming tyrants over their fellows and destroyers of civilization (Hayek [1974] 1989, 7). The populist critique of the establishment elite is not what constitutes the threat to a free society. It is the specifics of the populist program of inward-looking policies— of economic nationalism—that seek to erect barriers to trade, association, productive specialization, and peaceful social cooperation among dispersed and diverse individuals scattered near and far. The true liberal mindset, on the other hand, is one of cultivating and unleashing the creative powers of the free civilization. It celebrates human diversity in skills, talents, atti- tudes, and beliefs, and seeks to learn constantly from this smorgasbord of human delights in all things large and small, from different recipes to fine arts to fundamental beliefs and attitudes about the most sacred.[4] Liberalism is in theory and practice about emancipating individuals from the bonds of oppression. In doing so, it gives individuals the right to say NO (Schmidtz 2006). But while saying NO is critical to being able to break relationships of dominion, the positive program for liberalism is in creating greater scope for mutually beneficial relationships and thus opening the possibility for free and willing YESes in all acted-upon social engagements. Economic liberal- ism was an argument grounded in the mutual gains from association that could be realized with individuals of great social distance from each other, and in fact benefiting from cooperation with strangers as well as friends, and furthermore, expanding the scope by which strangers are turned into friends through mutually beneficial commercial relationships. The liberal argument was based in part in the doux commerce thesis, which is as much about civility and respect as it is about efficiency and profit.[5]

The liberal acknowledges the right of others to hold parochial attitudes in their restricted sphere and the right to say NO to potential relationships of mutual cooperation, but true liberals also recognize that this can only be possible within a *framework* of cosmopolitan liberalism. Saying NO in that context entails a cost that must be paid by the individual or group turning inward. They will bear the cost of forgoing the mutual gains from exchange and thus the benefits of productive specialization and peaceful social cooperation with others.

If, on the other hand, parochial attitudes grasp hold of the framework—which is what is currently at risk with this current populist threat—then those in power end up saying NO for the individual, and the creative powers of the free civilization will be curtailed and the growth of knowledge and wealth will be equally stunted. Parochialism kills progress by forcing attention in-group, rather than allowing, let alone, enabling individuals in their quest to seek new ways to learn and benefit from others. Turning inward means turning away from pursuing productive specialization and peaceful social cooperation in the global marketplace.

"The goal of the domestic policy of liberalism," the great economist and social theorist Ludwig von Mises wrote in *Liberalism*:

> is the same as that of its foreign policy: peace. It aims at peaceful coopera-
> tion just as much between nations as within each nation. The starting point
> of liberal thought is the recognition of the value and importance of human
> cooperation, and the whole policy and program of liberalism is designed to
> serve the purpose of maintaining the existing state of mutual cooperation
> among the members of the human race and of extending it still further. The
> ultimate ideal envisioned by liberalism is the perfect cooperation of all man-
> kind, taking place peacefully and without friction. Liberal thinking always has
> the whole of humanity in view and not just parts. It does not stop at limited
> groups; it does not end at the border of the village, of the province, of the
> nation, or of the continent. Its thinking is cosmopolitan and ecumenical: it
> takes in all men and the whole world. Liberalism is, in this sense, human-
> ism; and the liberal, a citizen of the world, a cosmopolite. ([1927] 1985, 76)

So how can there be any confusion on the relationship between liberalism and populism? True liberal radicalism has *nothing* in common with populist movements except a critique of the progressive elite establishment that has ruled the intellectual and policy world since World War II. This liberal critique of the progressive elite is grounded in sound economics and the grand and honorable tradition of political economy. It is not born in disillusionment and angry frustration.

Liberalism Is Liberal

There is a multiplicity of reasons why the liberal espouses virtues of openness, of acceptance, of above all else *toleration*. As Mises wrote in *Liberalism*, "What impels liberalism to demand and accord toleration is not consideration for the content of the doctrine to be tolerated, but the knowledge that only tolerance can create and preserve the condition of social peace without which humanity must relapse into the barbarism and penury of centuries long past" ([1927] 1985, 34).

Of course, Mises also argued that liberalism must be intolerant of intolerance. Those who seek to express their convictions through violence and disturbance of peace must be rebuked. The answer, however, is to be found in the liberal principle of tolerance and the free flow of ideas and beliefs. If the liberal principle of toleration makes it impossible to coerce others into one's cause, it also makes it impossible for other causes to coerce you. Even zealots, Mises reasons, must concede this point.

Serious thinking by true liberal radicals must emphasize the *positive* aspects of human sociability, of cooperation with those of great social distance, and of the civilizing aspects of commerce. The doux commerce thesis from Voltaire, Montesquieu, and Smith needs modern advocates in addition to scholars like Deirdre McCloskey (2006, 2010, 2016) who will address the questions of globalization, immigration, refugees, and the possibility for mutually beneficial exchange with those who think differently, worship differently, and live differently than you, as well as the nuts-and-bolts issues that are tied up with worldwide commerce in monetary policy, fiscal policy, and international law.

Our modern understanding of the technical economics, structural political economy, and deeper moral philosophy of Adam Smith is so flawed that such a basic common concern of the Scottish philosophers—that of creating the institutional conditions for a civil and compassionate society—is lost in the rendering. David Hume's focuses on private property, the transfer of property by consent, and the keeping of promises through contract are not rules that benefit only one segment of society at the expense of others, but instead form the general foundation for civil society and peaceful social cooperation.

Smith's analysis of the wealth of nations is not ultimately measured in trinkets and gluttonous acts of consumption, but by a rising standard of living that is shared by more and more of the general population. It is an empirical matter as to which set of institutions best achieves that task. But the concern with raising the living standards of the least advantaged in society is never far from view in any careful reading of liberal political economy from Adam Smith to Vernon Smith. The atomistic model of man—the caricature of neoclassical economics—has nothing to do with liberalism as understood by the classical political economist or the modern descendants of the mainline of political and economic thought.

Classical liberal political economists treat the individual not as atomistic, but as embedded within social settings—in families, in communities, in history. Yes, there is both the self-interest postulate and the "invisible hand" theorem, but these are not understood as the conventional critic wants to present them. The mainline of economic thought from Smith to Hayek has a rational-choice analytical structure to the questions of the logic of choice, but it is rational choice for mortals, not robots. And there are invisible hand processes discussed throughout the various works, but they depend on an institutional context to provide the filter processes that dictate the equilibrating tendencies exhibited. In short, the mainline of political economy from Smith to Hayek is one that does rational choice as if the choosers are human, and institutional analysis as if history mattered. No atomistic, egocentric prudence, only analysis is to be found in this work properly read.[6]

Furthermore, this mainline of political economy approach, while rejecting the moral claims to resource egalitarianism, is firmly grounded in analytical egalitarianism. Anyone who challenges the analytical egalitarian perspective is subject to scorn by Smith—for example, his proposition that the only difference between the philosopher and the street porter is in the eyes of the philosopher, or his warning cited earlier that the statesman who attempts to outguess the market would not only assume a level of responsibility he is incapable of judiciously exercising, but would also be nowhere as dangerous as in the hands of a man who thought himself up to the task.

Hume and Smith presented a structural argument in political economy intended to discover a set of institutions where bad men could do least harm if they were to assume positions of power. As Hume put it, when we design institutions of governance, we must presume that all men are knaves. And in a move that anticipated the modern political economy of both Hayek and Buchanan, Smith basically argued that our knavish behavior manifests itself in either arrogance or opportunism. The emphasis so far has been on the restraints that classical liberals hoped to establish on the abuse of power by political elites. However, it is just as important to stress the emancipatory aspect of the doctrine as well.

As Hayek writes in his essay "Individualism: True and False" ([1940] 2010), Smith and other classical liberal political economists were concerned "not so much with what man might occasionally achieve when he was at his best but that he should have as little opportunity as possible to do harm when he was at his worst." Hayek continues:

> It would scarcely be too much to claim that the main merit of the individualism which he and his contemporaries advocated is that it is a system under which bad men can do least harm. It is a social system which does not depend for its functioning on our finding good men for running it, or on all men becoming better than they now are, but which makes use of men in all their given variety and complexity, sometimes good and sometimes bad, sometimes intelligent and more often stupid.

And he concludes, "Their aim was a system under which it should be possible to grant freedom to all, instead of restricting it, as their French contemporaries wished, to 'the good and the wise'."

The liberal vision throughout its history has sought to find a set of institutions that would produce a society of free and responsible individuals, who have the opportunity to participate and prosper in a market economy based on profit and loss, and who live in, and are activity engaged in, caring communities.[7]

This is ultimately an empirical question. Empirical questions cannot be answered philosophically, but only through careful and thorough scholarship. Compassionate concern for the least advantaged must always be disciplined by analysis of how the institutional environment within which we live together structures the incentives people face in making decisions, and mobilizes the dispersed information throughout the social system that must be utilized in making decisions and learning from social interaction.

Liberalism constitutes an invitation to inquiry into the rules of governance that enable us, as fallible but capable human beings, to live better together; to realize the gains from social cooperation under the division of labor. True liberal radicalism exalts liberal virtues, and those liberal virtues undergird the institutions of liberal political economy.

Populist Critique of the Establishment

The rise of populist critique of the status quo in our time has multiple reasons—some in deep-rooted cultural frustration and disillusionment with the American dream, others in frustration with policy choices that have made the perception of their lives less prosperous and less secure. To address a problem requires the admission of a problem. Pointing out that these perceptions might not be the reality—while important facts to get right—is perhaps not the most productive response. If problems exist, we should look for the institutional reasons. Institutional problems demand institutional solutions, and liberal political economy has institutional solutions to offer.

The problem with the establishment elite in the democratic West is that the answer to social ills for over a century has been more government programs, and especially more government programs run by a trained policy elite who were largely immune from democratic feedback from the very populations these programs were designed to assist.

In *The Intellectual Crisis in American Public Administration*, Vincent Ostrom ([1973] 1989) detailed the transformation from democratic administration to bureaucratic administration during the Progressive Era. With this basic philosophical shift also came an institutional shift, as not only did the Progressive Era see the rise of the regulatory state, but also the rise of the administrative state, and in particular independent regulatory agencies with trained experts at the helm.

More recently, David Levy and Sandra Peart argue that this demand for, and more importantly claim to, expert rule resulted in an argument for the *Escape from Democracy* (2017). The consequences—as Hayek identified in his Nobel address and discussed earlier in this essay—were significant for the self-understanding of political economy, and the practical affairs of public policy and economic performance.

Unfortunately, the critique of the liberal order that the progressives peddled to justify the shift from democratic administration to bureaucratic administration was treated by intellectuals as separate and as such to be acceptable even if the proposed solution of expert rule was disappointing. The capitalist system was responsible for instability through industrial fluctuations, inefficiency through monopoly and other market failures, and injustice through income inequality and unfair advantages due to the accumulation of wealth.

So today, we find ourselves in a strange position where the populists are critiquing expert rule, but believe what the experts told them were the problems that plagued society and resulted in their disillusionment with the promise of progress.

The populist rhetoric argues that industrial workers are displaced by machines and lower-cost foreign labor, whether through firms relocating overseas or immigrants competing with them in the domestic labor market. And not only do these immigrants cut into their standard of living; but also a subset of them, we are told, are criminals and terrorists who threaten their very safety and the safety of those they love.

The populist rhetoric argues that the middle class and working-class population have been made to suffer through the irrational speculation of the investment bankers, who destroyed the livelihood, homes, and communities of ordinary citizens. The world as we know it, they are told from various corners, is one of a privileged few, where monopoly power dictates the prices they have to pay and monopsony power limits the wages they can reasonably expect from the market.

In populist economic nationalism—of both left and right—only government intervention can serve as the necessary corrective. We must restrict the free flow of capital and labor, we must counter monopoly power, and we must forcibly raise wages. Yet the populist criticizes the establishment elite in public policy while advocating an increased role of the government and its agencies to counter the social ills of instability, inefficiency, and inequality.

There is a fundamental contradiction in the populist critique of the establishment, both left and right, which is that government is failing them, but it is failing as it grows larger in scale and scope of activities. Yet precisely because it is failing, it must grow in scale and scope to address the failure.

Governments everywhere in the democratic West have grown bloated, and have deviated significantly from any constitutional principles of restraint. The progressive elite's critique of capitalism was grounded in a fear of the unhampered predatory capability of powerful private actors, but to curb private predation they enlisted a powerful centralized public authority. In doing so, they enabled the possibility of wide-scale public predation. But while it may be acknowledged at different times that the social ills that plague society manifest in public debt and inflation, they are tied less to overregulation, overcriminalization, overmilitarization, and so on, which are other manifestations of an ever-expanding scale and scope of governmental authority in the lives of citizens throughout the democratic world.

The truth is that the social ills that are faced throughout the world can be traced to this growth of government, which leads to the erosion of a contract-based society and to the rise of a connection-based society, entailing the entanglement of government, business, and society.

We have policies that don't promote competition, but instead protect privileged individuals and groups from the pressures of competition. We have financial institutions that have been able to privatize their profits while socializing their losses. We have governments (and their service agents) at the local to the federal level that face extremely soft budget constraints in fiscal decisions precisely because the monetary system imposes weak to nonexistent constraints. Government overreaches and oversteps everywhere and in everything so that pockets of liberalism provide growing freedom on some margins while "the road to serfdom" is literally being manifested on other margins—such as mass incarceration in the United States and the biases evident in the criminal justice system. Again, government fails because it grows, and it grows because it fails.

The reconstruction of the liberal project must begin with a recognition of these problems. Under the influence of the progressive elite, democratic countries have asked too much of government and in the process crowded out civil society and constrained the market society.

An answer is to be found in mechanisms to once more restrain the predatory capabilities of the public sector and unleash the creative entrepreneurship of the private sector. In the debate, this can be accomplished to some degree by convincing those in the progressive elite as well as those on the populist left and right that to engage in rigorous comparative institutional analysis, we must recognize that we are dealing not only with erring entrepreneurs but also with bumbling bureaucrats. The main institutional differences are that erring entrepreneurs pay a price for their failures, and they either adjust in response or some other entrepreneur will enter to make the right decision.

There is no direct analogue with respect to the bumbling bureaucrat. Public-sector activity seemingly just repeats the same errors over and over again, yet with expectation of different results. Not much learning is going on in that, at least not much learning if the ultimate goal of ameliorating or eradicating the social ill targeted is to be achieved. This is most evident in military affairs, but also in other "war" metaphors deployed from the War on Poverty to the War on Drugs to the War on Terror. It truly is the case that "War is the Health of the State," but these "wars" are definitely not a reflection of true liberal radicalism.[8] Militarism, even in metaphor, is at odds with liberalism.

Cosmopolitanism as an Answer

My answers to our current challenges are simple. Let's begin at the beginning—which for the liberal is basic human equality. We are one another's equals. There *should* be no confusion on this point. And if you are an advocate of liberalism and you find yourself "standing" (metaphorically or literally) alongside anyone asserting the superiority of one group over another, you should know you are in the wrong crowd and you need to move in opposition quickly to leave no doubt in their or others' minds.

Liberalism is liberal. It is an emancipation philosophy, and a joyous celebration of the creative energy of diverse people near and far. The liberal order is about a framework of rules that cultivates that creativity and encourages the mutually beneficial interaction with others of great social distance—overcoming such issues as language, ethnicity, race, religion, and geography.

We are fallible but capable human choosers, and we exist and interact with each other in a very imperfect world. No one of us, let alone any group of us, has access to the truth from the Almighty Above, yet we are entrusted to find rules that will enable us to live better together than we ever would in isolation. We bump into each other and we bargain with one another to try to ease the pain of bumping or to avoid bumping in the future.[9] But we must recognize that despite our basic human equality, we argue and we don't naturally agree with one another about how we are to live our lives.

So in our bumping and bargaining with one another, it is critical to keep in mind that we will soon face severe limits on what we can agree on.[10] In particular, we have little hope of coming to an agreement among dispersed and diverse individuals and groups over a scale of values, of ultimate ends that we should pursue. As Hayek put it in *The Road to Serfdom*:

> The essential point for us is that no such complete ethical code exists. The attempt to direct all economic activity according to a single plan would raise innumerable questions to which the answer could be provided only by a moral rule, but to which existing morals have no answer and where there exists no agreed view on what ought to be done. (1944, 101)

So if we rule out as impossible an all-inclusive scale of values on which we can agree, rather than seeking agreement on the ends to be pursued, our discussion will be limited to a discussion of the *means* by which a diversity of ends can be pursued within society. We can, in essence, agree to disagree on ultimate ends, but agree about the way we can acceptably engage with one another in disagreement. We are, after all, one another's equals, and each of us must be accorded dignity and respect as capable architects of our own lives. The liberal virtues of respect, honesty, openness, and toleration all entail a commitment to a way of relating to one another, not necessarily a commitment to agreement with one another about sacred beliefs or lifestyle choices, or what commodities we desire, or what occupation we want to pursue.

True liberal radicalism is about the *framework* within which we interact. The most critical aspect of a viable framework for liberal society is that it can balance contestation at all levels of governance with the necessity of organizing collective action so as to address troubling issues that cannot be adequately addressed through individual action.[11]

Let me unpack that sentence. The first task in thinking through a viable framework is to determine what problems demand collective action, and what problems can be addressed by alternative forms of decision-making. One of the great insights of Buchanan's theory of public finance was that *any theory* of public finance—whether classical liberal, progressive elite, or socialist planner—had to posit a basic political philosophy for no other reason than public finance is premised on some answer to the question of the appropriate scale and, more importantly, scope of government action.

Questions of the scale of government are not invariant with respect to questions of scope. As Keynes once remarked, you cannot make a fat man skinny by tightening his belt. Scope is about the range of responsibilities of government; scale is about the size of the governmental unit. The growth of government discussed earlier is primarily targeted at scope, but that in turn is reflected in scale. This expansion of scale and scope has pushed politics in the democratic West beyond the limits of agreement, and that explains both the dysfunctions and the disillusionment.

Questions of scope are philosophical as well as practical. But though philosophical, there is an institutional component due to the very fact that even wishful thinking must be operationalized in practice, and that requires institutions and organizations. The delineated scope of authority for the different units of government should match the externality the collective action is intended to address. To put this in the most commonsense way, we don't need the federal government to decide how to collect our garbage, and we probably shouldn't expect the local mayor to design a defense system against a nuclear attack.

Assuming we have solved these two structural problems of government—general rules to which we agree on how we relate to one another in our interactions as neighbors, and the delineated scope of responsibility and authority between local, state, and federal governments—we still have the problem of learning how to match citizen demand, expressions of voter preferences, and government policies and services. We have to postulate some *mechanism* for learning within the liberal order of politics that corresponds to the process that was identified within the marketplace. How do we get a sort of *learning liberalism* within this general structure?

In the marketplace, learning is guided by prices and disciplined by profit-and-loss accounting, but it is fueled by the rivalrous competitive process where one can be sure that if A doesn't adjust their behavior to learn from previously missed opportunity to realize the gains from trade or to realize the gains from innovation, then B will gladly step in to take their place. Can we get such contestation in the political process? It's not just a matter of contested elections, but contestation throughout the governmental process of service production and distribution. We cannot answer these questions without addressing the supply and demand of public goods, and thus the political process within democratic society.

The frustrations with the establishment elite are as deep seated for the true liberal radical as they are for the populist on the left or right. The status quo is neither desirable nor sustainable. The diagnosis of the reasons why the establishment elite has failed differ between the liberal and the populist, but the critique of expert rule is an area of overlap.

The liberal project has a history that stretches back centuries, and the true radical liberal has always been frustrated. Constitutional constraints bend when they are meant to pinch, especially in times of war. Delineated authority and responsibility are violated all the time, and not always due to the unwarranted interference of the federal into the affairs of the local, but in response to the state elected official strategically interacting with duly elected officials from other states to form a political cartel to benefit local interest groups at the expense of the general population.

Hayek asked his audience in 1949 to allow themselves to be utopian, and I think that is correct. We need to envision a liberal system that respects the general rules of engagement, but structures an intense and constant competition between government units. Bruno Frey (2001) presented a vision of government without territorial monopoly. His idea of overlapping competing jurisdictions may be one such idea of how to cultivate a learning liberalism. Work by Edward Stringham (2015) provides another vision, and Peter Leeson (2014) yet another.

What is common among all of these writers is that they offer arguments and evidence related to the operation of institutions and in particular the processes by which self-governance performs not only better than you think, but in many instances better than any reasonable approximation for how traditional government would perform in the circumstances described.

Hayek throughout his career proposed a series of institutional suggestions to bind monetary authority from engaging in the manipulation of money and credit, only to be met with frustration as his suggested method proved ineffective against the governmental habit. Perhaps then in the supply and demand of government goods and services, the governmental habit as well is a source of instability, inefficiency, and injustice, and thus frustration. If so, the reconstruction of the liberal project in the 21st century may need to turn to utopian visions as laid out by the writers mentioned earlier.

A humane liberalism, as well as a robust and resilient liberalism, may find its ability to be operationalized in an institutional structure of overlapping competing jurisdictions, and in a public discourse that respects the limits of agreement on ultimate values but insists on a general framework that exhibits neither discrimination nor dominion.

Conclusion

Liberalism is liberal. But to realize liberalism it has to be institutionalized. That means a general structure of government has to be at the forefront of the conversation. And that conversation is aided by the consequentialist reasoning of the discipline of political economy. What we have learned from this discipline is that there are great gains from pursuing productive specialization and peaceful cooperation among dispersed and diverse individuals. The greater the social distance, the more benefits we can realize in exchange, but also the more difficult to realize that exchange, given transportation costs, communication costs, and cross-cultural costs.

In short, transaction costs were high, so the great expansion of wealth in the modern world was due to institutional changes that lowered transaction costs and made possible the development of exchange relations with distant others (distant due to social factors or geographic reasons). Liberalism was one of the main vehicles that made that lowering of the costs of exchange a reality. Its doctrines celebrated trade, gave individuals decision rights over resources, freed individuals from the bonds of serfdom, and separated science from religious dogma. It was a slow and onerous process, and liberalism certainly wasn't consistently applied. But the spread of these ideas resulted in the unleashing of the creative powers of people across the globe.

Despite the obvious frustrations with the establishment elite, it is a simple fact that 2016 was the first year in recorded human history when less than 10 percent of the world's population was living in extreme poverty. This was realized in spite of the establishment elite's policies, and instead was due to the power of economic liberalism even when restricted and constrained. Smithian trade and Schumpeterian innovation simply offset and pushed ahead of the obstructions of government stupidity.[12] As Joel Mokyr (2016) likes to point out, there are tail winds and head winds, and as long as the tail winds are stronger than the head winds, progress is inevitable. Liberalism provides those tail winds.

The challenge for liberalism in the 21st century is the same as in the past—there will be conservative forces that provide the head winds. These conservative forces come in the form of the entrenched interests of the status quo establishment elite, and the populist movements on the left and the right, who, while criticizing the establishment, demand simply more of the same policies just in greater proportion—more government intervention, more regulation of industry, more restrictions on the movement of people, more restrictions on the flow of capital, and so on.

There can be no alliance between the liberal and the populist precisely because populism is illiberal. It is discriminatory, and it seeks not to limit power but to put different people in power. The natural ally of populism is planning and militarism.

It has fallen on the current generation of true radical liberals to stand up against the threats to basic human equality, to stand up against intolerance, to fear, to meddlesomeness. We must embrace Hayek's challenge and explore the philosophical foundations of a free society with a renewed excitement and invitation to inquiry. And we must, above all else, insist that liberalism is liberal in thought, in word, and in deed.

Notes

1. It is important to note that true liberalism differs greatly from the rhetoric of "litmus test" libertarianism, which is particularly unhelpful for thinking about what rules of social interaction enable us to live better together than we ever could in isolation. For a critique of what I call the error of "litmus test" libertarianism, see Boettke (2017).
2. See James Buchanan's address to the Mont Pelerin Society titled "The Soul of Classical Liberalism." These calls are not for a change in human nature, but for a cultivation of an understanding and appreciation of how a change in the rules that govern social intercourse can channel our behavior into productive and peaceful interactions.
3. The anti-globalization movement of the 2000s and the Occupy Wall Street protests in the wake of the global financial crisis of 2008 reflect the populist left, while the rise of the paleoconservatives, paleolibertarians, and economic nationalist segments of the alt-right movement represent the populist right. I am leaving out of the discussion the odious racial politics that is also intermingled here in the populist discussions in the United States and in Europe concerning immigration, refugees, and public policy.
4. I still find one of the most persuasive statements of the underlying attitudes of a liberal society to be Steve Macedo's *Liberal Virtues* (1990), and of the institutional

infrastructure that might follow to be Chandran Kukathas, *The Liberal Archipelago* (2003). The cultivating of mutual respect and dignity accorded to each that a liberal order must entail does, as my colleague Tyler Cowen argued in *Creative Destruction* (2002), turn on the homogeneity of some beliefs at the rules level of analysis, while the celebration of heterogeneity does at the within-rules level. It is a question ultimately of the relevant margins that operationalize cosmopolitan liberalism.

5. The work of my colleague Virgil Storr (2008) has developed this core thesis of liberal political economy in new and fascinating ways, and in the process drawing our methodological and analytical attention to foundational issues in the cultural science. See also Storr (2012).

6. See Boettke (2012); Boettke, Haeffele, and Storr (2016); and Mitchell and Boettke (2017).

7. The liberal vision is often misunderstood even by extremely intelligent folks, such as Samuel Freedman (2001) and Jeffrey Sachs (2012). Deirdre McCloskey has done great work in trying to set the record on liberalism straight, but all of us scholars within this tradition must take it upon ourselves to ensure that liberalism is able to be easily understood by folks such as Freedman and Sachs. For a critique of what I call the error of "litmus test" libertarianism, see note 1.

8. Among contemporary liberal political economists, Christopher Coyne's work on military affairs is in my opinion the most insightful. See Coyne (2008, 2013) and Coyne and Hall (2018).

9. The bumping-into-neighbors metaphor is from Schmidtz's (2006) brilliant *Elements of Justice*, as is the essential issue of the right to say NO to offered terms of exchange.

10. James Buchanan has shown that the "general welfare" approach to public policy is a nonsensical one throughout his career, beginning in 1949 with his first critique of the "fiscal brain."

11. The troubling issues are the social ills that plague human interactions, such as poverty, ignorance, and squalor. But the troubling issue in designing the framework is the potential for the powerful to exert their influence over the powerless and establish rules that provide them with a permanent advantage. So both "within any system" and "about any system" of governance we face tradeoffs of eliciting agreement and curbing political externalities. If our liberal system of government is to institutionalize our basic human equality in our ways of relating, then it must be designed so that neither discrimination nor dominion is permitted. Various classic works in the analytical tradition of political economy from a liberal perspective have tackled different aspects of these puzzles starting, of course, with F. A. Hayek, *The Constitution of Liberty* (1960); Buchanan and Tullock, *The Calculus of Consent* (1962); Ostrom, *The Meaning of Democracy and the Vulnerability of Democracies* (1997); and Munger, *Choosing in Groups* (2015).

12. See Boettke (2016) for a discussion of the interplay between Smithian and Schumpeterian forces for optimism and the stupidity of the governmental habit of obstructing the free flow of labor and capital and stifling entrepreneurial creativity and initiative. See also Coyne and Hall (2018).

References

Boettke, Peter J. 2012. *Living Economics*. Guatemala City: Universidad Francisco Marroquín.

———. 2016. "Pessimistically Optimistic." *The Independent Review* 20 (3): 343–46.

———. 2017. "True Liberalism Is About Human Compassion." Foundation for Economic Education, Atlanta, November 10.

Boettke, Peter J., Stefanie Haeffele, and Virgil Henry Storr, eds. 2016. *Mainline Economics: Six Nobel Lectures in the Tradition of Adam Smith*. Arlington, VA: Mercatus Center at George Mason University.

Buchanan, James M. 1949. "The Pure Theory of Government Finance: A Suggested Approach." *Journal of Political Economy* 57 (6): 496–505.

———. 2000. "The Soul of Classical Liberalism." *The Independent Review* 5 (1): 111–19.

Buchanan, James M., and Gordon Tullock. 1962. *The Calculus of Consent: Logical Foundations of Constitutional Democracy*. Ann Arbor: University of Michigan Press.

Cowen, Tyler. 2002. *Creative Destruction: How Globalization Is Changing the World's Cultures*. Princeton, NJ: Princeton University Press.

Coyne, Christopher J. 2008. *After War: The Political Economy of Exporting Democracy*. Stanford, CA: Stanford University Press.

———. 2013. *Doing Bad by Doing Good: Why Humanitarian Action Fails*. Stanford, CA: Stanford University Press.

Coyne, Christopher J., and Abigail R. Hall. 2018. *Tyranny Comes Home: The Domestic Fate of U.S. Militarism*. Stanford, CA: Stanford University Press.

Freedman, Samuel. 2001. "Illiberal Libertarians: Why Libertarianism Is Not a Liberal View." *Philosophy and Public Affairs* 30 (2): 105–51.

Frey, Bruno S. 2001. "A Utopia? A Government without Territorial Monopoly." *Journal of Institutional and Theoretical Economics* 157 (1): 162–75.

Hayek, F. A. [1940] 2010. "Individualism: True and False." in *The Collected Works of F. A. Hayek*. Volume 13: *Studies on the Abuse and Decline of Reason*, edited by Bruce Caldwell, 46–76. Chicago: University of Chicago Press.

———. 1944. *The Road to Serfdom*. Chicago: University of Chicago Press.

———. 1949. "The Intellectuals and Socialism." *University of Chicago Law Review* 16 (3): 417–33.

———. 1960. *The Constitution of Liberty*. Chicago: University of Chicago Press.

———. [1974] 1989. "The Pretence of Knowledge." *American Economic Review* 79 (6): 3–7.

———. 1979. *Law, Legislation and Liberty*. Volume 3: *The Political Order of a Free People*. Chicago: University of Chicago Press.

———. 1988. *The Collected Works of F. A. Hayek*. Volume 1: *The Fatal Conceit: The Errors of Socialism*, edited by W. W. Bartley III. Chicago: University of Chicago Press.

Kukathas, Chandran. 2003. *The Liberal Archipelago: A Theory of Diversity and Freedom*. Oxford: Oxford University Press.

Leeson, Peter T. 2014. *Anarchy Unbound: Why Self-Governance Works Better than You Think.* New York: Cambridge University Press.

Levy, David M., and Sandra J. Peart. 2017. *Escape from Democracy: The Role of Experts and the Public in Economic Policy.* New York: Cambridge University Press.

Macedo, Stephen. 1990. *Liberal Virtues: Citizenship, Virtue and Community in Liberal Constitutionalism.* Oxford: Oxford University Press.

McCloskey, Deirdre N. 2006. *The Bourgeois Virtues: Ethics for an Age of Commerce.* Chicago: University of Chicago Press.

———. 2010. *Bourgeois Dignity: Why Economics Can't Explain the Modern World.* Chicago: University of Chicago Press.

———. 2016. *Bourgeois Equality: How Ideas, Not Capital or Institutions, Enriched the World.* Chicago: University of Chicago Press.

Mises, Ludwig von. [1927] 1985. *Liberalism: The Classical Tradition.* Irvington-on-Hudson, NY: Foundation for Economic Education.

———. [1949] 1998. *Human Action.* Auburn, AL: Ludwig von Mises Institute.

Mitchell, Matthew D., and Peter J. Boettke. 2017. *Applied Mainline Economics: Bridging the Gap between Theory and Public Policy.* Arlington, VA: Mercatus Center at George Mason University.

Mokyr, Joel. 2016. *A Culture of Growth: The Origins of the Modern Economy.* Princeton, NJ: Princeton University Press.

Munger, Michael C. 2015. *Choosing in Groups: Analytical Politics Revisited.* Cambridge: Cambridge University Press.

Ostrom, Vincent. [1973] 1989. *The Intellectual Crisis in American Public Administration.* Tuscaloosa: University of Alabama Press.

———. 1997. *The Meaning of Democracy and the Vulnerability of Democracies: A Response to Tocqueville's Challenge.* Ann Arbor: University of Michigan Press.

Sachs, Jeffrey. 2012. "Libertarian Illusions." *Huffington Post,* January 15.

Schmidtz, David. 2006. *The Elements of Justice.* Cambridge: Cambridge University Press.

Smith, Adam. 1776. *An Inquiry into the Nature and Causes of the Wealth of Nations.* London: Routledge and Sons.

Stringham, Edward Peter. 2015. *Private Governance: Creating Order in Economic and Social Life.* New York: Oxford University Press.

Storr, Virgil Henry. 2008. "The Market as a Social Space: On the Meaningful Extra-economic Conversations That Can Occur in Markets." *Review of Austrian Economics* 21 (2/3): 135–50.

———. 2012. *Understanding the Culture of Markets.* Volume 31, *Routledge Foundations of the Market Economy,* edited by Mario J. Rizzo and Lawrence H. White. New York: Routledge.

Chapter 14

The Reception of Free to Choose and the Problem of the Tacit Presuppositions of Political Economy

I t is hard for today's students to appreciate the economic reality of the late 1970s, an economic reality of high unemployment, high inflation, and general economic malaise. This situation was true not only for the Rust Belt sections of the US economy, such as Pittsburgh's steel industry or Detroit's automobile industry, but also for the coal and energy industries as well as industrial manufacturing in general, all of which were in decline. This sense of economic malaise and political turmoil was not isolated to the United States. The United Kingdom was experiencing decades of economic decline, as well as social disruption due to strikes and violence. And the world learned of economic, political, and human rights crises throughout Latin America and Africa. India and China continued to languish in extreme poverty. The economies in Eastern and Central Europe and the former Soviet Union were also stagnating and falling behind even the stalling economies of the mature Western democracies of France and Germany. Economic malaise and political turmoil were a global phenomenon of the 1970s and early 1980s. Milton Friedman and Rose Friedman sought to explain the reasons for this sad economic reality with special reference to the public policy discussions in the United States.

Milton and Rose were veterans of both the scientific contestation in the economics discipline and the general clash of ideas among the intelligentsia and the public policy community. *Capitalism and Freedom* (1962) was an international best seller, and Milton Friedman's columns in *Newsweek* as well as elsewhere—including numerous appearances on TV and radio—made

---

Revised version of presentation at a special meeting of the Mont Pelerin Society at the Hoover Institution, Stanford University, January 2020.

him by the late 1970s perhaps the most recognized economist in all of the United States, and perhaps the world. His 1976 Nobel Prize, of course, also solidified his reputation in the public imagination. In fact, it is perhaps no exaggeration to say that other than John Maynard Keynes, no economist in the 20th century achieved simultaneous scientific and public acclaim as did Milton Friedman. And Friedman, who obviously possessed a sharp analytical mind, was gifted with a quick wit and a charming personality, which made him such an engaging guest on TV, from the *Phil Donahue Show* to *Book Talk* on C-SPAN. Others are not so gifted. This rare set of gifts I will return to at the end of this chapter.

My central thesis concerns the concept of the "tacit presuppositions of political economy" that are held at any specific historical epoch. Thomas Sowell has brilliantly worked with the idea of "visions"—in particular the constrained versus unconstrained vision—but this is a slightly different idea. Joseph Schumpeter had also earlier contrasted "vision" with "analysis," and insisted that while in science and scholarship we judge contributions mainly by critical examination of analysis (logical and empirical), there is a vital place in science and scholarship for recognizing vision as the essential preanalytic cognitive act that provides the questions for us to ask, and the raw material from which we commence our analysis.

But even here, the concept of "tacit presuppositions" is slightly different. The concept comes from James M. Buchanan, and it relates to the unquestioned lived reality of the relevant population under investigation[1]—what they "take for granted" to be the reality of the situation. It is this "taken for granted" that determines how new ideas are heard, received, understood, and reacted to. Wresting control of that "taken for granted" and in the process shifting the "tacit presuppositions of political economy" was Milton and Rose Friedman's great gift, and *Free to Choose* (1980) is a perfect illustration.

John Stuart Mill, in an essay on the "Claims of Labour" in 1845, postulated that when ideas are introduced without the appropriate circumstances, they just fade into the background, and when circumstances arise but there is a lack of ideas to frame and guide the moment, opportunities for change will be missed. *But* when the right ideas meet up with the appropriate circumstances, social change can be rapid and decisive. The Friedmans make a similar claim about the "tide of opinion" and how that must precede the shift in policy. Policy ideas which are considered outside the bounds of the reasonable in one era will be considered commonsensical in another era, depending on the shift in the tide of opinion. "A tide of opinion," they write, "once it flows strongly, tends to sweep over all obstacles, all contrary views. Equally, when it has crested and a contrary tide sets in, that too tends to flow strongly" (1980, 272).

Textbook economic models often work best when unique individuals are minimized in their influence on outcomes. That makes analytic sense as the focus is on market theory and the price system. But as various theoretical conundrums that have been exposed in basic theory, this analytical move has a cost—namely, the loss of our ability to understand market makers and trendsetters, in other words, the entrepreneur as the prime mover in the competitive market process. In our understanding of the history of social change, I would argue, we make a similar mistake if we discount the power of specific individuals and focus instead on abstract ideas and momentary circumstances. In the clash of ideas just as in the contestation of the market, there are pivotal people at pivotal times.

Milton Friedman was such a pivotal person, and he changed the world because of it. He was able to do that because his unique talents enabled him to wrest control of the "tacit presuppositions of political economy" of a historical era, and as Andrei Shleifer (2009) summarized as "The Age of Milton Friedman," which he dates from 1980 to 2005. That era, Shleifer adds, was characterized by a sharp rise in global living standards, while by all statistical indicators, life expectancy, educational attainment, and the establishment of democracy improved across the globe, and absolute poverty declined globally. That there is a dispute about this, I would argue, is one of the strongest pieces of evidence in favor of the power of the concept of "tacit presuppositions of political economy."

This chapter will proceed as follows. Section 2 will discuss the reception of *Free to Choose* in real time circa 1980–1982 prior to Friedman successfully shifting the tide of opinion. I focus on reviews by Robert Heilbroner and Kenneth Arrow in an effort to capture the tacit presuppositions of political economy that were in place in the post–World War II period that Friedman had to buck up against throughout his scientific career and in his career as a public intellectual. Section 3 will discuss Friedman's wresting control of the tacit presuppositions and the global impact of that, first with the reforms in China (Deng Xiaoping), Britain (Margaret Thatcher), and the United States (Ronald Reagan), followed by the collapse of communism in Eastern and Central Europe and the former Soviet Union, and finally the reforms among the Nordic countries, as well as India, East Asia, Latin America, and Africa.

The ideas in *Free to Choose* concerning the power of the market and the tyranny of controls spread throughout the globe, and a new era of economic freedom and international commerce lifted mankind to new heights of improvement in living standards and provided the "great escape" from poverty. It is a fact that must always be acknowledged when debating the merits of this era of globalization that in 2015, for the first time in human history, less than 10 percent of the world's population was living on less than $2 per day. This decline in extreme poverty in absolute terms must never been forgotten as we contemplate the human condition. But it is also not the end of the story, as I will discuss in section 4, because our era faces different challenges, and those "tacit presuppositions in political economy" have once more shifted due to discontent with globalization, the consequences of the global financial crisis, and concerns with inequality and injustice. This challenge is a significant one for those of us influenced by the ideas in *Free to Choose* as educators, as scholars, and as citizens. After discussing these challenges, I will conclude the chapter with a reminder of the main lessons from *Free to Choose* and a call to embrace the radical liberalism of F. A. Hayek, Milton Friedman, and James Buchanan by adopting its core principles for our age.

Reception of Free to Choose

Both *Capitalism and Freedom* (1962) and *Free to Choose* (1980) were in the same intellectual tradition as Hayek's *The Road to Serfdom* (1944) and *The Constitution of Liberty* (1960). As such, these were foundational texts of the intellectual motive forces of the Mont Pelerin Society. *Capitalism and Freedom* sold over half a million copies in the English-language edition and was translated into 18 different languages. The *Times Literary Supplement* rated it one of the 100 most influential books since World War II. *Free to Choose* was the best-selling nonfiction book of 1980, and was subsequently translated into over 20 languages throughout the world. And the TV series *Free to Choose* introduced these ideas to multiple generations through PBS distribution and later classroom use by professors.

Reception studies is an emerging discipline in intellectual history. I am not claiming to do a full "reception study" of *Free to Choose*, but instead a very select analysis to stress this point about the "tacit presuppositions of political economy." To do so, I will look at some highly select reviews to demonstrate the intellectual consensus that the Friedmans were challenging and to which they effectively countered and reversed. I have selected to highlight Robert Heilbroner's review in the *New York Review of Books* entitled "The Road to Selfdom," Kenneth Arrow's review in the *New Republic*, and Christopher Lehmann-Haupt's review in the *New York Times*. I will also point to the professional consensus within economics circa 1980, as reflected in the review in the *Journal of Economic Literature*.

The key issue to keep in mind, as the Friedmans themselves stress, is how the Great Depression framed the discussion in the minds of the intellectual class. I would also add that the previous era of late-19th-century capitalism, and the first 15 years of the 20th century, and the concern with monopoly, the exploitation of the workers, the disregard for the health of consumers, and the general sense of economic and political injustice permeated the discussion among intellectuals and policymakers. Some of these concerns with laissez-faire capitalism can be factually contested, and in fact have been by a variety of economists and historians, but that is different from wresting control of the tacit presuppositions. As I will stress throughout this essay, in our discussions over the power of ideas and lived historical experience, we are always dealing with a problematic past and a troubling present. How scholars and intellectuals learn to disentangle the various causes from the obvious correlations and use sound theory to get the factual record straight is always one of the most difficult and treacherous tasks of the social scientists. But it is a task we must undertake if we hope to improve our understanding of the human condition.

This is particularly true if we remember, as Hayek taught us, that economics is a uniquely *human science*, where we are what we study, and thus our purposes, plans, expectations, and actions make up our subject, and the object of our efforts must be primarily to render intelligible in terms of human purposes the social phenomena we purport to study, such as the marketplace. This means, as Hayek stressed, the facts of the social sciences are what people believe and think them to be. Thus, while framing effects are vital in all scientific and scholarly endeavors, they become that much more critical in the human sciences. As Fritz Machlup once put it, economics is a science just like the natural sciences except that in the economist's case "matter can talk." As we study the molecules and postulate the underlying principles of their motion and interaction, they speak back to us, and loudly if we care to listen. We are privileged as it were to be in this situation. The chemist or the physicist isn't so lucky to have this direct access to intentionality and thus the ultimate causal factor in their analysis of phenomena.

If all facts are theory impregnated as this implies, then all interpretations will be slanted in this or that direction, requiring us to be very careful with our logic in our theoretical constructions and transparent with our data analysis. Clarity of exposition actually takes on a moral imperative in the human sciences if progress is going to be made, and strict rules of engagement must be adhered to otherwise the clash of ideas will result, not in a new consensus, but in the rather unproductive exercise of cataloging arguments as right, left, or center. Part of the motivation of Friedman's insistence that there aren't any schools of economic thought, but instead only "good economics" and "bad economics" was to overcome this tendency to catalog one another rather than engage one another.

But finding the best terms of engagements is often easier said than done. One key idea can be attributed to Max Weber, who seemed to be faced with impossible barriers to conversation within the German academy. He suggested a simple rule of thumb: scholars should restrict their analysis to the logical coherence and empirical consequences of the use of certain chosen means for the attainment of given ends from the point of view of the advocate of those ends. In other words, scholars do not debate ends, but only the relative effectiveness of various means to the achievement of those ends. This was the path toward *positive analysis*, and enabled scholars to escape the endless quarrel over normative goals in social arrangements and public policy. In this way, social science could strive for objectivity in analysis, and thus be of service to mankind as a tool for social understanding, and as a critical guide in public policy.

It is not my purpose to enter into a long discussion of methodology of the social sciences by stressing both subjectivism and value-free analysis, but I thought it was important to put forward only because Friedman always couched his policy discussion in terms of value freedom. His goal was to demonstrate that the frustration with various public policies was not because the intentions were unworthy. To the contrary, these public policy intentions were most worthy, but ill served by the policy means chosen to achieve those ends. I will come back to this shortly, but first let me just say that this emphasis on unintended consequences (both good and bad) was a major stumbling block in the real-time reception of *Free to Choose*. The book was a challenge to perceived aspirations of the New Deal and the Great Society not so much in terms of their aspirations for the public good, but for the inability of the chosen policy path to achieve that public good. Intentions, the Friedmans argued, were not the same thing as achieving, and that is disturbing to the sensibilities of those who believe they have devised the right policy to fix the serious problems that have been identified. And, in fact, the Friedmans' challenge was often harsher than mere ineffectiveness, but that the policies chosen actually exacerbated the social problem. Such a conclusion surely had to be incredulous.

Christopher Lehmann-Haupt (1980) begins his *New York Times* review with a note that the Friedmans are part of a "small but preserving band of spokesmen who have adhered to the tenets of free enterprise ever since, and despite, the coming of the New Deal." In contrast to the teachings of Adam Smith and the contemporary doctrines of free enterprise, Lehmann-Haupt informs his readers that those of us "who have been raised at the foot of the New Deal have been taught that the manipulations of Adam Smith's invisible hand were not always so benign—that ever since the Industrial Revolution began, the invisible hand produced a minority of victims—the young, the old, the sick, the uneducated—which became a majority with the coming of the Great Depression of the 1930s." He then pronounces simply that the "Friedmans pronounce this view of history a myth."

After summarizing the argument in *Free to Choose*, Lehmann-Haupt states that perhaps "10 or 20 years ago such arguments would be greeted by the public with all the seriousness reserved for a pamphlet picked up at Knott's Berry Farm."[2] But he quickly adds that today (circa 1980), it is obvious that the arguments found in *Free to Choose* have a "great deal going for them" in this historical context, and that he expects that the Friedmans will "open the debate." The position laid out in *Free to Choose*, Lehmann-Haupt states unequivocally, can no longer be seen as some minority view.

In contrast, both Arrow (1980) and Heilbroner (1980) inform their readers that the Friedmans are incapable of presenting both sides of an argument. Heilbroner, unlike the *New York Times* review, starts by telling his readers that a "large number of people are yearning to hear" the message the Friedmans have to offer. The resentment that was once directed at Big Business is now directed at Big Government. Thus, *Free to Choose* is a book in tune with the times "whether the arguments and diagnoses are cogent or not." There are few among its potential readers, Heilbroner opines, who will be willing to mull over the arguments presented, and instead will unfortunately take what the Friedmans have to say as a matter of faith. And Milton and Rose Friedman will not disappoint the faithful, as their argument on first read will appear to be one of "overwhelming logic" and "unanswerable evidence." The case made for the Smithian market and Jeffersonian government is completely convincing *until* one considers what is left out of the narrative constructed throughout *Free to Choose*. The Friedmans present only a one-sided argument and leave out any nuance and qualifications that would muddy the presentation. This tactic, Heilbroner argues, is so frustrating and disingenuous that reasonable critics are reduced to the position of just throwing up their hands, no room for reasoned discussion being left.

Rather than the history the Friedmans tell, what if, Heilbroner insists, we follow the great social theorists of capitalism such as Karl Polanyi and recognize that the capitalist system was not grounded in voluntary choices and mutual benefit. Instead, the modern capitalist system was a "product of a violent process of social displacement." Economists like the Friedmans can talk all they want about productive specialization and peaceful social cooperation in theory, but the capitalist reality is one of an "unstable and unwelcome structure of social and economic relationships." Capitalist society is far more dynamic and disruptive than the Friedmans want their readers to see, and they also smuggle in moral judgments without being explicit in their introduction, according to Heilbroner. Due to disproportionate distributions of power in society, the simplistic voluntary-exchange model conceals the need for countervailing forces in relations between management and labor, and between business and society if we hope to achieve a humane society. This is particularly damaging in the Friedmans' discussion of equality, which in the end, Heilbroner says, violates our sense of justice and violates modern conventions. Heilbroner sums up his opinion of the book as follows: "*Free to Choose* is to serious economic and political debate what fundamentalist preaching is to Bible scholarship."

Sadly, I would argue that Arrow's review is even harsher in its assessment. Arrow's first complaint is that the Friedmans nowhere elaborate the costs associated with following their path to policy change given the current status quo, nor do they admit the possibilities of negative consequences that might follow in the wake of the adoption of their proposals. Arrow seems to imply that true professional economists have a moral responsibility to the public to be more circumspect and evenhanded in their presentation. The fact that the Friedmans do not is grounds for serious doubt in the exercise.[3]

Furthermore, Arrow insists to his readers that they recognize that the Friedmans do not rely on the libertarian principles of justice and political economy one might find in say Robert Nozick's *Anarchy, State, and Utopia*, so their case must rely on *economic reasoning*. *Free to Choose* does not contain a deontological case for freedom, but a utilitarian-consequentialist argument. But Arrow is quick to point out, such an argumentative basis is a far weaker defense of laissez-faire. "They are also aware," Arrow writes, "that economic theory shows that the market cannot always be successful achieving efficiency" (1980, 26). Externalities, public goods, monopoly power, macroeconomic instability, inequality, all ensure that markets fail to achieve ideal levels of efficiency in exchange and in production.

The various intellectual gymnastics that the Friedmans engage in to make their argument about the power of the market and the tyranny of controls, Arrow tells his readers, is littered with instances of fallacious argument making *Free to Choose* a "textbook example of false logical reasoning" and their lack of concern with questions of the distribution of income appears as "heartless" (27). Lacking in logic and in compassion, unfortunately, the Friedmans also engage in a "cavalier" reading of economic history in the effort to make their case. Another serious flaw is that the work makes "no reference to the social reality of classes" except to indict the "new class" of bureaucrats, academics, and journalists who benefit from government largesse. All the time making this argument, the Friedmans appear completely unconcerned with the dysfunctions in the market and in politics that result from concentrations in wealth. Arrow, in fact, uses the example of the Friedmans' skepticism toward government funding of science and their championing of private philanthropy and flips the argument, suggesting that private donors of science will bias the research in the interest of the donor rather than the pursuit of truth.

Overall, Arrow ends his review of *Free to Choose* stating clearly that he was disappointed by the lack of a guiding principle to public policy deliberations, a failure to consider the costs of policy changes being proposed, and the one-sided selection of arguments and evidence in the presentation. In short, while there is value to be found in the Friedmans' "itemization of government failures: industrial regulation that is primarily in the interests of the special interest groups regulated, inefficient post offices, disappointing schools, welfare 'messes,' the failure of public housing," this does not follow from their presentation of economic principles or the broad sweep of history that they provide (28). One must remember, Arrow states, that there is a long list of social problems related to the free market that *Free to Choose* simply fails to wrestle with. Though he doesn't explicitly say it, readers could easily be excused if the main takeaway from the review they got was that the book simply cannot be trusted, and as such, should be dismissed rather than debated.

I have belabored these reviews because they speak to the difficulties of getting the basic message the Friedmans want to offer to the intelligentsia of 1980. Their tacit presuppositions of political economy were just so at odds. For example, in Arrow's litany of social problems, he lists questions about consumer lack of knowledge and labor's weak bargaining power, and the claim, remember, is that the Friedmans supposedly do not address these issues. Yet any close reading of *Free to Choose* would see immediately that these are central questions raised and answered in chapter 7 ("Who Protects the Consumer?") and chapter 8 ("Who Protects the Worker?").

Moreover, starting with the introduction, the Friedmans constantly remind their readers that perfection in human affairs is simply not an option; we must face not only past imperfections, but future imperfections. There is no Dr. Pangloss in the Friedmans' view of capitalism. As they state, "In an imperfect world there were still many evils" (1980, xviii). The idea was to find a set of institutions that would disperse power, rather than concentrate it, and would minimize the downside risk of the imperfections of this world. There was a danger to strong government in terms of freedom and prosperity, and the checks on guaranteeing that only the "right people" would be in charge of that strong government were not as robust as wishful thinking had hoped. Wishful thinking is no substitute for hard-nosed analysis in political economy.

The tensions in the liberal project, and the costs and benefits of social change, are stated clearly and weighed throughout—from the introduction to the conclusion in *Free to Choose*.[4] Arrow just doesn't find the Friedmans' analysis persuasive, but that isn't how he argues. Instead, Arrow wants to insist that the Friedmans don't address these fundamental social questions. Why? It is my hypothesis that Arrow doesn't engage in the "reasonable individuals of good faith can disagree" sort of dialogue with the Friedmans because he cannot see their answers as ones within the reasonable set of possible answers to these serious social questions. The "taken for granted" bounds of reasonable opinion were established by Arrow in the post–World War II consensus, and the Friedmans are challenging that consensus.[5]

Wresting Control of Tacit Presuppositions

One must remember that *Free to Choose* is really the persistent and consistent application of basic economic reasoning to analyze the consequences of changes in public policy on the performance of the economy. The book building on *Capitalism and Freedom* also develops the argument about the interrelationship between economic and political freedom. The biggest differences in the central argument between the 1962 book and the 1980 book are the addition in the latter of ideas developed by F. A. Hayek on the nature of the price system and spontaneous order, and ideas developed by James Buchanan on the economic analysis of politics, or what came to be known as public choice and constitutional political economy. But boiled down to its bare essentials, the Friedmans are simply asking that public policies be incentive compatible with basic economic motivations. Asking policy proposals to not require mythical beings populating the world for the policies to yield the results desired is not too big a logical leap.

And the reality is that when the Friedmans sat down to write *Free to Choose*, the stagnation and economic malaise were the reality that all were experiencing. Slowing growth and declining productivity raised doubt that private initiative could continue to overcome the dysfunctions caused by an overgoverned society. We were trapped in the unenviable situation where government grew because it failed, and it was continually failing because it was growing in scale and scope over the economic life of the people. The Friedmans were warning their audience that this growth of government and the politicization of our lives would eventually destroy both our prosperity and our freedom. Whereas Adam Smith taught us that individuals pursuing their own self-interest within a system of property, contract, and consent could promote the general interest in society, the experience in the 30-year period following World War II demonstrated that "individuals who intend only to promote the general interest are led by the invisible political hand to promote a special interest that they had no intention to promote" (Friedman and Friedman 1980, 281). Something had to change.

Free to Choose provides the reader with some suggested constitutional changes that would in principle guarantee our economic and political liberties. But in following through consistently with their approach, the clash of ideas must be engaged first and the tide of opinion must be decisively turned. Milton and Rose Friedman believed that people were "waking up" and that individuals are "recognizing the dangers of an overgoverned society, coming to understand that good objectives can be perverted by bad means, that reliance on the freedom of people to control their own lives in accordance with their own values is the surest way to achieve the full potential of a great society" (297).

The Friedmans were champions of clarity of exposition, so their argument is not too hard for anyone to hear, but as we have seen, it was much more difficult to actually be listened to. Over the next decades, the Friedmans' message not only would be heard but would be listened to—from China, the United Kingdom, and the United States to throughout the entire globe. Both *Capitalism and Freedom* and *Free to Choose* would influence political leaders and finance ministers, as well as dissidents and community activists to challenge the monopoly of power held by governments from the big debate over capitalism versus socialism to the smaller debate about public school versus choice in education. The direct and indirect influence Friedman exerted throughout the globe during the 1980–2005 period is simply staggering (see Boettke 2004; Shleifer 2009).

Bob McTeer, former head of the Dallas Fed, summarized the impact of Milton Friedman as follows:

> Friedman recognizes the power of the invisible hand of free enterprise to create wealth and jobs, while warning that the heavy hand of government will bring nothing but stagnation. He has argued for a monetary policy to stabilize prices and keep inflation low. Most important, Friedman has made economics a moral matter as well as one of productivity, jobs, and growth. Economic freedom, he reminds us, is every bit as precious as the other freedoms we treasure. (2004, ix)

During the period between 1962 and 1980, one can see slow but persistent changes in the standard textbooks in economics where Friedman's ideas are presented to students from the elementary to the advanced level. The Keynesian consensus breaks down in theory and practice, and central planning is rejected as a guiding principle for developed and developing economies.

The tacit presuppositions of political economy by 1990 decidedly shifted away from the taken-for-granted notions of inefficiency, instability, and injustice

of capitalism to one that saw capitalism as the creative force behind wealth creation and the tearing down of monopolistic privilege through entrepreneurial
innovation. Socialist presumptions that had so influenced what intellectuals
believed from the late 19th and most of the 20th century were pushed into the
background during the age of Milton Friedman. It would be difficult for me to
argue that they disappeared, as the resentment toward the bourgeois class and
the fear of market exploitation and market instability were omnipresent in the
educational establishment, as well as in popular culture. It remained the case
that the greatest fear of capitalism was mass unemployment, and the greatest
resentment of capitalism was the idle rich. It was just that the typical answers
that were given ever since the Great Depression were worn-out explanations,
and the contending perspectives of monetary mischief by central banks were
treated as worthy hypotheses to be reckoned with in empirical investigation
of macroeconomic volatility and economic growth.

There was during the 1960s and 1970s a renewed appreciation for the
power of the market and the dysfunctions of political intervention in the
market with respect to wage and price controls, industrial organization and
antitrust, and social programs and fiscal responsibility. In many ways by
the late 1980s, all of Milton Friedman's basic ideas with respect to public
policy and the power of markets and the tyranny of controls were accepted
as within the realm of reasonable opinion. And the seismic changes that
took place in the 1980s culminating in the collapse of communism and the
transition to capitalism must never be understated. Friedman's ideas were
influencing public discourse and policy initiatives from China to Estonia,
and from the Nordic countries to Latin America.

But as the 1990s progressed and the difficulties of postcommunism
became more obvious, Friedman himself began to question the lesson to
be learned from this experience. First, he stressed that while he sincerely
believed that, in the realm of ideas, the basic Smithian program he presented
had won the day based on impeccable logic and unimpeachable evidence,
he did admit that market-oriented thinkers of the conservative and classical liberal variety had often lost the battle of public policy implementation.
This was critical because lesson number one in public policy was to adopt
incentive-compatible policies, but lesson number two was to pursue incentive-
compatible strategies for the implementation of strategies.

As Dennis Robertson wrote years earlier, if for our explanations in
political economy we rely on the benevolence of the actors to achieve the

outcomes, we will both be left waiting forever to achieve the desired outcomes, and exhaust the benevolence that actors actually have in their possession in the futile effort to achieve those outcomes. Alternatively, rather
than requiring sacrificial beings, if we instead rely on the ordinary motives
of men and women and seek ways to align incentives in a way where doing
good is consistent with achieving good, we avoid those situations where we
end up doing bad by doing good (see Coyne 2013). If we align incentives
right, then we can escape the dysfunctions of the overgoverned society and
realize the "Good Society" that Walter Lippmann, F. A. Hayek, and Milton
Friedman all talked about. But by failing to win the day on implementation,
the contradictions and conflicts of the transition period have come to define
the experience of the 1980–2005 era as much as the great growth in wealth
and generalized prosperity.

Real existing capitalism does exhibit cronyism as well as creative destruction. That empirical reality in the 2000s created impressions and issues in
sustaining the control over the tacit presuppositions of political economy
along the lines the Friedmans fought so hard to pull in their direction. This
was solidified after the global financial crisis in 2008, and the policy responses
followed over the past decade in response. Those in politically privileged
positions were presumed to be bailed out, while those who lacked political
privilege access were left to fend for themselves in the hypercompetitive
world of global capitalism. The tacit presuppositions reversed back, I am
arguing, to the pre–*Free to Choose* era, and that presents the challenge we
must all face today.

The Challenge of Our Age

As a 19-year-old in my second year of college, but repeating my freshman
year over, I was exposed to economics. The year was 1979. What was my
experience with the world, not on the blackboard, but out the window? First,
the 1970s were difficult times economically and politically. Prior to my teens,
I did experience the turbulent times of the 1960s, but as a child would. I grew
up in the suburbs just outside of Newark, New Jersey, and my grandparents
lived close to Asbury Park down at the Jersey Shore.

My youth saw friends' older brothers sent off to fight in Vietnam, others
who missed the draft because of college deferment, and many older siblings
that started to question the entire purpose of the Vietnam War and the social

conventions of their parents. Watergate followed, and Nixon, Ford, and then Carter were objects of ridicule more so than symbols of leadership and hope. The images, for good or bad, from my youth are of Nixon saying, "I am not a crook" and his flying off in the helicopter after he was forced out of office in disgrace; of Ford, a former All-American college athlete, stumbling down the stairs of Air Force One; and Carter appearing on TV in a cardigan sweater invoking the Boy Scouts to check the thermostat in your home so as not to waste natural gas. Seriously, that happened! Combine that with a stagnating economy with high unemployment, with inflation, and with long lines to get gasoline.

When I sat in economics class and was introduced to basic supply and demand, it was as if I had been given a magic set of eyeglasses that now allowed me to see the world as it was and it gave me a sense at the ripe old age of 19 that I was starting to understand how the world worked. My "taken for granted" presuppositions were forged in a world where New York City was bankrupt, where the US economy was stagnant, and our politicians were corrupt at worst and buffoons at best. Communism did not offer an alternative as they cheated in sports, and were led by an old and decrepit cadre starting with Brezhnev.

Just as described by the Friedmans, the world in which I was educated in economics was the opposite of the world that Depression-era college students experienced. The intellectuals educated in the 1900–1950 period saw monopoly exploitation, financial speculation lead to ruin, mass unemployment, and gross social injustice. I saw those things as well; but rather than seeing the source as emanating from the acts of voluntary market exchange, I came to see them as the natural by-product of government policies that produced perverse incentives and distorted signals, and that when studied in-depth favored particular groups at the expense of others. Between 1979 and 1999, my studies and my experiences reinforced these priors. It was my taken-for-granted picture of the world. The Friedmans helped produce that, but they were not alone, and they were certainly aided in that framing by the lived reality of economic and political life both in the United States and abroad.

When I started teaching economics, most of my students had that same experience. I taught my first classes on my own in 1985, and the youngest person in that class would have been born around 1968. When I moved to George Mason University in 1998, my youngest students would have been born around 1980. They had all witnessed in their lives the collapse of communism, the birth of democratic countries, and the economic wealth created by globalization. But by 2008, those students were born around 1990, and their taken-for-granted background had shifted. They grew up during the era of tensions in the Middle East, the difficulties with postcommunism, the protests against globalization, and a growing concern with climate change. What they don't have is any lived memory of the failure of communism and the hope of postcommunism.

Fast forward to 2019, and those students were born around 2002. What they know is not the shock of 9/11, but the experience of a permanent war economy. They were coming of age intellectually when the global financial crisis hit, and more accurately after the narratives about that crisis were formed. This current generation—at least some of them—have grown up believing that wealth is ill-gotten due to privilege or pure random luck, that the wealthy are too myopic to consider the future costs of irreversible climate change, that markets are plagued by inefficiency, instability, and injustice. The global financial crisis in immediate impact might have been closer to the 1970s stagnation than the 1930s financial ruin, but a decade later and the impact on those "tacit presuppositions of political economy" is in fact closer to the 1930s.

The Friedmans had a framework for understanding why the promise of the 1980s gave way to the frustrations experienced with stalled and failed reforms in their book *The Tyranny of the Status Quo* (1984). The great awakening to the dangers of overgoverned society was only an idea awakening, but the reality of political change means defeating the "iron triangle" of interests that form during the period of government growth and benefit from the existing political arrangement (1984, 165ff). Unfortunately, their work on the frustrations with market reforms did not resonate with readers as their earlier work did. The cronyism of the capitalism that the current generation of youth identifies with the US economic system is a reality. We live in the rent-seeking society that Buchanan, Tollison, and Tullock (1980) warned of, and that Randy Holcombe (2018) and Michael Munger (2019) have respectively diagnosed recently. Promissory politics leads to predatory governments, just as the Friedmans taught, but the challenge of our age is that the young see the predation in the seeking of protection of privilege by business interests, rather than in the politicians, bureaucrats, and intellectuals who seek to expand the power of the state by securing those privileges for those monied interests.

One way to think about this that might help and highlight the challenge we face as educators, scholars, and communicators is to parse the issue of predation. We can all agree that predation is a fundamental problem in political economy. From Adam Smith's *The Wealth of Nations* ([1776] 1976) to Daron Acemoglu and James Robinson's *Narrow Corridor* (2019), the problem of curbing predation is fundamental in understanding the political economy of development, and of achieving a good society defined as one of religious, political, and civil liberties and generalized prosperity—in short, a society defined by productive specialization and peaceful social cooperation.

Predation comes in the form of *private* predation, as individuals exercise their power over others, and exploit them to their advantage. But predation also comes in the form of public predation, where those in positions of power use the full force of the law and the apparatus of coercion (including police and military) to rule over others and make them subjects rather than citizens. And here is the puzzle, in order to curb private predation, we create public authorities to police us, but in so doing we create the very possibility of public predation that we then must keep in check through constitutional efforts that must empower yet constrain. Again, political economists from Smith to Acemoglu and Robinson all understood this fundamental paradox of governance.

But where the tacit presuppositions of political economy kick in is not in recognizing this conundrum, but in our priors about the resolution to it. For ease of exposition, let's limit the discussion strictly to the question of optimism and pessimism about the ability for private governance to self-police private predation, and the ability of constitutional checks and balances to effectively bind the governmental habit of public predation. Because of the frustrations with the failed policies of the 1960s and 1970s, and demonstrated in the stagnation of the late 1970s when the Friedmans wrote *Free to Choose*, the tacit presupposition of my generation was that private predation would be easier to self-police than checking public predation via constitutional constraints.

To this generation, however, I contend it is the opposite, namely, because the faith in curbing government predation isn't to be found in constitutional restraint but in the selection of "right people." The only thing preventing this "right people" answer, according to this now-common narrative, is the willful and corrupt action of political opponents to fix the rules of the election, or manipulate the minds of voters through misinformation and

262 · THE STRUGGLE FOR A BETTER WORLD

sowing confusion and discord. As a result, we are prisoners to a political system populated by evil people empowered by stupid people who have been manipulated by those in power and the monied interests who work with them. If more people were allowed to vote, and if more voice was given to the voiceless, we would see more power transfer from the powerful to the powerless, and the public sector would reflect true democratic values of fairness and justice. We are one another's dignified equals, except when we lie, cheat, and steal to get what we want. So if we eliminate the lying, the cheating, and the stealing, what we get from democratic processes is what we will want—presumably a more just and humane society.

For those of us who believe in liberal political economy, we have a challenge, and the only way to meet this challenge head-on is to strive to be scientists, educators, and communicators at the Friedman level of clarity of argument and carefulness and thoroughness in empirical analysis. It requires patience, devotion to craft, and quickness of mind and gentleness of spirit. Friedman was a unique talent, and the skill set he exhibited must be adapted to our present age, but it must be displayed by many if there is any hope of turning the tide again. With great challenges comes a great opportunity for those prepared to take advantage of it. The best thing the Mont Pelerin Society (MPS) has done over the past decade, in my opinion, is to cultivate programs for the next generation of thought leaders, and from within that crowd perhaps will emerge precisely that pivotal person for these pivotal times. In terms of our global reach and recruitment of young scholars, often from previously underrepresented fields and locations, MPS is attempting to discover those talented scholars, educators, public intellectuals, and policymakers that are up to the challenge. This is something we must continue to do and do even better over the next decades if we are to meet the challenges of our age.

Conclusion

It will do no good in our effort to engage the current generation and to wrest back control of the tacit presuppositions of political economy to deny the problems they see as critical to the world. On issues from racial injustice to environmental degradation, we must be willing to grapple as Milton and Rose Friedman did in *Free to Choose* with the imperfections of this world and thus the great evils that are revealed. The political and economic systems of the Western democracies suffered from perverted incentives and distorted signals, and, as a result, the market process does not operate as it should to spur enterprise, to guide actors in their decisions, to lure them with profit, and to discipline them with loss. The power of the market has been muted, while the tyranny of controls has expanded since 9/11 and 2008.

There is much wisdom in Adam Smith's argument that great nations are never ruined by private misconduct, but they can be by public misconduct. Smith was also right to stress that the power of innovation can quite often overcome the impertinent obstructions which government erects to hinder productive specialization and peaceful social cooperation. As he wrote in *The Wealth of Nations*:

> The uniform, constant, and uninterrupted effort of every man to better his condition, the principle from which public and national, as well as private opulence is originally derived, is frequently powerful enough to maintain the natural progress of things toward improvement, in spite both of the extravagance of government, and of the greatest errors of administration. Like the unknown principle of animal life, it frequently restores health and vigor to the constitution, in spite, not only of the disease, but of the absurd prescriptions of the doctor. ([1776] 1976, 325)

But there also must be a tipping point where the perversity of the incentives and the distortions in the signals are so significant and the deformation of the economic system is so severe that the correction cannot avoid being deeply problematic and painful. As liberal thought leaders, are we prepared to grapple with the fallout of the bad public policies our own analysis has warned us about for decades?

We must always remember as true radical liberals that we inherited a problematic past, and a troubling present. Immanuel Kant told us, and Isaiah Berlin adopted it as his motto, that out of the crooked timber of humanity, nothing straight can ever be made. We are imperfect beings living in an imperfect world stumbling along with the aid of very imperfect institutions. As liberals, how we respond to this will dictate our success. James Buchanan (1991) explained how the great classical liberals of the 19th century missed their opportunity due to their failure to develop a theory of justice that answered the challenges of their day. Frank Knight pondered on multiple occasions whether liberals would have the intellectual courage and wherewithal to meet the challenge created by the Great Depression and the communist and fascist threat. And, of course, Hayek spent the second half of his career trying to answer this challenge and it largely motivated his efforts with the Mont Pelerin Society. We as heirs to this intellectual project can do no less.

This chapter was originally written as part of a Special Meeting of the Mont Pelerin Society celebrating the 40th anniversary of a meeting held on these grounds in 1980. That meeting was held at the cusp of a revolution spearheaded by Milton and Rose Friedman's *Free to Choose*, and it ushered in "The Age of Milton Friedman." It is right that we celebrate this chapter in our society's past. But as we meet today, we must remember that our situation intellectually is less like 1980 and more like 1938 (Walter Lippmann Colloquium) or 1947 (Mont Pelerin).

The tacit presuppositions of political economy have shifted once more and away from our ideas. Books are continuously released these days criticizing the Mont Pelerin Society, and in broader strokes, the entire economics profession in its complicity with regard to the global financial crisis, the prioritizing of capital over labor and democracy, and the preoccupation with growth over the environment. Each day, new studies in the New History of Capitalism are published, discussed, and built on in history, philosophy, political science, sociology, cultural studies, communications, global affairs, and area studies departments. In short, economics has been effectively surrounded by all the associated disciplines in the social sciences and humanities by critics. The reality is that not all the criticisms are wrong, and many, in fact, are right. But practically speaking, the reality is that any argument from within economics that hopes to effectively counter must begin with where they are, not where we are.

Hayek's career is instructive from this point of view. When he moved to the London School of Economics in the early 1930s, he gave as his inaugural address "The Trend of Economic Thinking," and a major lesson of that address is that if you think like a neoclassical economist, then the arguments for planning will appear very problematic to you (see Hayek 1933). Only those who reject the economic way of thinking could advocate for such a path. Unfortunately for Hayek, by the end of the 1930s, the standard argument for planning was couched precisely in the most neoclassical of language. This led him, I argue in my recent book on Hayek (Boettke 2018), to make two simultaneous turns in the 1940s away from technical economics and toward (a) the examination of the institutional framework within which economic life takes place, and (b) the philosophy of science, which, due to a wrong turn, had turned a blind eye toward the institutional framework and the essential dynamic nature of the market system and, in particular, the guiding role of relative prices and the functional significance of profit-and-loss accounting.

Hayek's great discoveries in economics as reflected in works—such as "Use of Knowledge in Society" (1948), as well as his political books such as *The Road to Serfdom* (1944), *The Constitution of Liberty* (1960), and *Law, Legislation and Liberty* (1973, 1976, 1979)—all follow from this research path he was forced to embark on with his examination of the "Abuse of Reason" (see Hayek [1952] 1979, 979). For our purposes, however, it is important to stress that Hayek took this intellectual journey not alone, but with his fellow members of the Mont Pelerin Society. Liberal political economy was reconstructed with their hands from 1947 to 1980, culminating in so many ways with the publication of the Friedmans' *Free to Choose* and the 1980 meeting at Hoover that we are celebrating with this special gathering.

In conclusion, I want to suggest that those here at this meeting must continually learn from the Friedmans, and from Hayek, and from Buchanan, but apply those lessons to our age, and the challenges we face today with the same creativity and commitment that these great intellectual leaders did. Respectfully, I want to suggest that the challenges the next generation of thought leaders must face are more difficult than those faced in the 1970–1980 period. The students sitting in our classrooms today do not have the same taken-for-granted lived experiences that I had.

They don't know in their heart of hearts that "socialism sucks," that government is "a parliament of whores," or that the welfare state is "losing ground." They believe they know that markets are inefficient, unstable, and unjust. They believe in their heart of hearts that markets are corrupting of our morals and destructive to the "good society."[6] Thus, now more than ever, we must remember Hayek's words by which he began *The Constitution of Liberty*:

> If old truths are to retain their hold on men's minds, they must be restated in the language and concepts of successive generations. What at one time are their most effective expressions gradually become so worn with use that they cease to carry a definitive meaning. The underlying ideas may be as valid as ever, but the words, even when they refer to problems that are still with us, no longer convey the same conviction; the arguments do not move in a context familiar to us; and they rarely give us direct answers to the

questions we are asking. This may be inevitable because no statement of an ideal that is likely to sway men's minds can be complete: it must be adapted to a given climate of opinion, presuppose much that is accepted by all men of the time, and illustrate general principles in terms of issues with which they are concerned. (1960, 1)

It is now up to the next generation of scholars, educators, and communicators involved with the Mont Pelerin Society to do the heavy work of restating and reconstructing the liberal principles of justice and political economy and offer a vision of the good society for our times. Let's hope that among you there is someone, and hopefully a number of you, who are as clear of thought, as firm in their convictions, and as convincing in argumentation as Milton and Rose Friedman were in *Free to Choose*.

Notes

1. Buchanan first develops the idea in his work with Richard Wagner *Democracy in Deficit* ([1977] 1999) and the idea of the Harvey Road presumptions that frame and give rise to the Keynesian revolution. But the idea of "tacit presuppositions of political economy" is more fully worked out in his work on postcommunism; see Buchanan (1997).
2. The Knott's Berry Farm reference is to the conservative political pamphlets designed to inform the general public about the benefits of the free enterprise system that were on display at this famous theme park and store.
3. One of the Friedmans' great strengths is their constant willingness to take on the strongest criticisms of the market economy and to raise the comparative analysis of the self-correcting mechanisms of the market in the wake of a variety of imperfections, and the difficulties of implementing political solutions. Their book is a constant exercise in comparative institutional analysis between the for-profit private sector, the nonprofit private sector, and the public sector in addressing a variety of social ills. So Arrow's dismissal of *Free to Choose* for being unwilling to weigh both sides of the argument in economic policy and social philosophy just seems to be disingenuous.
4. In his *Journal of Economic Literature* review of *Free to Choose*, Donald Yankovic (1981) stresses this point. As he says, rather than being the one-sided argument that critics such as Heilbroner and Arrow claim, the book has many instances where the Friedmans draw attention to counterarguments to their position (and he lists page numbers from the beginning to the end of the book). For the litany of dysfunctions of government regulations, there is also a litany of abuses in the marketplace that must be addressed. The Friedmans are calling for a comparative institutional analysis in *Free to Choose*. In his concluding paragraphs, Yankovic sums up his understanding of the Friedmans' argument: "Whether self-protection and competition

in markets, or the regulatory instruments of government are most appropriate to deal with these evils are areas of controversy. Reasonable men of good will can be expected to disagree. The book provides an excellent point of view for considering this issue. After all, one does not abandon the principle that liberty is always to be preferred when one is convinced by reasoning and evidence that certain evils of the marketplace are too great to expect even enlightened and virtuous citizens to cope with them" (570).

5. In 1982, *Capitalism and Freedom* was reprinted and Milton Friedman wrote a preface, where he states clearly, "Its views were so far out of the mainstream that it was not reviewed by any major national publication." It is "inconceivable that such a publication by an economist of comparable professional standing but favorable to the welfare state or socialism or communism would have received a similar silent treatment" (vi). My point in quoting this passage from Friedman is not to highlight the bias in academia and media, but to suggest that the silent treatment was due to the tacit presuppositions. One example is the Friedman position on competition in schools and voucher programs, which at one time were considered unthinkable, then became widely appreciated, and now are subject to efforts to discredit and delegitimize. From the tacit presuppositions of political economy perspective, the critical issue is what is considered in, and what is considered out, of the reasonable bounds of consideration. As those boundaries of the reasonable shift, so will the reception of challenging ideas.

6. I recommend most enthusiastically the book by Virgil Henry Storr and Ginny Seung Choi (2019) titled *Does the Market Corrupt Our Morals?* In tone and attitude, I believe this book is a model of how to engage today's students in a way that might persuade them of the merits of the market society. I would also recommend Paul Rubin's (2019) recent book *The Capitalism Paradox* for similar reasons.

References

Acemoglu, Daron, and James Robinson. 2019. *The Narrow Corridor*. New York: Penguin Press.

Arrow, Kenneth. 1980. "Book Review of *Free to Choose*." *New Republic*, March 22, 25–28.

Boettke, Peter J. 2004. "Milton and Rose Friedman's *Free to Choose* and Its Impact in the Global Movement toward Free Market Policy: 1979–2003." In *The Legacy of Milton and Rose Friedman's Free to Choose: Economic Liberalism at the Turn of the 21st Century*, edited by Mark A. Wynne, Harvey Rosenblum, and Robert L. Formaini. Dallas, TX: Federal Reserve Bank of Dallas, 137–52.

———. 2018. *F. A. Hayek: Economics, Political Economy and Social Philosophy*. New York: Palgrave Macmillan.

Buchanan, James M. 1991. *The Economics and Ethics of Constitutional Order*. Ann Arbor: University of Michigan Press.

————. 1997. *Post-Socialist Political Economy*. Cheltenham, UK: Edward Elgar.

Buchanan, James M., Robert D. Tollison, and Gordon Tullock, eds. 1980. *Toward a Theory of the Rent-Seeking Society*. College Station: Texas A&M University Press.

Buchanan, James M., and Richard E. Wagner. [1977] 1999. *Democracy in Deficit: The Political Legacy of Lord Keynes*. Indianapolis: Liberty Fund.

Coyne, Christopher J. 2013. *Doing Bad by Doing Good*. Palo Alto, CA: Stanford University Press.

Friedman, Milton, and Rose Friedman. 1962. *Capitalism and Freedom*. Chicago: University of Chicago Press.

————. 1980. *Free to Choose: A Personal Statement*. New York: Harcourt Brace Jovanovich.

————. 1982. *Capitalism and Freedom*. Reprint with new preface. Chicago: University of Chicago Press.

————. 1984. *The Tyranny of the Status Quo*. New York: Harcourt Brace Jovanovich.

Hayek, F. A. 1933. "The Trend of Economic Thinking." *Economica* 40 (May): 121–37.

————. 1944. *The Road to Serfdom*. Chicago: University of Chicago Press.

————. 1948. "The Use of Knowledge in Society." *Individualism and Economic Order*. Chicago: University of Chicago Press, 77–91.

————. [1952] 1979. *The Counter-Revolution of Science: Studies on the Abuse of Reason*. Indianapolis: Liberty Fund.

————. 1960. *The Constitution of Liberty*. Chicago: University of Chicago Press.

————. 1973. *Law, Legislation and Liberty*. Volume 1: *Rules and Order*. Chicago: University of Chicago Press.

————. 1976. *Law, Legislation and Liberty*. Volume 2: *The Mirage of Social Justice*. Chicago: University of Chicago Press.

————. 1979. *Law, Legislation and Liberty*. Volume 3: *The Political Order of a Free People*. Chicago: University of Chicago Press.

Heilbroner, Robert L. 1980. "The Road to Selfdom." *New York Review of Books*, April 17.

Holcombe, Randall G. 2018. *Political Capitalism*. New York: Cambridge University Press.

Lehmann-Haupt, Christopher. 1980. "Books of the Times." *New York Times*, January 14.

McTeer, Robert D. 2004. "Preface." In *The Legacy of Milton and Rose Friedman's Free to Choose: Economic Liberalism at the Turn of the 21st Century*, edited by Mark A. Wynne, Harvey Rosenblum, and Robert L. Formaini, ix–xi. Dallas, TX: Federal Reserve Bank of Dallas.

Mill, John Stuart. 1845. "The Claims of Labour." *Edinburgh Review*, April, 498–525.

Munger, Michael C. 2019. *Is Capitalism Sustainable?* Great Barrington, MA: American Institute for Economic Research.

Rubin, Paul. 2019. *The Capitalism Paradox: How Cooperation Enables Free Market Competition*. New York: Bombardier Books.

Shleifer, Andrei. 2009. "The Age of Milton Friedman." *Journal of Economic Literature* 47 (1): 123–35.

Smith, Adam. [1776] 1976. *An Inquiry into the Nature and Causes of the Wealth of Nations.* Chicago: University of Chicago Press.

Storr, Virgil Henry, and Ginny Seung Choi. 2019. *Do Markets Corrupt Our Morals?* New York: Palgrave Macmillan.

Yankovic, Donald. 1981. "Review of Free to Choose." *Journal of Economic Literature* 19 (June): 568–70.

Chapter 15

Competition, Discovery, and the Pursuit of Happiness: The Case for International Liberalism in Our Time

I am myopically an academic by training and temperament, so when I was given the great honor to become President of the Mont Pelerin Society (MPS) in 2016, I have since spent a great deal of time reading about the history of the society (Hartwell 1995), spending time in archives, and reading contemporary "histories" and critical commentary on the society in an effort to gauge where we have been, and to take a glimpse of where we may be going. It did conveniently coincide with research I was doing for a book on F. A. Hayek that was just published in September. But in doing that research, one could not help but notice the parallels in the challenges that Hayek and his contemporaries faced and challenges now facing this generation of liberal thinkers. It is eerie actually as militarism, protectionism, and restrictions on the mobility of people and resources define our age every bit as much as they defined Hayek's.

Yet we also can witness the tremendous benefits when peace and freedom are introduced even when limited to a relative scale. In *F. A. Hayek: Economics, Political Economy and Social Philosophy* (2018b), I argue that one way to view Hayek's project was that he, like others in the Viennese context, was part of a quest for exact thinking in demented times. One answer was provided by the Vienna Circle, the other was provided by Hayek. But demented times they were wrestling with, and demented time we find ourselves wrestling with when we contemplate the fate of people in Myanmar and Venezuela, or the refugee crisis in Europe, or the immigration debate in the United States, or the discontent one reads about with regard to modern democratic society,

Remarks made at the 2018 general meeting of the Mont Pelerin Society, Gran Canaria, Spain, September 30–October 5. Originally published in *Mont Pelerin Society Newsletter* 74 (2019): 8–16.

271

or the general experiences one has in the ongoing discussions discrediting previously trusted institutions of news media, educational institutions, and the criminal justice system in say, for example, the United States. We definitely could use some exact thinking in these demented times. This is one of the reasons why Steven Pinker's *Enlightenment Now* (2018) or Hans Rosling's *Factfulness* (2018) demand our attention.

When the Walter Lippmann Colloquium was organized in 1938 to the first meeting of MPS in 1947, the challenging task before the true liberal was to meet the intellectual critiques of the private property order based on the claims that the market economy inherently tended to produce monopoly power and macroeconomic volatility. Counterarguments had to be soberly developed, and the liberal project had to be reconstructed anew out of the ruins of World War II for a new generation of thinkers and actors.

In an attempt to meet those challenges, Hayek in 1939 developed a plan for interstate federalism, which could create a common market and permit the free flow of labor and capital, and in so doing promote peaceful social cooperation among the different "language communities" or "nationalities" of Europe. His essay is an optimistic reconstruction of 19th-century liberalism as a counter to the policies followed in Europe in the 1920s and 1930s. Competition, Hayek argued, would provide the necessary filtering mechanism for social cooperation under the international division of labor. This international division of labor would be the source of wealth creation, generalized prosperity, and lasting peace. As he argued: "It is, after all, only common sense that the central government in a federation composed of many different people will have to be restricted in scope if it is to avoid meeting an increasing resistance on the part of the various groups which it includes" ([1939] 1948, 264–65). Hayek then asks, "But what could interfere more thoroughly with the intimate life of the people than the central direction of economic life, with its inevitable discrimination between groups?" (265). The free movement of goods, individuals, and money across national boundaries has important implications for a federation. Competition will "limit to a great extent the scope of the economic policy of the individual states" (265). The abolition of economic barriers will bring with it more efficient exchange and production as the mutual gains from trade will be exploited, guided by freely adjusting relative prices, and the innovations of technological progress will be induced through the lure of profit. With so much discussion today challenging trade and migration, it seems high time for a renewed discussion of proposals for such a scheme as Hayek envisioned.

At the time of the founding of MPS, one of the major concerns expressed in the original draft of the statements of the society's aims was the misuse of history to discredit and scandalize, and the mismeasurement in history to mischaracterize. It was this misuse of history, after all, that negatively affected the attitudes of intellectuals toward capitalism and classical liberalism, and resulted in the rise of nationalism and odious racial doctrines during the first decades of the 20th century. In science, truth tracking should matter. Bad econometricians can be accused of p-hacking, but bad historians do their own version of that, or worse. The early MPS discussions and Hayek's edited volume *Capitalism and the Historians* (1954) were an effort to counter that trend, and bring reason and evidence to the forefront in the analysis of every student of society.

But today, we face a similar problem with the rise of the history of capitalism literature. This work takes the form of, on the one hand, intellectual history of capitalism—with MPS actually receiving a special critical treatment in a narrative about neoliberalism—and economic history of capitalism, on the other hand—where colonialism, slavery, and the factory system receive special emphasis. And in the minds of many of these contemporary historians, the point is to link both, and, in so doing, discredit and delegitimize capitalism, and the theorists of capitalism, with the exception of capitalism's critics, such as Karl Marx, John Maynard Keynes, and Karl Polanyi.

In the world of practical affairs, this critique has led to a weakening of the voice for true liberalism and radical capitalism among the intellectual class and in university and college lectures outside the discipline of economics, and we have seen throughout the world a rising threat of right-wing and left-wing populist nationalism without effective countervoices rising to meet the challenge.

The alternative in the minds of most intellectual commentators, even among economists,[1] remains elitist progressivism, but such a program suffers from Hayek's "fatal conceit" and thus represents no alternative whatsoever. In fact, as Hayek argued in "The Pretence of Knowledge" ([1974] 1989), it is this elitist progressivism—and the alliance between statism and scientism on which it is based—that has actually made such a mess of things that the populist critique has emerged and resonates with so many in popular discourse. But what is required for our time, as it was for Hayek's time, is a rejuvenated and full-throated defense of liberalism—international liberalism as developed by Ludwig von Mises, Hayek, and Lionel Robbins in the 1920s–1950s.

I would like to recommend to this generation of "students of society" to spend some time reading Lionel Robbins. Between 1930 and 1950, in particular, Robbins wrote some of the most clearheaded books in economic science and in economic policy. He is a fascinating character to study. The massive biography on Robbins written by Susan Howson runs over 1,000 pages. That might be overkill, but in a very real sense not really. He really is that fascinating of a mind and that important of a thinker.

Robbins was thrust into a leadership role at the London School of Economics and Political Science at an early age. Robbins was uniquely positioned in that he was trained in the intellectual tradition of Edwin Cannan and thus at the intersection of classical political economy and modern neoclassical economics. And he could read and absorb German. As a young man, he had read Mises's *Socialism* and was impressed. He also was impressed with Mises's work on the logical status of economic science. He was instrumental as well in bringing the theory of industrial fluctuations developed by Knut Wicksell and Ludwig von Mises to the English audience, and offered it as an alternative to underconsumption theories and the emerging "New Economics" of Keynes. In fact, it was an article by a young F. A. Hayek criticizing the underconsumption theories of the US economists William Trufant Foster and Waddill Catchings that inspired Robbins to invite Hayek to the London School of Economics to give the lectures that would be published as *Prices and Production*, and eventually to Hayek's professorship at the LSE.

During the decade of the 1930s, the Hayek-Robbins seminar would become one of the international hubs of research in economics. Hayek-Robbins shared a commitment to presenting *a unified body of economic thought*, in which the various "schools" of economics would fade into the background and the substantive propositions of "what economics as science taught" would be emphasized.[2] Critical to this exercise was, of course, the clarification of the logical status of economic theory, and in particular the pure logic of choice as distinct from the nexus of exchange that constitutes the market order. The "economic calculus" as Hayek would term it, was a necessary, but not sufficient component to the explanation of the market order based on private property and freedom of contract embedded in a rule of law. The *institutional infrastructure* that was such an integral part of the classical political economist system of thought had to be moved from the background to the foreground of modern economic analysis if progress was going to be made.

During these "years of high theory," the debates were intense and the stakes were very high as liberalism was under assault intellectually, and in a very real sense European civilization was threatened with destruction by the militarism of fascism and of communism. Against the backdrop of the ongoing economic stagnation of the Great Depression and rising tensions from nationalism and militarism, there arose the debate with Keynes over macroeconomic volatility, and with the market socialists, such as Oskar Lange and Abba Lerner, on the efficiency of socialist planning. Other debates included imperfect competition and the welfare economics of externalities and monopoly power.

These were indeed years of high theory, and Hayek and Robbins were a formidable team basically defending the classical laissez-faire argument as developed by Cannan and Mises the generation before. Critical to this argument, however, was a deep intellectual commitment to articulating the necessary *institutional framework* for the liberal order to emerge and operate effectively. That framework consisted of private property and the rule of law. But *if* this institutional framework could be established and maintained, then the liberal economic order of the competitive market could be relied on to deliver maximize efficiency and improvements in the material conditions of mankind.

By the late 1930s, it was obvious that international liberalism was on retreat. The market economy, it was argued, was inefficient, unstable, and unjust, and government planning was the panacea of the age. Sound familiar? It should. But back to the late 1930s. Lionel Robbins decided to step up and provide the counterargument. As Henry Hazlitt pointed out in his August 1, 1937, *New York Times* review of *Economic Planning and International Order*, the "brilliant exception" to the tenor of the times was Lionel Robbins. Liberalism without apology was the answer to the social ills that plagued the world economy. Robbins dedicates his book to the memory of Edwin Cannan, and in more than 300 well-written pages he makes the case that "not capitalism, which rightly conditioned, is a safeguard of liberty and progress, but nationalism, which tends to poverty and conflict, is the cause of our present distresses" (1937, 327). Again, I ask, sound familiar? It should. And as such, we need renewed defenses of international liberalism for our times.

"The principle of international liberalism," Robbins writes, "is decentralization and control by the market" (1937, 224). Planning, on the other hand, Robbins argues, has proven itself to lead to "waste and insecurity," and thus "now there seems reason to doubt that the practicability of a comprehensive planning from the centre which does not destroy just that which it was intended to preserve" (221). Civilization was at stake, and sober economic analysis was perhaps the best response. For it is the technical principles of economics that enable the analyst to assess the impact of alternative institutional arrangements of the ability of individuals to realize productive specialization and peaceful social cooperation. "We should not claim for liberalism," Robbins insisted, "that the world it could produce would be perfect. . . . But we may claim that, with all its deficiencies, it would still provide a safeguard for happiness and spontaneity more efficient than any other which has yet been suggested" (268).

Robbins reminds his readers that international liberalism should not be seen as a panacea any more than international socialism. The imperfections of man will always be with us. The question is about the rewards and penalties that guide the continual adjustment and adaptation. What matters is that participants are not protected in the market system from the consequences of their decisions, and that these participants also have options to exchange with others, to work with others, to pursue new avenues of enterprise or consumption. This reality of choice and exit imposes a discipline on the system. International liberalism does not promise that all of humanity will love each other overnight. Perhaps we imperfect beings never will. But what international liberalism does seek to do is to persuade us that "cooperation between the different members of humanity is advantageous for the furtherance of individual ends" (326). From this simple mechanism for efficiency, however, grows stronger consequences that turn us away from the "spiritual sickness of nationalism" and the "antics of guttersnipe racialism" and toward the cosmopolitanism of the international division of labor and social cooperation through mutually beneficial trade. "The ideals of Athens," Robbins states, "still challenge the ideals of Sparta."

The issue of international liberalism was very much on the minds of the individuals who met a decade after Robbins's book was published in April 1947 to found the Mont Pelerin Society. It is often forgotten that it was indeed Lionel Robbins who wrote the Statement of Aims for MPS. It is clear from Robbins's statement that MPS was established to cultivate a constructive and critical dialogue among serious students of society concerning the nature of liberalism. It is also clear how central to that dialogue economic analysis of the competitive market economy is if progress is going to be made in our understanding. But make no mistake, this dialogue was going to focus on "the problem of the creation of an international order conducive to the safeguarding of peace and liberty and permitting the establishment of harmonious international economic relations."

That was the purpose in 1947, and it remains the purpose today. So to avoid any confusion, though, it is critical to read the final paragraph of the statement: "The group does not aspire to conduct propaganda. It seeks to establish no meticulous and hampering orthodoxy. It aligns itself with no particular party. *Its object is solely, by facilitating the exchange of views*, among minds inspired by certain ideals and broad conceptions held in common, to contribute to the preservation and improvement of the free society" (emphasis added).

Some of you know that my undergraduate teacher of economics was Dr. Hans Sennholz at Grove City College; he is the person most responsible for me becoming an economist. Dr. Sennholz was a longtime member of MPS, and in fact I remember fondly his tales of his battles at the meetings when he returned. Vigorous debate and discussion, he would report, about monetary theory and policy, about fiscal policy, about regulations, and about the global market for goods and services. Sennholz painted a picture of a vibrant community of scholars working hard to figure out the best way to think and argue about the benefits of the private property order and the free-enterprise system.

Many of you probably do not know who Dr. Sennholz was, and those who do will most likely remember him as a hard-money—gold standard— advocate. But what you might have forgotten is that his first book *How Can Europe Survive?* (1955)—written as his doctoral thesis under the direction of Ludwig von Mises at New York University in the 1950s—is a defense of international liberalism, and the sort of interstate federalism that Hayek (and Mises) had argued for in the 1930s and 1940s. The hope for Europe—a hope for postwar reconstruction and a system of lasting peace and prosperity— would turn on the ability to establish a common market and a system of interstate federalism. The free mobility of labor and capital was critical to mobilizing the initiative and tapping into the dispersed knowledge throughout the region, and will lead to the efficient use of resources and wealth creation.

Besides Hayek and Robbins, Mises was a longtime proponent of international liberalism. In his book *Liberalism* published in 1927, Mises argued simply that "liberalism is, in this sense, humanism; and the liberal, a citizen of the world, a cosmopolite" ([1927] 2005, 76). And he added, "It is from the fact of the international division of labor that liberalism derives the decisive, irrefutable argument against war" (78). Lasting peace follows from the free mobility of capital and labor, and the rejection of all forms of nationalistic chauvinism.

Also on the eve of World War II, Mises ([1939] 1990) penned the essay "The Disintegration of the International Division of Labor," where he argued that not only did economic theory from Adam Smith, and especially David Ricardo, forward demonstrate that free trade produced the highest productivity of capital and labor, but that any effort to prohibit trade must lead to a reduction in the output of capital and labor. Moreover, prohibitions on trade give rise to nationalism and militarism, while international liberalism results in peace and prosperity. It is the free mobility of capital and labor that ensures individuals will pursue productive specialization, and realize peaceful social cooperation among individuals of great geographic and social distance.

Sennholz's book (1955) was pursuing the logic of Mises's argument for the context of Europe in the immediate aftermath of World War II. There is a lot to be learned by revisiting these efforts, and critically assessing their strengths and weaknesses.

My argument is simple: there is much to learn by examining anew the works of Mises, Hayek, Robbins, and Sennholz for the trouble we find ourselves grappling with today—a world of institutional transformations that have had bumps along the way in postcommunism; of globalization and its discontents; of global financial crises; of looming fiscal reckoning for the social democratic countries; and of a legitimation crisis in democratic governments. These, and many others, are the tensions of our time. True radical liberalism if it is going to be relevant to the intellectual discourse—let alone as a guiding ideology for practical affairs—must not shy away from tackling the tensions. Nor can it assume these tensions will easily repair themselves. Instead, the task before us is one of serious scholarly exploration and articulation of the mechanisms by which competitive forces in economics and politics can ameliorate these tensions, and prod and induce individuals using nothing more than their ordinary motivations to act in concert with one another to realize productive specialization and peaceful social cooperation.

Liberalism, it must be reasserted, is *liberal*. It is an emancipation philosophy. It promises to free all from the bonds of oppression and the indignity of domination. We are one another's equals before the law—dignified human beings. Trade is the vehicle of our deliverance; it is not only how wealth is created, but how strangers are transformed into friends. Trade-tested betterment, as Deirdre McCloskey likes to stress, results in the escape from wretched poverty and debilitating ignorance.

But this comes from the spread of certain ideas. And as we have been discussing all week, competition is how we discover, and through liberty is how we learn. This is true in economics, but also outside the realm of the market. As Hayek argued in *Law, Legislation and Liberty*:

> Quite generally outside as well as inside the economic sphere, competition is a sensible procedure to employ only if we do not know beforehand who will do best . . . *competition is thus, like experimentation in science, first and foremost a discovery procedure.* No theory can do justice to it which starts from the assumption that the facts to be discovered are already known. There is no pre-determined range of known or 'given' facts which will ever all be taken into account. All we can hope to secure is a procedure that is on the whole likely to bring about a situation where more of the potentially useful objective facts will be taken into account than would be done in any other procedure once we know. (1979, 68, emphasis added)

The institutional environment must be one that promotes competition, and builds in nodes of contestation throughout the entire system. And this discovery process and the learning process it engenders give rise to our pursuit of happiness. Liberty leaves room for us to translate aspirations into achievements. As Hayek wrote in *The Constitution of Liberty*:

> It is often objected that our concept of liberty is merely negative. This is true in the sense that peace is also a negative concept or that security or quiet or the absence of any particular impediment or evil is negative. It is to this class of concepts that liberty belongs: it describes the absence of a particular obstacle—coercion by other men. It becomes positive only through what we make of it. It does not assure us of any particular opportunities, but leaves it to us to decide what use we shall make of the circumstances in which we find ourselves. (1960, 19)

"Competition, Discovery, and the Pursuit of Happiness" should be seen as a joyous celebration of the ability of individuals to realize productive specialization and peaceful social cooperation with others of great geographic and social distance. As Adam Smith long ago pointed us to—that human propensity to truck, barter, and exchange is the source of our salvation from poverty, ignorance, and squalor. Trade is the fountain of progress, and the institutions that make the expansion of trade possible—private property and the rule of law—provide the safeguards for liberty. Human betterment results when liberty and progress are safeguarded by the institutional regime of international liberalism.

It is important, however, for me to stress that international liberalism has never been fully realized due to nationalism and other parochial forces at work. We have escaped the horrors of international communism, but not really fully escaped from the inefficiencies and injustices of modern mercantilism. Even in 1937, it was important for Robbins to point out: "International liberalism is not a plan that has been tried and failed. It is a plan that has never yet had full chance" (1937, 233). The chaos of his time, he argued, was a result of the retreat from even the partial pursuit of a regime of international liberalism in the 19th century. Privileges doled out by the powerful to create monopolies and restrict trade were the norm then, as they are today, as documented in the work of scholars from Gordon Tullock to Luigi Zingales. What we can see is when, relatively speaking, the privilege to restrict becomes itself restricted, the disposition of resources does not follow the demands of the monopolists, but the demands of the consumers and wealth is created and lives of millions (and perhaps billions) improve. This shift results from the power of ideas to overcome the narrow interests of the privileged and the powerful.

The Economist has recently run a series of articles on the political philosophy of liberalism, and its critics and its alternative formulations.[3] We must speak with a strong voice and reaffirm that liberalism is an emancipation doctrine—emancipating humanity from the intolerance of dogma, from the bonds of slavery, from the arbitrary use and abuse of power by the privileged class. Its weapons of emancipation are ideas of basic human equality before the law and the dignity of every individual, and the mechanisms of competition and of mutually beneficial exchange.

Thank you for this great honor to serve as President of MPS, and as one of my other teachers—James Buchanan (MPS President, 1984/86)—often said, "Onwards and upwards."

Notes

1. Or perhaps I should say *especially* among economists. One of the most serious issues with the Vienna Circle response to the quest for exact thinking in demented times is that the alliance between scientism and statism effectively transformed economics from a science of social understanding to a science of social control. But what if economics is incapable of achieving as a science what would be required to be a science of control, yet the public sector demands that the science proceed as if it can? This is one of the main themes explored in Hayek's Nobel lecture "The Pretence of Knowledge" ([1974] 1989). Also see my Southern Economic Association presidential address "Economics and Public Administration" (2018a).

2. In various writings, for example, *Living Economics* (2012), I have referred to this unified body of economic thought as *mainline economics*, and contrasted it with *mainstream economics*. Also see *Mainline Economics: Six Nobel Lectures in the Tradition of Adam Smith* (2016, edited with Stefanie Haeffele and Virgil Henry Storr) and *Applied Mainline Economics* (2017, written with Matt Mitchell).

3. See *The Economist* issues for August 4, August 9, August 18, August 23, August 30, and September 6, 2018. Theorists discussed include John Stuart Mill, Alexis de Tocqueville, John Maynard Keynes, Joseph Schumpeter, F. A. Hayek, Karl Popper, Isaiah Berlin, John Rawls, Robert Nozick, and illiberal critics such as Jean-Jacques Rousseau, Karl Marx, and Friedrich Nietzsche. Absent from the discussion are thinkers such as Ludwig von Mises and Frank Knight, and Milton Friedman and Buchanan, let alone more contemporary "students of society." Nevertheless, this discussion in *The Economist* indicates the fundamental longing for intellectuals and citizens to ponder the great questions about the liberalism, the political order of a society of free and responsible individuals, and the institutional foundations for a sustainable self-governing democratic society. This is the conversation that we must be having if we have any hope of achieving peace, justice, and liberty.

References

Boettke, Peter J. 2012. *Living Economics: Yesterday, Today, and Tomorrow*. Oakland, CA: The Independent Institute.

———. 2018a. "Economics and Public Administration." *Southern Economic Journal* 84 (4): 938–59.

———. 2018b. *F. A. Hayek: Economics, Political Economy and Social Philosophy*. New York: Palgrave Macmillan.

Boettke, Peter J., Stefanie Haeffele, and Virgil Henry Storr, eds. 2016. *Mainline Economics: Six Nobel Lectures in the Tradition of Adam Smith*. Arlington, VA: Mercatus Center at George Mason University.

Hartwell, R. M. 1995. *A History of the Mont Pelerin Society*. Indianapolis: Liberty Fund.

Hayek, F. A. [1939] 1948. "The Economic Conditions of Interstate Federalism." Reprinted in *Individualism and Economic Order*. Chicago: University of Chicago Press.

——, ed. 1954. *Capitalism and the Historians*. Chicago: University of Chicago Press.

——. 1960. *The Constitution of Liberty*. Chicago: University of Chicago Press.

——. [1974] 1989. "The Pretence of Knowledge." *American Economic Review* 79 (6): 3–7.

——. 1979. *Law, Legislation and Liberty*. Volume. 3: *The Political Order of a Free People*. Chicago: University of Chicago Press.

Hazlitt, Henry. 1937. "Economic Planning as a Panacea." Book review. *New York Times*, August 1.

Mises, Ludwig von. [1927] 2005. *Liberalism: The Classical Tradition*. Indianapolis: Liberty Fund.

——. [1939] 1990. "The Disintegration of the International Division of Labor." In *Money, Method, and Market Process*, edited by Richard M. Ebeling, 113–36. Boston: Kluwer.

Mitchell, Matthew D., and Peter J. Boettke. 2017. *Applied Mainline Economics: Bridging the Gap between Theory and Public Policy*. Arlington, VA: Mercatus Center at George Mason University.

Pinker, Steven. 2018. *Enlightenment Now: The Case for Reason, Science, Humanism, and Progress*. New York: Penguin Random House.

Robbins, Lionel. 1937. *Economic Planning and International Order*. London: Macmillan.

Rosling, Hans. 2018. *Factfulness*. New York: Flatiron Books.

Sennholz, Hans F. 1955. *How Can Europe Survive?* New York: Van Nostrand.

Chapter 16
Pessimistically Optimistic about the Future

After being a professional economist for over 30 years, I am pessimistically optimistic about our economic future. My bottom line is optimistic because, like the great Julian Simon (1983), I believe that the ultimate resource is the human imagination and that the great diversity of human ingenuity and creativity will help us find our way out of the numerous troubles that we have made and may make for ourselves. But I am pessimistically optimistic because the dominant mental models that human beings deploy to make sense of their interaction with each other and with nature are so fundamentally flawed and grounded in zero-sum and negative-sum moral intuitions.

We systematically underestimate the costs of blocking trading opportunities with one another and of curtailing the creative powers of the entrepreneurial spirit, and we systematically overstate the benefits of attempting to curb the excesses of self-interest through collective action by state power. I am an optimist because of the creativity of individuals and the power of the market; I am a pessimist because of the moral intuitions hard-wired into humans through our evolutionary past in small-group settings and the tyranny of government controls in the affairs of men. The logical outcomes of both are fundamentally opposed: complete and unregulated trade with all or isolation and war against all. Human history, I contend, can be seen as the long drama of these two forces battling it out to determine which norms of interaction will be dominant. Put another way, we can follow the Smithian propensity to truck, barter, and exchange, or we can follow the Hobbesian propensity to pillage and plunder. Optimism comes from Smithian propensities winning out over Hobbesian ones, whereas pessimism comes from the Hobbesian propensities sweeping aside the Smithian ones.

Originally published in *The Independent Review* 20, no. 3 (2016): 343–46.

Which force will ultimately determine our future path will be a function of ideas. Economic logic and reality are not subject to popular vote any more than the law of gravity or the physical laws governing the flow of water in a river. Reality simply is not optional. But politicians, pundits, and the public often communicate a message as if economic policy is a question of popular will. There is no doubt that populations can vote for this or that economic policy, but whether the policy decided on will have the intended desirable consequences is not a matter of good wishes. Policy effectiveness is a consequence of recognizing the relevant tradeoffs that individuals face in their decisions about the use of scarce resources and pursuing the opportunities for gains from trade and gains from entrepreneurial innovation.

Certain policies are compatible with realizing productive specialization and peaceful cooperation, and others are not. Bad ideas about humans and nature produce bad public policies about the way humans interact with one another and with nature, which in turn have bad economic results. In contrast, good ideas lead to good policies, which in turn produce good results. The economic miracle of the Western world was a by-product of ideas and institutions that produced high-powered incentives, quality informational signals, and disciplining feedback so that the gains from social cooperation under the division of labor were realized. The lingering poverty in much of the world is a result of ideas and institutions that prevent the realization of gains from social cooperation.

As we contemplate the future of economic policy, the questions we must ask are: Which ideas and institutions will prevail? Are we looking at a future where property, contract, and consent will be foundational to the social order? Or will our future be one where ideas that challenge the very legitimacy of property, deny the freedom of contract, and claim that consent is but an illusion ultimately define the conventional wisdom of the age? Tomorrow will be better than today provided that property, contract, and consent remain pivotal ideas in the social order—that is, the rights of others are respected, promises are kept, and those rights are exchanged or those promises are modified only if both parties agree to the transfer or modification.

We are very imperfect beings who interact with one another in a very imperfect world, but our institutional environments aid us in stumbling our way through to a better world. As Adam Smith remarked in *The Wealth of Nations*:

> The natural effort of every individual to better his own condition, when suffered to exert itself with freedom and security, is so powerful a principle, that it is alone, and without any assistance, not only capable of carrying on the society to wealth and prosperity, but of surmounting a hundred impertinent obstructions with which the folly of human laws too often incumbers its operation. ([1776] 1976, 49–50)

For our purposes, at least two aspects of this Smithian claim must be addressed. The first is the business of what it means to exert our individual initiative with freedom and security. The second is the possibility of identifying a tipping point when those impertinent obstructions simply cannot be surmounted.

By stating things in this way, I think, we can begin to identify the probability of whether our future will be bleak because we eliminate the individual's freedom to choose and in so doing adopt not a hundred obstructions to market transactions but hundreds of thousands. What is the probability that the United States will follow a policy path that will kill the proverbial goose that lays the golden egg, as happened in the socialist experiments of the 20th century in the Soviet Union and China or as experienced in the past decade in Venezuela and Greece? For the democratic West, I say the probability is extremely low, for reasons discussed later, so my pessimism is constrained to the observation that we will continue to muddle through with some form of crony capitalism or mercantilism. Our wealth will not be what it could be. We will continue to suffer from macro volatility and micro distortions, but the erring entrepreneurs will outpace the bumbling bureaucrats in realizing mutually beneficial exchanges and coming up with creative entrepreneurial innovations in production and distribution of goods and services. We will, as Smith argued, be carried to wealth and prosperity even in the face of the impertinence of human folly motivated by the wrong moral intuitions and the meddlesome preferences of those who hope to lord over others.

To communicate this point to audiences, I have often asked them to envision a horse race between three horses: (a) a Smithian horse representing the gains from exchange, (b) a Schumpeterian horse representing the gains from innovation, and (c) a Stupid horse representing government meddling in the voluntary affairs of humans in the effort to control the economy. As long as the Smithian and Schumpeterian horses are outrunning the Stupid horse, the economy will continue to progress despite the restrictions under which it must operate. But if we ever allow the Stupid horse not only to gain ground on the Smithian and Schumpeterian horses by shackling them with restrictions on trade and regulations on innovation but also to overcome them, then our economic future will indeed be bleak. The United States isn't at that stage yet, but it might reach that stage if right reason is rejected and emotional appeals substitute for logic and evidence.

Stupidity gains ground if and only if an alliance is forged between wrong ideas and opportunistic political interests. So the economist's task is to debunk popular fallacies and expose the special interests that benefit from the bad policies at the expense of the general populace. Economists must be forever vigilant in their role as public educators—both in and out of the classroom. As I said before, economic reality is not optional—voting for any economic policy by democratic majority does not mean it is a good policy. The worthiness of economic policy measures can be determined on the basis of only one criterion: do the economic policies proposed result in wealth and prosperity or not? The answer is not arrived at through democratic procedures but through the science of economics and the art of political economy.

In the future, many possible factors will affect the world of affairs—war is perhaps the most obvious, but there are also natural disasters such as earthquakes and hurricanes. But even in the face of these factors, the critical variable under our command is public policy responses. We should not compound the fury of nature, for example, with the folly of the human being. The policies of economic freedom will dampen the calls for war as trading partners seek to avoid such costly engagements, whereas economic nationalism tends to breed war. In a probabilistic sense, the likelihood of a major war between the Western democratic states is negligible, and thus the biggest threat to our economic future rests with bad ideas and meddlesome preferences. This means we muddle through, confronting not only periodic volatility and distortions wrought by perverse incentives but also episodic technological breakthroughs and innovations in exchange and production, as well as the opening up of new markets, both foreign and domestic.

The great political economist James Buchanan often described himself as a pessimist when he looked to the future but an optimist when he looked back because surely the world should be worse off than what it is. My position is slightly different and might be characterized as "pessimistic optimism." As I said, my optimism is grounded in the force of argument from Adam Smith to Julian Simon about the creative forces of the human imagination. My pessimism is equally grounded in the force of argument from Thomas Hobbes to James Buchanan about the war of all against all and the self-serving capacity of political interests. Squeeze these intellectual arguments together—Smith and Hobbes, Simon and Buchanan—and what you get is optimism about productive specialization and peaceful cooperation being realized by diverse populations, plus a tempered pessimism due to the desire of many to rule over others and the attempt to control the economy. The upshot is that the economic future of my grandchildren will be bright compared with the world we live in today. But it will not be the post-scarcity world envisioned by Keynes or the apocalyptic future envisioned by many conservatives. Instead, it will be a better world than today, but not as good a world as it could have been had individuals come to understand the tyranny of politics and ineffectiveness of economic policies of control and had been more receptive to freedom of choice and the power of the market.

References

Simon, Julian. 1983. *The Ultimate Resource*. Princeton, NJ: Princeton University Press.
Smith, Adam. [1776] 1976. *An Inquiry into the Nature and Causes of the Wealth of Nations*. Chicago: University of Chicago Press.

Conclusion
Liberalism, Socialism, and Our Future

Injustice is not built to last. Each generation must rise to the challenge of answering the cries of the powerless and giving voice to the voiceless, in the unending quest to ensure that we do everything within our capabilities to establish a humane and just society. Anything short is a demonstration of a lack of understanding of our shared humanity. We are one another's dignified equals, and justice demands that equals be treated equally.

Human beings are imperfect, and our institutions are imperfect. That is simply reality. Perfection is not an option for us. As Immanuel Kant argued long ago, and Isaiah Berlin adopted as a motto, out of the crooked timber of humanity nothing straight can ever be made. But that doesn't mean we acquiesce in the face of that imperfection. We can, and must, constantly strive to do better in our quest to establish a more humane and just society.

This is where economic reasoning enters as an essential tool in both understanding the human condition and striving to achieve a better world. Simply put, constraints matter. Human action always takes place against given constraints. Consequences follow from actions, and not all consequences are as intended. Scarcity, choice, and the necessity of tradeoffs are at the core of the first lesson of economics. But the recognition of *unintended consequences* of purposive human action—both beneficial and detrimental—is critical in our quest for understanding social systems of exchange, production, and distribution. These unintended consequences must be taken into account in our deliberations over alternative institutional arrangements in the hope that we can achieve a social system that delivers peace and prosperity, that satisfies the conditions of equality and justice, and that minimizes human suffering and maximizes the opportunities for human flourishing.

For their helpful comments and criticisms on an earlier draft, I gratefully acknowledge Rosemary Boettke, Rosolino Candela, Jessica Carges, Chris Coyne, and David Prychitko. The usual caveat applies.

Simply intending these components of a "Good Society" is not enough. Immature modes of reasoning—for example, bad people do bad things; good people do good things—must be replaced by the more mature and disciplined reasoning of "invisible hand" explanations. As discussed in several of the essays in this collection, this mode of analysis commences with a focus on purposive human actors, but then places those actors within specified institutional filters. The social scientist then examines the "mechanism" in operation in these alternative institutional filters through a study of the structure of incentives and the flow of information they generate.

In a market society, for example, property, prices, and profit and loss work in concert with one another to produce the positive and negative feedback that result in a continuous stream of new and fresh knowledge that individuals discover, utilize, and learn from in coordinating their plans with one another through time. The influence these economics forces at work impose on the relevant human actors produces systematic tendencies that prod and guide actors either to pursue productive specialization and realize peaceful social cooperation through exchange, or—in the absence or attenuation of the institutions of property, prices, and profit and loss—to move toward the misallocation of scarce resources and missed opportunities for mutual gains from trade, and ignorance of least-cost technologies in production. The wealth and poverty of nations turn on the adoption of institutions. But so do the questions of equality, liberty, and justice.

Joseph Stiglitz in his *Whither Socialism?* argues, "The dream of a better world here on earth has been a central theme in the development of Western civilization since the Reformation" (1994, 269). The history of the translation of these utopian visions into social experiments in the 20th century "should make us cautious in the confidence with which we hold our views, and cautious in our appeal to 'science' to justify our beliefs about the organization of society." But, Stiglitz argues, we cannot commit the alternative intellectual sin and insist that we live in the best of all possible worlds. The struggle to solve the problems that plague our world must continually be waged. And Stiglitz is correct to ask "whether the insights on modern economic theory and the utopian ideas of the nineteenth century can be brought closer together?" (277).

One of my teachers, James Buchanan, often quoted his teacher Frank Knight, in our classes—"To say a situation is hopeless is to say it's ideal." Since Buchanan was firmly committed to the idea that improvement in human affairs could result from a change in the rules of the game, or as he put it, by shifting to the constitutional level of analysis, there was an implied corollary to the Knightian quip. Since obviously the current situation is less than ideal, the situation must not be hopeless. Improvement was indeed possible through constitutional rearrangement. There is freedom, as Buchanan put it, through constitutional contract.

While Hayek adopted the Humean dictum of using reason to whittle down the claims of reason, and thus a more evolutionary approach in *The Constitution of Liberty* and *Law, Legislation and Liberty*, Buchanan was more Hobbesian and sought to provide the underlying "Reason of Rules" and the "Logical Foundations" to "The Calculus of Consent."[1] For my purpose here, though, the important element to stress in their respective efforts in the second half of the 20th century was their rejection of the modern trend in economic and political economy thinking toward a theory of social control, and their underlying commitment to the Smithian plan of equality, liberty, and justice. But that liberal plan had to be reconstructed, as well as restated, and not merely reprinted, for their time. The task at hand wasn't limited to salvaging the old books of Adam Smith, John Stuart Mill, and Ludwig von Mises, nor even to saving the ideas of classical liberalism, but of refining and advancing the science and art of political economy in the modern age. As Hayek begins *The Constitution of Liberty*:

> If old truths are to retain their hold on men's minds, they must be restated in the language and concepts of successive generations. What at one time are their most effective expressions gradually become so worn with use that they cease to carry a definite meaning. The underlying ideas may be as valid as ever, but the words, even when they refer to problems that are still with us, no longer convey the same conviction; the arguments do not move in a context familiar to us; and they rarely give us direct answers to the questions we are asking. ([1960] 2011, 1)

Those of us influenced by these ideas must take that message of Hayek seriously for *our time* in the 21st century.

As I mentioned in my introduction, at the present time (summer 2020), economic and political liberalism faces both a *severe test* in the form of a public health crisis and a *severe challenge* in the form of the antithetical doctrines fueled by odious racism, nationalism, and intolerance. The test is an old one for liberalism in that it highlights the tensions in the project of collective action to address externalities and supply public goods. Whenever we must choose in groups, the fundamental question emerges of how individuals can be free while subject to wills other than their own. Liberalism is not silent on this question; in fact, it was largely born from wrestling with this puzzle of freedom and authority and in addressing the appropriate constitutional design question.[2] Similarly, the challengers to liberalism—both prior to its inception and after—have always been grounded in odious doctrines of a parochial nature whether based on race, ethnicity, creed, or gender.

The cosmopolitan liberal project is the opposite of these collectivist doctrines, and begins instead with the insistence that the dignity of each human being must be respected. Within the liberal order, each of us has a moral obligation to respect the dignity of our fellow citizens. The cosmopolitan aspect of that liberal order is reflected in an inclusive and expansive definition of fellow citizens. In the extreme, the position I maintain is that of true radical liberalism, that citizenship would reflect the entire planet. The cosmopolitan liberal ideal is that we are "strangers nowhere in this world." We are in fact citizens of the world, free to move, free to transact, free to associate, free to believe, free to love, as we want, where we want, and with whom we want, as long as we do not infringe on the rights of others to do similarly. The liberal order is a tolerant society, and liberal citizens cultivate a cosmopolitan attitude toward others who differ from them.

Liberalism is *liberal,* and the liberal expresses *liberality*—an openness to change and new ideas and new experiments in living. The liberal order is an *open society*, a social and political arrangement that when organized correctly exhibits neither discrimination nor permits domination in public or private space. It is a system that is designed at its core to be absent of any privileges granted to some and not to others.

Enough with abstract theory/philosophy. We must face the fact that we don't live in a world of open borders, with peace and prosperous international commerce, and a political, legal, and social order that doesn't have privileges embedded in its very structure. We are often not tolerant of "others," our institutions do not perfectly reflect liberal values, and citizens do not perfectly exhibit liberality in their attitudes and practices.

At best, in the developed economies of the globe, we have a quasi-mercantilist order that has produced a managed global network of trade and commerce; at worst, we have a system of power and privilege that has been in perpetual war with other nation states. This system at its "best" has—due to pockets of liberal commerce—raised the living standards of billions over the course of the past 50 years.

If we take the current definition of extreme poverty, which is living on or below $1.90 a day, then in 1990, there were 1.9 billion (or 36 percent of the global population) living in extreme poverty. In 2015, that number had fallen to 730 million (or 9.9 percent of the global population). That was the *first time* in recorded human history that less than 10 percent of the global population was living in extreme poverty. Let that sink in a minute. Then think a bit more about what that means in terms of human well-being. We do not eat economic growth rates! But economic growth brings with it better nutrition, better healthcare, better education, greater access to opportunities for women and people of color, more freedom from arbitrary coercion, and so forth. It is not a panacea for all the world's ills, but economic growth and development may be a necessary condition for human flourishing even if it is not a sufficient one.[3]

Projections are that if modern economic growth—which is fueled by trade and technology—was to continue on trend, by 2030 the number of people living in extreme poverty would be reduced to fewer than 500 million. But those projections were made before the rise of a new wave of xenophobia, nationalism, and the restrictions on the free flow of goods, labor, and capital due to a rise of populist regimes in Europe, North America, and Latin America, and then pursued with even more vehemence in the wake of the emergence of the COVID-19 global pandemic.

Angus Deaton described the contemporary period of globalization and economic development as *The Great Escape* (2013). But while Deaton tells his readers about the remarkable improvements in global wealth, health, and well-being, he also stresses the problem of global inequality both between rich and poor countries, and within rich countries as some segments of the population fall behind the general trend. It is important to correct two false impressions. The rich did not get rich at the expense of the poor. And while the rich did get richer, in study after study we learn that the poor tended to get richer faster than the rich got richer. The poor are "escaping" from extreme poverty and experiencing vast improvements in their lives, and they are doing so at a faster rate than the rich have seen their life circumstances improve. Just imagine the improvements that could be realized if we had a true cosmopolitan liberal order that championed the free movement of people and capital throughout the globe. But still, even with this intellectual correction to the contemporary conversation concerning globalization, much suffering remains, and the COVID-19 global pandemic threatens to heighten human suffering.

The cries of injustice and the tragedy of human suffering all demand our attention. The older among the current generation of young and intellectually aware individuals (roughly 40 years old) only know the pale rhetoric of liberalism, having been raised on a steady diet of criticisms of neoliberalism and capitalism, and having had to grow up in a reality (in the United States) where since 2001, there has been an ongoing and seemingly never-ending War against Terrorism that has not only committed our troops overseas but has robbed us of civil liberties and privacy at home.[4] The median age (30-something) among the current generation of young citizens came to intellectual awareness as the Global Financial Crisis of 2008–2009 hit home, families were affected, and financial prospects were derailed. Between 2010 and 2020, the youngest members of the current generation of college students and recent graduates entering the workplace (20-something) have witnessed growing political division in society, almost to the point where any sort of civil discourse seems impossible between the contending perspectives in public policy. They have grown up with social media and seen the amazing explosion of information available to them at their fingertips, but they have also been witnesses to the potentially dire consequences of the spread of misinformation and cyberbullying.

The current generation (old, median, young) understands that the value of a college education per se has declined relative to its cost. Again, it is important to clarify misperceptions because the rate of return for a college education is still very favorable for those who choose certain majors (e.g., computer science and engineering), while very low for those who pursue other educational routes. Market conditions may change, shifting the rate of return on the human capital investment to reflect changes in social conditions. The college experience is, pre-COVID-19, more than occupational training. And in aggregate, college graduates still do much better in terms of lifetime earnings than non-college graduates. Nevertheless, it must be admitted that the cost of education is significant and the student debt problem is real. This generation I have been discussing (those in their 40s, 30s, and 20s) has less savings, less home ownership, and less long-term economic security than previous generations. And their frustrations and anger are directed at what they have been told is the ruling capitalist system, and to a considerable extent at the guardians of that current system—*economists.*[5]

In the socialist manifesto *Bigger Than Bernie* (2020), Meagan Day and Micah Uetricht explain that what matters is not Bernie Sanders's personal electoral fate, but that he has set in motion a movement for socialist reform that in their opinion cannot be stopped. He has helped to reinvigorate "class struggle" in America, and socialist ideas are no longer relegated to the sidelines in popular culture and political discourse. Their message has a sense of urgency as well as elation tied to it. If, they argue, rabidly racist and xenophobic politics is going to be defeated in America, then it will be because of the rise of a modern socialist movement; a *democratic socialist* movement. Capitalist exploitation, empowered by privatization and austerity, not only produces needless human misery, but is driving the planet to the brink of environmental catastrophe.

The answer, according to Day and Uetricht, is straightforward. We must pursue public policies that guarantee "justice, equality, security, and shared prosperity in the form of free education, affordable housing, free high-quality health care, full employment, a secure retirement, and a clean environment for all" (1). High ideals. The reason we have not achieved these high ideals, in their opinion, is because of monied interests in politics that perpetuate the capitalist system, the reckless pursuit of profit over the welfare of people, and the neoliberal theories of economists that supposedly came to dominate public policy in the 1970s and increased in influence globally through the 1980s. "The rise of neoliberalism has been disastrous for workers in the United States and helped defeat and dismantle the movements that won so many gains in the New Deal era and the 1960s" (22).

The serious problem, they contend, is that even the Democratic Party sold out to neoliberal ideology, monied interests, and the professional economists who championed the ideology and thwarted the working-class struggle from below. Sanders in his failed presidential bids demonstrated that the democratic socialist message can inspire people and unite them in solidarity in the struggle against the injustice and inequality of the capitalist system. The drive for equality and justice that the democratic socialist demands "excites working people's passions and raises their class consciousness, and inspires them to dream of a better world" (211).

This narrative contains many flaws, but challenging each of them and providing the correcting arguments and evidence are beyond the scope of this concluding essay.[6] Though let me just reference a recent book by Geoffrey Hodgson that should give pause to a significant part of this narrative from perhaps the most sympathetic perspective that one might find—Geoffrey Hodgson's *Is Socialism Feasible?* (2019). As Hodgson argues, the bold and inspiring idea of socialism "suffers from a number of fundamental problems" that are "revealed by theoretical analysis and confirmed by the experience" with the socialist experiments of the 20th century. And it is critical to point out that attaching the intended modifier *democratic* doesn't achieve what modern socialist activists think it does for the simple reason that "socialists have often promised a substantial expansion and enrichment of democracy." Unfortunately, "things always turn out differently, despite their intentions, because of the centralist logic of big socialism" (72–73).

There is, however, enough truth in the critiques of the existing crony-capitalist system, and enough falsehood spread among the economically illiterate of the intellectual class related to the critical theoretical and empirical observations in the debate over socialism and capitalism, that it is relatively easy to sustain this fallacious narrative. This becomes especially true as the experience of real-existing socialism of the 20th century fades into historical memory. In an effort to sustain the falsehoods, the contemporary intelligentsia often condemn the responses most commonly offered by classical and modern political economists to address the serious social ills of our time—not with reason and evidence, but with emotion and ad hominem attacks. This reinforces the cycle of despair as programs are devised to address social ills, and the social ills persist and, in many instances, grow worse.

Rational discourse would focus on means/ends analysis and the critical questions of incentive alignment and informational transmission to guide adaptation, adjustment, and social learning of how best to organize affairs to address the pressing issues in the most effective manner possible. But rational discourse is not encouraged in the modern age of anger, resentment, and despair.[7] Arguments are ignored or dismissed without critical engagement, and evidence is either ignored or worse distorted to construct the preferred narrative. The post-truth world of "truthiness" creates a serious challenge to rational deliberation and discourse between contending perspectives.[8]

The critical point I want to stress is that because this current generation has *no knowledge* of the horrors of socialism, except what they might read in a history book, nor do they have *any experience* with the high bouts of inflation and unemployment that brought down the Keynesian consensus in the 1970s; as a result, they are ill-equipped to ferret out the falsehoods and adjudicate between contending perspectives. It is not their fault. They lack the context, and they lack the training. Their teachers and professors in philosophy, politics, economics, and history have failed them. They do not possess the arguments or evidence that would aid in formulating an *effective* and *robust* response to the cries of injustice and the tears of human misery that plague our society. Without that knowledge and command of the evidence, the current generation not only may propose solutions that fail to address the root cause of social ills, but also, in pursuing those mistaken solutions enthusiastically and with such passion, as if they have found the definitive solutions, may unintentionally exacerbate the very ills they are hoping to eradicate. This would be a tragedy.

It is not a new form of tragedy, but sadly an old one. As Hayek warned in *The Road to Serfdom*, "Is there a greater tragedy imaginable than that, in our endeavor consciously to shape our future in accordance with high ideals, we should in fact unwittingly produce the very opposite of what we have been striving for?" ([1944] 2007, 5). And it is all the more tragic the more passionate and confident the advocates are in their beliefs that this is the only path forward to achieve equality and justice.

Economists, Paul Rubin (2019) has argued, have failed in their educational mission because they have miscommunicated their core message. There is no doubt, Rubin suggests, that the economic way of thinking focuses on choice within constraints and the vital role played by competitive forces in bringing about efficient solutions. But that is not, and should not be, the main lesson from Adam Smith to James Buchanan. The main lesson of economics is the mutual gains from trade and the peaceful social cooperation under the division of labor that a modern commercial society engenders. Motivated by Rubin's book, I published a book of essays titled *The Four Pillars of Economic Understanding* (2020), where I argue that with the increasing attacks on economics—some legitimate, others misplaced—it is time for a renewed commitment by teachers of economics to take up the communication challenge with students of this generation and teach them the best of what the discipline of economics has to offer through the years, and not the sterility of optimization and equilibrium modeling exclusively. We must tap into the natural curiosity of our students and open them to the ongoing and fascinating conversation that constitutes worldly philosophy. And above all, if we are inviting them to be active participants in a contested conversation, we must demonstrate by our own behavior and cultivate in them the fundamental virtue of civility in discourse.

A collection of essays by Edward Shils was published posthumously under the title *The Virtue of Civility* (1997). In one of his more relevant essays for our current contexts, "Civility and Civil Society: Good Manners between Persons and Concern for the Common Good," Shils divides political discourse and practice into "ideological politics," "machine politics," and "interest politics." On the one hand, ideological politics is grounded in the "us versus them" mentality of a final struggle and definitive judgment. Machine politics, on the other hand, is best reflected in the spoils system and the bureaucratization of the leadership of political parties. Interest politics, however, can devolve into machine politics, or mature into a politics of responsibility. It takes something outside of the political process itself, and a general disposition in the social order, for the practice of the politics of responsibility to rise to prominence in the everyday life of a modern liberal democratic society. A critical aspect of that disposition is civility. Such civility fades into oblivion under ideological politics, where only one notion of the higher good is to be recognized and only those who truly believe are dignified and purified, while all others are irredeemably defective and the solution for the defects is extirpation, suppression, or exile. Machine politics does not exhibit any such philosophical rejection of the other, but a practical rejection because politics is reduced to a zero-sum game where one party gains only at the expense of the other party. Thus, civility fades again once the party affiliation becomes the basis for the spoils.

In a liberal democratic society, though, civil society plays the role of the informal governor, which regulates both the economy and the government. Civility is the critical social glue that permits social cooperation among diverse and conflicting factions. The totalitarian societies of the 20th century all destroyed civil society in their countries, and with that, the countervailing forces against the devolution into either ideological politics or machine politics, or some atrocious combination of both as in the Stalinist and post-Stalinist Soviet Union. Shils contends that all large and heterogenous societies stand in need of civility to operate. "Civility," he argues, "is an attitude and a mode of action which attempts to strike a balance between conflicting demands and conflicting interests. Liberal democracy is especially in need of the virtue of civility because liberal democracy is more prone to bring latent conflicts into actuality, simply because it permits their open pursuit" (76).

The lack of civility that defines our current age in US politics is striking. Political polarization has grown so stark in the past decade that the Pew Research Center maintains a web page tracking the extent of the divide and the consequences.[9] The divide has produced a corresponding distrust among those on opposite sides and, as a result, an increase in the lack of civility in our public spaces. The rancor is especially seen in the federal government and the interaction with media. Shils's observations were prescient. The center of government and society, Shils argued, must be more civil than the peripheries. "It is dangerous for the internal peace and good order of society if the centers are very uncivil internally and in their relations with each other. A civil society is imperiled if there is a low degree of civility within and between its centers" (86). The importance of the virtue of civility cannot be stressed enough in the workings of a free and democratic society. "I should emphasize," Shils writes, "that the institutions of civil society—representative government, competitive political parties, periodic or regular elections, secret ballot, universal suffrage, a free press, freedom of association, assembly and petition or representation, independent institutions of learning and institutions of private property and freedom of contract—are absolutely necessary for a civil society. Without these institutions, there is no such thing as civil society" (87).

As I stressed in my introduction, Deirdre McCloskey in *Why Liberalism Works* (2019) is striving to encourage an ongoing conversation among adults where they can continually learn together. Remember what I said earlier about liberality; liberality is about openness to new information and to change. In short, liberality is about lifelong learning. Such ongoing learning through social interaction and true conversation presupposes certain institutions, and those institutions dovetail with the liberalism I have been exploring throughout the essays in this volume.

Liberalism is far from a perfected doctrine, and it is nowhere practiced to perfection. But its absence means we devolve into ideological politics, machine politics, or both. Socialism is the antithesis of liberalism; thus it is incoherent with respect to democratic values in practice. Placing the modifier *democratic* in front of the word *socialism* in a polemical tract does not address the logical incongruence of the two ideas in any practical implementation. Our own lack of civility in the United States at this time is because of the explicit rejection of liberalism and the adoption of nationalism on the one hand and socialism on the other, with the result that we have unleashed both ideological politics and machine politics, and have squeezed out the politics of responsibility and squashed civil society. Civility has lost its proper place as a restraining power in the public sphere of the United States. We must fix this issue for the sake of our future.

I am going to end this concluding essay by reaching back to my own roots in the writings of my dissertation adviser Don Lavoie.[10] While I was studying with Don, he published a landmark study on the socialist calculation debate, *Rivalry and Central Planning* ([1985] 2015), and a more wide-ranging book in political economy and social theory, *National Economic Planning: What Is Left?* ([1985] 2016). These works of Lavoie have informed my scholarly career at every step along the way. His teaching influenced my methodological perspective, my analytical approach, and my social philosophical commitments. He was "my teacher" and I was "his student," and I remain that to this day, almost 20 years after his tragic death.

I honestly believe Lavoie's work is a perfect conversation starter with the new generation of students who are searching for answers as they too struggle for a better world. The radical seeks, Lavoie stresses, not merely to change the current personnel in power, but to change the foundational institutions in society. And liberal radicalism, the true progressive left according to Lavoie, seeks to "transform institutions in such a way as to make the very exercise of power by one human being over another extinct" ([1985] 2016, 233). The socialist movement expressed high ideals of equality and justice, but they misdiagnosed the social disease and provided the wrong treatment and cure. It was the failure to learn the lessons of economics that paved the way for this betrayal of the high ideals of the progressive left during the age of socialism. As Lavoie argues:

> It is not correct to say that planning was modified from its Marxist origins to take on its modern, noncomprehensive forms. It would be more accurate to say that comprehensive planning and the radical movement it inspired were utterly defeated and replaced root and branch by an entirely different idea with an entirely different heritage, by a movement driven not by popular resistance to oppression but by ruling groups themselves. The radicals' chief purpose was not just modified but completely reversed: from ending all wars and exploitation to conducting a world war of unprecedented destruction; from avoiding the monopoly power of big corporations that they feared unrestricted competition would permit, to handing these corporations the very weapons they needed (and could not have gotten under a free market)

to secure monopoly power for themselves. The Left, in short, was duped into cloaking the corporations' monopoly-building agenda in its progressive-sounding anticorporate rhetoric. ([1985] 2016, 220)

And the current enthusiasm for socialist means to address the social ills that continue to plague our current society threatens once more to derail the struggle for our better world. We cannot succeed in our dual quest to understand the human condition and effectively address the injustice we hope to eradicate if we turn our backs, Lavoie stresses, on "what logic and economic science tells us we should do" ([1985] 2016, 232–33).

Economic science imposes an intellectual discipline on us by insisting that we pay close attention to not only the logic of choice, but also the situational logic of alternative institutional arrangements. By pursuing the economic way of thinking persistently and consistently, we come to understand the functional significance of the private property order and the price system for coordinating the diverse and often divergent plans of individuals. The market process—through the prodding of property, guiding of prices, luring of profits, and disciplining of loss—provides the required incentives wrapped in signals for constant social learning by the participants. As Lavoie put it:

> The evolution of the economy would be driven by the unplanned flux of market competition regulated only by the principles of natural law. Social progress was to be the indirect consequence of the competitive engagement of human minds with one another, not the direct result of the conscious planning of any single organization of minds. It was to be a society where no person was to coercively rule over another but where each one was to be persuasively influenced by others. ([1985] 2016, 215–16)

Unfortunately, socialist intellectuals either ignored or rejected the teachings of the classical and modern economists about spontaneous order and social cooperation under the division of labor. Rather than embrace the market process, they sought to replace it either with comprehensive (Marxism) or noncomprehensive (Market Socialism) planning. The policy chosen was designed to eliminate the "anarchy of production" and substitute a "rationalization of production" through scientific management of economic life. The adaptability and adjustment processes mediated through the competitive entrepreneurial market process and steered by the activity of consumers were to be substituted with socialist planning authorities. "The essence of planning," Lavoie argues, "as it is practiced is to sabotage this very feature of markets, to slow down or prevent the revision of established routines. These rigidification policies are implemented by using the traditional mercantilist tools for government interference into the competitive process: licensing restrictions, wage and price controls, credit allocation, and the dispensing of subsidies to special interest groups" ([1985] 2016, 221–22). The modifier *democratic* doesn't fix this. As Lavoie further elaborated, "Planning in practice constituted nothing more nor less than governmentally sanctioned moves by leaders of major industries to insulate themselves from risk and from the vicissitudes of market competition. It was not a failure to achieve democratic purposes; it was the ultimate fulfillment of the monopolistic purposes of certain members of the corporate elite" ([1985] 2016, 225).

As stated earlier, the contemporary demand for a socialist solution to our contemporary woes—and there are serious issues to contend with—results, in my assessment, from a failure of educators to communicate widely to the general public the core teachings of economic science and the lessons from economic history of the 19th and 20th centuries. Instead, bad theory and distorted history direct the general public's passion and outrage in a tragic direction. The tragedy—as Hayek warned us in the quote from *The Road to Serfdom* I gave earlier—is that in their effort to address demands for social justice, they perpetuate injustice. "Planning," Lavoie states, "does not accidentally deteriorate into the militarization of the economy; it is the militarization of the economy. . . . The theory of planning was, from its inception, modeled after feudal and militaristic organization. Elements of the Left tried to transform it into a radical program, to fit into a progressive revolutionary vision. But it doesn't fit. Attempts to implement this theory invariably reveal its true nature. The practice of planning is nothing but the militarization of the economy" ([1985] 2016, 230).

The power of Lavoie's analysis in *National Economic Planning* is conveyed throughout his book as he discusses the underlying governing dynamic mechanisms of the three main social arrangements: Tradition, Market, Planning. He demonstrates the poverty and misery of Tradition, and the impracticality and tragic consequences of Planning. That leaves us with Market, and in particular the radical liberal vision of commercial society and free association among individuals. We must be willing to think through to a vision of a "workable utopia." As Lavoie makes the case:

Many, perhaps most, utopias that have inspired people in the past have been inherently unachievable, and their pursuit has often led to immeasurable social harm. But there is really no alternative for anyone who recognizes the gross injustices of our modern world—and, for that matter, of virtually the whole of human history—but to lie down and resign oneself in defeat or to try to get up and devise a new utopia, a new vision of a fundamentally different world with which to reinspire an international movement. For if we settle for anything less than this, if we try to work within the constraints imposed by the current regimes, we are playing into the hands of the existing power structure and are destined to repeat the tragic story of the twentieth-century Left. ([1985] 2016, 234)

The essays in this volume should be viewed as an invitation to inquiry. None should be viewed by anyone, and certainly weren't intended by me, to be definitive statements. They are conversation starters, not conversation enders. The struggle is ongoing and never-ending in science and in society. This means, however, that we must also face up to our imperfections—our troubling past and our difficult present. If we don't, we are doomed.

Building on the work of Mises, Hayek, Buchanan, and Lavoie, the essays in this volume try to tackle various aspects of the argument for a true radical liberalism. "Our task now," Lavoie suggests, "is to complete the American revolution. Unlike the failed Marxist utopia of Planning, the Jeffersonian, Market-guided society is a workable idea, an ideal that when properly understood is far more consistent with the humanitarian and internationalistic values of the Left" ([1985] 2016, 238). Lavoie, and I, are not blind to the gross inconsistencies in the American experience. But the *principles* are not to be rejected because of the imperfections and immorality of men. If the principles are workable, then it would be a grave error to reject them. Rather than reject, we argue that our task today is to admit "exceptions to the principles that otherwise guided that revolution were allowed which kept America from fully achieving its ideal. For example, equal rights were incompletely extended to women and withheld altogether from blacks and Native Americans. . . . Such remnants of coercion were not only inconsistent with the general principles that fueled the American revolution but were also ultimately to prove the causes of most of the nation's problems—and shame—since. It was this incompleteness that let Americans massacre Indians, enslave blacks, and restrict the rights of women" (Lavoie [1985] 2016, 238).

Liberalism has nothing to do with the maintenance of the status quo. The constant adaptation and adjustment to change, and the continuous evolution of social mores that promote peaceful cooperation and wealth creation, represent the greatest threat to the citadels of power and privilege. The goals of social justice will be best served by the free forces of market competition, and will be ill-served by the renewed calls for socialist planning that inevitably devolve into the permanent war economy of a militaristic state. True liberal radicalism, as we have stressed, was born in the struggle for emancipation from dogma, from subjugation, from violence, from poverty. The goal was to find the set of institutions that would minimize human suffering and maximize the opportunities for human flourishing—a system that could empower and grant freedom to all, rather than a select few. The liberal plan of equality, liberty, and justice would deliver autonomy, prosperity, and peace. Foreign military entanglements would end, and peaceful and mutually beneficial entanglements of trade would be pursued instead. Interventionism in domestic economic and foreign political affairs would be rejected, and the principles of noninterventionism both at home and abroad would be the governing principles. Such a complete liberalism has yet to be instituted, but it follows from the consistent and persistent application of the teachings of economics and political economy to the practical affairs of our world.[11]

As the essays in this collection reveal, I am neither a cynical pessimist who believes such a vision of cosmopolitan liberalism is an unrealizable dream, nor am I a naïve optimist who believes the ideal society is easily achieved if we show goodwill toward one another. The "Good Society" of true radical liberalism is an ideal, not a speculative utopia but a guiding principle for what ought to be. Economic science is the tool we use to examine how the guiding principles can be realized through institutions that align incentives and discover, utilize, and disseminate the relevant knowledge to participants in the social order so they can coordinate their plans with one another. In this way, we can find the set of institutions that enables individuals to pursue productive specialization and realize peaceful social cooperation through exchange. Autonomy, prosperity, and peace.

Liberalism promises a more harmonious world, a less violent world, a more prosperous world, a better world. Achieving such a world is worth the struggle.

Notes

1. See Brennan and Buchanan (1986) and Buchanan and Tullock (2008).

2. See the Old Testament, 1 Samuel 8, where Israel asks for a king; or *The Epic of Gilgamesh* from ancient Mesopotamia and the need for countervailing forces to check the abuse of power by central authority; or Plato and the puzzle of who is to guard the guardians; and then trace to the Enlightenment exercise of Montesquieu and John Locke, and eventually David Hume and Adam Smith, and then the constitutional project of the American Founders in The Federalist Papers and the drafting of the Constitution of the United States of America.

3. See Tyler Cowen's *Stubborn Attachments* (2018); also see Cowen's Arrow Lecture from 2019 (https://ethicsinsociety.stanford.edu/events/economic-growth-moral -imperative). On the cultural as well as economic benefits of globalization, see Cowen's *Creative Destruction: How Globalization Is Changing the World's Cultures* (2002).

4. I cannot recommend highly enough the work of Christopher Coyne. See in particular Coyne's *After War* (2008) and *Doing Bad by Doing Good* (2013), and more recently Coyne and Hall, *Tyranny Comes Home* (2018). The importance of the topic for understanding the human condition is in this instance matched by the brilliance of the insights. These are must additions to the personal library of every citizen who hopes to be an informed participant in the democratic deliberation over the collective choices that hold the fate of civilization in balance during this modern era of violence and conquest.

5. One could describe the past decade or more as an age of anger, resentment, and disillusionment, and it is shared by the older generation as well. See Eric Lonergan and Mark Blyth (2020) and Case and Deaton (2020).

6. One of the most important ideas in social science is the concept of value freedom in analysis where ends are treated as given, and the theorists restrict their analyses to the critical examination of the effectiveness of chosen means to the obtainment of those given ends. Socialism, according to Hayek, was the noblest and most influential of the collectivist doctrines, but it was fundamentally flawed. It is a false ideal, according to Hayek, not because of the values on which it is based, but "because of a misconception of the forces which have made the Great Society and civilization possible. The demonstration that the differences between socialists and non-socialists ultimately rest on purely intellectual issues capable of scientific resolution and not on different judgements of value appears to me one of the most important outcomes of the train of thought pursued in this book" (1973, 6).

7. Look at the way Paul Krugman chooses to engage with those who differ from him in applied public policy judgments, as evidenced by his book *Arguing with Zombies* (2020) and compare with the philosopher Daniel Dennett's rules of intellectual engagement for a rational and productive conversation as presented in his book *Intuition Pumps and Other Tools of Thinking* (2013, 33): "How to compose a successful critical commentary: 1. You should attempt to re-express your target's position so clearly, vividly, and fairly that your target says, 'Thanks, I wish I'd thought of putting it that

way.' 2. You should list any points of agreement (especially if they are not matters of general or widespread agreement). 3. You should mention anything you have learned from your target. 4. Only then are you permitted to say so much as a word of rebuttal or criticism." Krugman violates *every* rule of rational and productive engagement when he writes about "Knaves, Fools and Me" (2013) or lists his own rules of engagement in *Arguing with Zombies*. His attitude as a public intellectual is a betrayal of his responsibility as a Nobel Prize winner and much more problematic precisely because he is a gifted writer with a knack of communicating widely beyond his scientific peers. I will address this issue of responsibility shortly.

8. The most egregious example of this is Nancy MacLean's *Democracy in Chains* (2018), which I have tried to provide a measured review of, stressing the tragic missed opportunity her work represents (see Boettke 2019). But the real tragedy is that she is far from alone in pursuing this style of work in assessing contending perspectives on capitalism and society.

9. See Pew Research Center's web page "Political Polarization," https://www.pewresearch.org/topics/political-polarization/.

10. See, for example, my remarks at Lavoie's memorial service in 2001 (https://donlavoie.org/remembering-don-lavoie-a-student-perspective-by-p-boettke/).

11. Hayek writes: "Utopia, like ideology, is a bad word today; and it is true that most utopias aim at radically redesigning society and suffer from internal contradictions which make their realization impossible. But an ideal picture of a society which may not be wholly achievable, or a guiding conception of the overall order to be aimed at, is nevertheless not only the indispensable precondition of any rational policy, but also the chief contribution that science can make to the solution of the problems of practical policy" (1973, 65).

References

Boettke, Peter J. 2019. "The Allure and Tragedy of Ideological Blinders Left, Right, and Center: A Review Essay of Nancy MacLean's Democracy in Chains." In *Research in the History of Economic Thought and Methodology*, edited by Luca Fiorito, Scott Scheall, and Carlos Eduardo Suprinyak, 123–47. Bingley, UK: Emerald Publishing.

———. 2020. *The Four Pillars of Economic Understanding*. Great Barrington, MA: American Institute for Economic Research.

Brennan, Geoffrey, and James M. Buchanan. 1986. *The Reason of Rules: Constitutional Political Economy*. Cambridge: Cambridge University Press.

Buchanan, James M., and Gordon Tullock. 2008. *The Calculus of Consent: Logical Foundations of Constitutional Democracy*. Ann Arbor: University of Michigan Press.

Case, Anne, and Angus Deaton. 2020. *Deaths of Despair and the Future of Capitalism*. Princeton, NJ: Princeton University Press.

Cowen, Tyler. 2002. *Creative Destruction: How Globalization Is Changing the World's Cultures.* Princeton, NJ: Princeton University Press.

———. 2018. *Stubborn Attachments: A Vision for a Society of Free, Prosperous, and Responsible Individuals.* San Francisco: Stripe Press.

Coyne, Christopher J. 2008. *After War: The Political Economy of Exporting Democracy.* Stanford, CA: Stanford University Press.

———. 2013. *Doing Bad by Doing Good: Why Humanitarian Action Fails.* Stanford, CA: Stanford University Press.

Coyne, Christopher J., and Abigail R. Hall. 2018. *Tyranny Comes Home: The Domestic Fate of U.S. Militarism.* Stanford, CA: Stanford University Press.

Day, Meagan, and Micah Uetricht. 2020. *Bigger Than Bernie: How We Go from the Sanders Campaign to Democratic Socialism.* London: Verso.

Deaton, Angus. 2013. *The Great Escape: Health, Wealth, and the Origins of Inequality.* Princeton, NJ: Princeton University Press.

Dennett, Daniel C. 2013. *Intuition Pumps and Other Tools for Thinking.* New York: W. W. Norton.

Hayek, F. A. [1944] 2007. *The Road to Serfdom: Text and Documents—The Definitive Edition.* Edited by Bruce Caldwell. Chicago: University of Chicago Press.

———. [1960] 2011. *The Constitution of Liberty: The Definitive Edition.* Chicago: University of Chicago Press.

———. 1973. *Law, Legislation and Liberty.* Volume 1: *Rules and Order.* Chicago: University of Chicago Press.

———. 1976. *Law, Legislation and Liberty.* Volume 2: *The Mirage of Social Justice.* Chicago: University of Chicago Press.

Hodgson, Geoffrey M. 2019. *Is Socialism Feasible? Towards an Alternative Future.* Cheltenham, UK: Edward Elgar.

Krugman, Paul R. 2013. "Knaves, Fools, and Me (Meta)." *New York Times Blog*, April 28.

———. 2020. *Arguing with Zombies: Economics, Politics, and the Fight for a Better Future.* New York: W. W. Norton.

Lavoie, Don. [1985] 2015. *Rivalry and Central Planning: The Socialist Calculation Debate Reconsidered.* Arlington, VA: Mercatus Center at George Mason University.

———. [1985] 2016. *National Economic Planning: What Is Left?* Arlington, VA: Mercatus Center at George Mason University.

Lippmann, Walter. 1938. *The Good Society.* London: Routledge.

Lonergan, Eric, and Mark Blyth. 2020. *Angrynomics.* New York: Columbia University Press.

MacLean, Nancy. 2018. *Democracy in Chains: The Deep History of the Radical Right's Stealth Plan for America.* New York: Viking.

McCloskey, Deirdre N. 2019. *Why Liberalism Works: How True Liberal Values Produce a Freer, More Equal, Prosperous World for All.* New Haven, CT: Yale University Press.

Rubin, Paul H. 2019. *The Capitalism Paradox: How Cooperation Enables Free Market Competition*. New York: Bombardier Books.

Shils, Edward. 1997. *The Virtue of Civility: Selected Essays on Liberalism, Tradition, and Civil Society*. Edited by Steven Grosby. Indianapolis: Liberty Fund.

Stiglitz, Joseph E. 1994. *Whither Socialism?* Cambridge, MA: MIT Press.

About the Author

Peter J. Boettke is the vice president and director of the F. A. Hayek Program for Advanced Study in Philosophy, Politics, and Economics at the Mercatus Center, as well as the BB&T Professor for the Study of Capitalism and University Professor of Economics and Philosophy at George Mason University. He is also a Distinguished Fellow at the Institute for Humane Studies. He specializes in Austrian economics, economic history, institutional analysis, public choice, and social change.

Boettke has authored and coauthored 14 books, including his most recent *The Four Pillars of Economic Understanding*, and is editor of the *Review of Austrian Economics*, series editor of the New Thinking in Political Economy book series, and coeditor of the Cambridge Studies in Economics, Choice, and Society.

Boettke is a former Fulbright Fellow at the University of Economics in Prague, a National Fellow at Stanford University, and a Hayek Visiting Fellow at the London School of Economics. He has held visiting academic positions at the Russian Academy of Sciences in Moscow and the Stockholm School of Economics, among other institutions. Before joining the faculty at George Mason University, Boettke taught economics at New York University.

Boettke's work has earned him numerous awards, including best article in Austrian economics at the Society for the Development of Austrian Economics, a doctorate honoris causa in social sciences from Universidad Francisco Marroquin in Guatemala, and an honorary doctorate from Alexandru Ioan Cuza University in Romania.

Boettke received his PhD from George Mason University.

Index